신흥교역국의 통관환경 연구

브라질

한국조세재정연구원

2014년 11월 15일 1판 1쇄 인쇄
2014년 11월 15일 1판 1쇄 발행

지 은 이	세법연구센터 / 한국조세재정연구원
발 행 인	이헌숙
표　　지	김학용
발 행 처	생각쉼표 & 주)휴먼컬처아리랑
	서울특별시 영등포구 여의도동 45-13 코오롱포레스텔 309
전　　화	070) 8866 - 2220 FAX • 02) 784-4111
등록번호	제 2009 - 000008호
등록일자	2009년 12월 29일

www.휴먼컬처아리랑.kr
ISBN 979-11-5565-096-7

신흥교역국의 통관환경 연구

브라질

한국조세재정연구원

※ 본 보고서는 브라질 관세제도의 대부분을 담기 위해서 노력하였으나 지면의 부족 및 시간상의 제약으로 인해 부족한 부분이 있다.

또한 가급적 최신의 내용을 수록하기 위하여 노력하였지만, 사회·경제 상황에 따라 세제에 변화가 빈번하여, 가장 최신의 내용을 본 보고서에 반영하는 데에는 한계가 있었다.

따라서 본 보고서는 브라질의 관세에 대한 최소한의 길라잡이임을 밝히며, 보다 정확하고 구체적인 사항은 브라질 연방 세무국 및 재무부의 출판물 및 홈페이지와 관련 법령을 참조할 것을 권장함. 특히 민감한 사안에 대하여는 반드시 관련 법령을 통해 확인할 필요가 있으며, 불명확한 부분에 대해서는 관련 관세전문가의 도움을 받을 것을 강조하고자 한다.

본 보고서의 내용은 저자들의 개인적인 의견이며, 한국조세연구원의 공식적인 견해와 무관함을 밝혀 둔다.

목 차

I. 개 관··· 9
  1. 일반 개황 ··· 9
  2. 경제 개황 ··· 11
    가. 브라질의 주요 경제 지표 ·· 11
    나. 브라질의 수출입 동향 ·· 13
    다. 브라질의 외국인 투자 동향 ·· 16
  3. 우리나라와 브라질의 교역 관계 ·· 18
  4. 브라질의 자유무역협정(FTA, Free Trade Agreement) 현황 및 동향 ········ 22
  5. 브라질의 AEO 유사 제도(Blue Line 제도) ··· 26

II. 외국의 통상환경 보고서 ··· 28
  1. World Bank의 『Doing Business 2011』 ··· 28
  2. 미국 국별 무역장벽 보고서(National Trade Estimate Report on Foreign Trade
     Barriers: NTE 보고서) ·· 30
    가. 관세분야 ·· 31
    나. 수입허가·관세평가·무역조치 ·· 32
    다. 수출 보조금 ·· 33
    라. 정부 조달 ·· 33

III. 브라질의 통관 환경 ·· 35
  1. 통관 행정 개요 ··· 35
    가. 통관 행정 조직 ··· 35
    나. 관세 ·· 37

다. 관세특혜제도 ·· 41
　2. 수입 통관 절차 ·· 42
　　가. 수입허가 ·· 43
　　나. 수입신고 ·· 45
　　다. 물품검사 후 화물 출고 ·· 45
　3. 수출 통관 절차 ·· 46
　　가. SISCOMEX 업체 등록 단계 ·· 46
　　나. 수출신고 단계 ·· 47
　　다. 물품검사・심사 단계 후 통관 완료 ·· 47

Ⅳ. 통관 절차별 고려 사항 ·· 48
　1. SISCOMEX 등록 및 NCM 분류 단계 ·· 49
　　가. 통관 절차상 특이사항 ·· 49
　　나. 애로 사례 및 업무상 유의점 ·· 49
　2. 수입허가 취득 및 행정처리 단계 ·· 51
　　가. 통관 절차상 특이사항 ·· 51
　　나. 애로 사례 및 업무상 유의점 ·· 52
　3. 수입신고 단계 ·· 54
　　가. 통관 절차상 특이사항 ·· 54
　　나. 애로 사례 및 업무상 유의점 ·· 54
　4. 물품검사 단계 ·· 55
　　가. 통관 절차상 특이사항 ·· 55
　　나. 애로 사례 및 업무상 유의점 ·· 56
　5. 물품반출 및 환급 단계 ·· 57
　　가. 통관 절차상 특이사항 ·· 57
　　나. 애로 사례 및 업무상 유의점 ·· 57

참고문헌 ·· 58

부 록·· 59
　부록 Ⅰ. 비즈니스 팁·· 59
　부록 Ⅱ. 주요 유관 기관 정보·· 65
　부록 Ⅲ. 법령 정보·· 68
　부록 Ⅳ. 조세 체계·· 74
　부록 Ⅴ. Names and Acronyms··· 79
　부록 Ⅵ. 인증 주관 기관 및 시험기관··· 80
　부록 Ⅶ. GSTP 혜택 품목·· 84

표 목차

〈표 Ⅰ-1〉 브라질 국가 개황 ·· 11
〈표 Ⅰ-2〉 브라질의 주요 거시경제 지표 ·· 13
〈표 Ⅰ-3〉 주요기관의 브라질 신용등급 평가추이 ································ 13
〈표 Ⅰ-4〉 브라질의 수출입 추이 ·· 14
〈표 Ⅰ-5〉 브라질의 주요 수출국 현황 ·· 15
〈표 Ⅰ-6〉 브라질의 주요 수입국 현황 ·· 15
〈표 Ⅰ-7〉 브라질의 연도별 FDI 추이 ·· 16
〈표 Ⅰ-8〉 UNCTAD/BDO 외국인 투자희망국 순위 ···························· 17
〈표 Ⅰ-9〉 한-브라질 연도별 투자 현황(신고기준) ····························· 18
〈표 Ⅰ-10〉 최근 대(對)브라질 교역량 및 무역수지 ··························· 19
〈표 Ⅰ-11〉 최근 대(對)브라질 10대 수출 품목 ·································· 20
〈표 Ⅰ-12〉 최근 대(對)브라질 10대 수입 품목 ·································· 21
〈표 Ⅰ-13〉 브라질의 무역협정 체결 현황 ·· 25

〈표 Ⅱ-1〉 브라질의 무역 분야 순위 비교 ·· 29
〈표 Ⅱ-2〉 브라질 수출입 소요 기간 및 비용 ······································ 30
〈표 Ⅱ-3〉 기타 브라질 비관세 장벽 ·· 34

〈표 Ⅲ-1〉 브라질 수입시 과세되는 최종가격 도출 예 ······················ 40

〈표 Ⅳ-1〉 브라질 통관 절차별 유의사항 ·· 48
〈표 Ⅳ-2〉 브라질 제소 및 규제내역 ·· 51

그림 목차

[그림 Ⅲ-1] 통관 행정 조직 ·· 36
[그림 Ⅲ-2] 브라질 연방세무국 조직도 ··· 37
[그림 Ⅲ-3] 브라질의 수입 통관 절차 ··· 42
[그림 Ⅲ-4] 자동발급(수입허가 불필요) 및 자동발급 불가(수입허가 필요)물품의 통관
           절차 ··· 44
[그림 Ⅲ-5] 수입신고 후 물품검사 과정 ·· 46

I. 개 관

1. 일반 개황[1]

☐ 정식국명은 브라질연방공화국(República Federativa do Brasil)이며, 공식 언어는 포르투갈어임
  ○ 라틴아메리카에서는 유일하게 1531년부터 포르투갈 식민지에서 발전한 나라로 1822년 포르투갈 왕가(王家)를 받드는 왕국으로 독립하여 1889년 노예제도를 폐지하고 공화제가 됨
  ○ 아메리카 대륙에서 유일하게 포르투갈어를 사용하며, 포르투갈어 사용국가로는 세계에서 가장 많은 인구수를 가진 나라이기도 함

☐ 인구는 약 1억 9,100만명이며, 민족은 백인(48.4%), 흑백혼혈(43.8%), 흑인(6.8%), 기타(1.2%)로 구성됨
  ○ 백인은 포르투갈계, 독일계, 이탈리아계, 스페인계, 폴란드계 등이며 기타 1.2%에는 일본계, 아랍계, 인디오가 있음

☐ 국토의 총 면적은 8,547,403.5㎢로 남아메리카 중앙부에 있는 나라임
  ○ 대부분 평원지형이며, 한반도의 약 37배인 동시에 세계 제5위를 기록할 만큼 넓은 면적을 가지고 있음
  ○ 아마존(Amazon)평원은 국토면적의 약 60%를 차지하며 아마존강의 길이는 7,000km임

☐ 북부 및 북동부 일부 지방의 경우 적도성 기후를, 북동부 일부를 비롯하여 중서부와

---

[1] 외교통상부, CIA country profile Mexico

남동부 일대가 열대성 기후를 나타내며 남부는 아열대기후를 보이고 있음
- 국토의 92% 이상이 남회귀선 위쪽에 위치하여 전체적으로는 열대 기후로 분류되며, Paraná, Santa Catarina, Rio Grande do Sul 등 남부 3개 주(州) 및 상파울루 주 남부 지방만이 온대기후에 속함

□ 행정구역은 1개 연방구(distrito federal)와 26개 주(estado)로 이루어져 있으며, 브라질리아(Brasilia)에 수도를 두고 있음
- 과거에는 리우 데 자네이루(Rio de Janeiro)가 수도였으나, 1960년부터 브라질리아(Brasilia)로 수도를 이전함

□ 정치체제는 연방주의와 3권 분립주의 원칙에 의해 연방정부와 주정부에 통치권한을 분배하고 있으며 각기 입법부, 사법부, 행정부가 존재함
- 대통령(Dilma Vana Rousseff)이 국가수반이며, 연방의회는 양원(상원 81석, 하원 513석)제임
- 연방정부의 주요 권한은 외교 관계, 국제 교역, 이민정책 수립, 국경 관리, 국제기구 참여, 국방, 화폐 발행, 사회 발전계획 수립 등임
- 주정부는 연방 헌법을 침해하지 않는 범위에서 주 헌법을 제정하고, 연방정부와 주정부가 공동으로 다루어야 할 노사 관계, 환경, 조세 문제 등은 연방법과 주법이 공동으로 규정함

□ 화폐단위는 헤알(Real)[2]이며, 자유변동환율제를 채택하고 있음
- 헤알(Real)은 1994년 화폐 개혁 이후 탄생했음
- 지폐로는 1헤알, 2헤알, 5헤알, 10헤알, 20헤알, 50헤알, 100헤알, 동전으로는 1센타보(Centavo), 5센타보, 10센타보, 25센타보, 50센타보, 1헤알이 사용되고 있음

---

[2] 1달러당 1.8헤알(2011월 9월 기준)

〈표 Ⅰ-1〉 브라질 국가 개황

항목	내용
공식국명	브라질연방공화국(República Federativa do Brasil)
수도	브라질리아(Brasilia)
국가형태	1개 연방구, 26개 주
국토면적	8,547,403.5km²(한반도의 37배)
위치	남미
인구	1억 9,100만명(2010)
정부형태	대통령 중심제
정부성향	보수 온건 좌파
대통령	지우마(Dilma Vana Rousseff) 대통령(2011년 1월 취임)
의회	양원제(상원 81석, 하원 513석)
인종	백인(48.4%), 흑백혼혈(43.8%), 흑인(6.8%), 기타(1.2%)
언어	포르투갈어

자료: 한국수출입은행, 『세계국가편람』; CIA country profile Brazil

2. 경제 개황[3]

가. 브라질의 주요 경제 지표

☐ 2010년 브라질의 경제성장률은 7.5%로 24년 만에 가장 높은 증가율을 보임
  ○ 미국발 글로벌 금융위기로 인해 2009년 경제성장률은 -0.7%를 기록하였음
  ○ 금융위기에도 불구하고 2010년의 높은 경제성장률 시현은 대선에 따른 정부지출 증가, 2014년 월드컵 및 2016년 올림픽 개최 특수에 따른 투자 확대 등의 요인이 긍정적으로 작용함

☐ 2010년 국내총생산(GDP)은 3조 6,750만헤알(약 2조 2,138억달러)이었음

---

3) 한국수출입은행, 브라질 통계청, 브라질 중앙은행

○ 브라질의 경제규모는 구매력 기준으로 프랑스와 영국을 제치고 세계 7위이며, 중남미 국가들 중 1위임

□ 2010년 소비자 물가지수(IPCA)[4]는 5.9%로 전년 대비 1.6% 포인트 상승함
  ○ 2009년 IPCA는 4.3%로 목표치인 4.5%를 달성하였으나, 2010년에는 목표치 기준 1.4% 초과됨
  ○ 2010년 IPCA 목표치가 초과되어, 예상 물가지수를 상회한 원인은 브라질 중앙은행의 기준금리 인하와 경기회복으로 분석됨
  ○ 향후 IPCA 목표치를 달성하기 위해서 경상경비 절감 등 긴축재정 기조에 돌입할 것으로 예상됨

□ 헤알화 고평가로 브라질 제조업 경쟁력이 약화되는 문제가 발생하고 있음
  ○ 2005년 달러당 2.43헤알을 기록했던 환율이 2011년 8월기준 1.55까지 하락하여 헤알화가 고평가 됨
  ○ 무역수지 흑자기조, 외국인투자 확대, 주식시장 외국인 투자자금 유입 확대 등에 따라 헤알화 강세현상이 나타나고 있음

□ 브라질 경제의 끊임없는 화두인 소득불평등 문제는 여전히 심각한 수준이며, 경제성장을 저해하는 요인으로 지적되고 있음
  ○ 2006년 세계은행보고서에 따르면, 브라질은 중남미 국가 중 소득불균형이 가장 심한 국가로 조사되었음
  ○ 브라질의 지니계수[5]는 0.6에 가까운 수치로, 우리나라의 두 배 이상이며 지역간 계층간 격심한 소득불평등을 보이고 있음

---

4) 소비자가 구입하는 상품이나 서비스의 가격변동을 나타내는 지수
5) 소득이 어느 정도 균등하게 분배되는가를 나타내는 소득분배의 불균형 수치로, 지니계수는 0과 1 사이의 값을 가지는데, 값이 0에 가까울수록 소득분배의 불평등 정도가 낮다는 것을 뜻함. 보통 0.4가 넘으면 소득분배의 불평등 정도가 심한 것으로 봄

〈표 Ⅰ-2〉 브라질의 주요 거시경제 지표

(단위: 달러, %)

구분	2007	2008	2009	2010
경상 GDP (10억달러)	1,366.5	1,650.7	1,598.4	2,030.5
1인당 GDP	7,283	8,706	8,348	10,504
경제성장률	5.4	5.1	-0.2	7.5
물가상승률	4.5	5.9	4.3	5.9
실업률	9.3	7.9	8.1	7.1
대미달러환율	1.77	2.34	1.74	1.67

주: 브라질중앙은행(BCB) 2010년 연말기준환율
자료: 브라질중앙은행(BCB), 브라질통계청(IBGE)

〈표 Ⅰ-3〉 주요기관의 브라질 신용등급 평가추이

평가기관	2007	2008	2009	2010
한국수출입은행	B2	B2	B2	B2
OECD	3	3	3	3
S & P	BBB-	BBB-	BBB-	BBB-
Moody's	Baa1	Baa3	Baa3	Baa2
Fitch	BBB-	BBB-	BBB-	BBB

자료: 한국수출입은행

나. 브라질의 수출입 동향

☐ 2009년 브라질의 대외수출은 전년 대비 22.7% 감소한 1,530억달러를 기록함
  ○ 대외수출 부진요인은 미국, 아르헨티나 등 주요 수출시장의 경기부진과 헤알화 강세 현상에 따른 브라질제품의 수출경쟁력 하락이었음

☐ 2010년 수출실적은 2,019억달러, 수입실적은 1,816억달러를 기록하며 역대 최고치였던 2008년 수준을 상회함

○ 수출은 전년 대비 32% 증가, 수입은 42% 증가함
○ 교역량이 감소했던 2009년과 달리, 2010년에는 수출입 모두 크게 증가하였으나, 수출보다 수입 증가율이 높아서 무역수지는 253억달러에서 203억달러로 감소
○ 전체 수출 중 철, 석유, 설탕 품목이 54%의 비중을 보였고 동 상품의 수출증가로 전년 대비 수출량이 급증함
○ 수입은 국내시장의 활성과 헤알의 강세로 인한 수입상품의 경쟁력 증가에 기인함

〈표 Ⅰ-4〉 브라질의 수출입 추이

(단위: 백만달러, %)

연도	수출		수입		무역수지
	금액	증감률	금액	증감률	
2005	118,309	22.6	73,545	17.1	44,785
2006	137,470	16.2	91,396	24.3	46,074
2007	160,649	16.9	120,621	32.0	40,028
2008	197,942	23.2	173,196	43.5	24,746
2009	152,994	-22.7	127,647	-26.3	25,347
2010	201,915	31.98	181,648	42.31	20,266
2011(1-6)	118,304	32.65	105,350	29.58	12,954

자료: WTA 2011

□ 주요 수출입국은 중국과 미국으로 전체 점유율의 25%를 상회하는 수준임
  ○ 수출: ① 중국(점유율 15.1%) ② 미국(10.04%) ③ 아르헨티나(8.76%) ④ 네덜란드(5.37%) ⑤ 독일(4.04%) ⑥ 일본(3.20%)
  ○ 수입: ① 미국(점유율 14.85%) ② 중국(13.23%) ③ 아르헨티나(8.25%) ④ 독일(6.83%) ⑤ 한국(4.95%) ⑥ 일본(3.91%)

〈표 Ⅰ-5〉 브라질의 주요 수출국 현황

(단위: 백만달러)

순위	국명	금액			점유율(%)		
		2008	2009	2010	2008	2009	2010
	전체	197,942	152,994	201,915	100	100	100
1	중국	16,403	20,190	30,785	8.29	13.2	15.25
2	미국	27,423	15,601	19,307	13.85	10.2	9.56
3	아르헨티나	17,605	12,784	18,522	8.89	8.36	9.17
4	네덜란드	10,482	8,150	10,277	5.3	5.33	5.07
5	독일	8,850	6,174	8,138	4.47	4.04	4.03
6	일본	6,114	4,269	7,140	3.09	2.79	4.54
7	영국	3,791	3,723	4,627	1.92	2.43	2.29
8	칠레	4,791	2,656	4,258	2.42	1.74	2.11
9	이탈리아	4,765	3,016	4,235	2.41	1.97	2.10
10	러시아	4,652	2,868	4,152	2.35	1.88	2.06
11	스페인	4,045	2,637	3,867	2.04	1.72	1.92
12	베네수엘라	5,150	3,610	3,853	2.6	2.36	1.91
13	한국	3,118	2,622	3,760	1.58	1.71	1.86
14	멕시코	4,281	2,675	3,715	2.16	1.75	1.84
15	프랑스	4,125	2,905	3,576	2.08	1.9	1.77

자료: WTA 2011

〈표 Ⅰ-6〉 브라질의 주요 수입국 현황

(단위: 백만달러)

순위	국명	금액			점유율(%)		
		2008	2009	2010	2008	2009	2010
	전체	173,196	127,647	181,648	100	100	100
1	미국	25,626	20,028	27,039	14.8	15.69	14.89
2	중국	20,040	15,911	25,593	11.57	12.47	14.09
3	아르헨티나	13,257	11,281	14,426	7.66	8.84	7.94
4	독일	12,025	9,865	12,552	6.94	7.73	6.91
5	한국	5,412	4,818	8,422	3.13	3.78	4.64
6	일본	6,806	5,367	6,981	3.93	4.21	3.84
7	나이지리아	6,706	4,760	5,919	3.87	3.73	3.26
8	이탈리아	4,612	3,663	4,837	2.66	2.87	2.66
9	프랑스	4,678	3,615	4,799	2.7	2.83	2.64
10	인도	3,563	2,190	4,242	2.06	1.72	2.34
11	칠레	4,161	2,615	4,091	2.4	2.05	2.25
12	멕시코	3,125	2,783	3,858	1.8	2.18	2.12
13	영국	2,551	2,407	3,154	1.47	1.89	1.74
14	타이완	3,536	2,413	3,104	2.04	1.89	1.71
15	스위스	2,246	2,050	2,864	1.3	1.61	1.58

자료: WTA 2011

다. 브라질의 외국인 투자 동향

□ 거대한 시장규모, 풍부한 노동력 등 여타 중남미 국가에 비해 상대적 투자 매력도가 큰 시장임

□ 브라질 2010년 FDI 금액은 484억달러로 전년 대비 86.7% 증가함
  ○ 2008년 451억달러의 정점 후, 2009년에 259억달러로 급감하였으나, 2010년에 484억달러로 다시 급증하여 사상최대치를 기록함

〈표 Ⅰ-7〉 브라질의 연도별 FDI 추이

(단위: 백만달러, %)

연도	2005	2006	2007	2008	2009	2010
FDI 금액	15,066	18,822	34,585	45,058	25,949	48,438
증감률	17.0	24.9	83.7	30.3	42.4	86.7

자료: 브라질 중앙은행

□ UNCTAD[6]과 BDO[7]에 따르면 브라질 월드컵 축구대회(2014)와 리우 데 자네이루 하계올림픽(2016) 개최로 향후 2020년까지 지속적인 해외직접투자의 증가가 예상됨
  ○ UNTAD의 "World Investment Prospects Survey 2010-2012"에 따르면, 236명의 국제 경영자 설문조사 결과, 브라질이 3번째 투자유망 국가로 집계되었음
  ○ 또한, 영국 BDO International 컨설팅사가 237명의 국제 사업가들을 대상으로 인터뷰한 내용을 발표한 자료[8]에서도 브라질은 향후 투자 유망국가 중 4위로 기록됨

□ 브라질에 투자를 희망하는 국가 중 하나인 중국의 FDI 유입속도가 급격히 증가하고 있음
  ○ 2010년 대(對)브라질 중국의 FDI 총액은 170억달러로 전체의 35%의 비율을 보임

---

6) UN 무역개발협의회
7) BDO International
8) 2010.10.28

○ 중국의 급속한 경제발전을 지탱하기 위한 자원확보 차원에서 브라질의 광산과 토지를 매입하기 위한 자금으로 분석됨

<표 Ⅰ-8> UNCTAD/BDO 외국인 투자희망국 순위

순위	1	2	3	4	5	6	7	8	9	10
UNCTAD	중국	인도	브라질	미국	러시아	멕시코	영국	베트남	인니	독일
BDO	중국	인도	미국	브라질	러시아	중동	영국	독일	멕시코	아프리카

자료: UNCTAD, BDO 2010

☐ 반면, 브라질 인프라 부족은 FDI 유치의 가장 큰 장애 요인으로 지적되고 있음
  ○ 인도와 러시아에 비해서는 브라질의 인프라가 다소 앞서있는 것으로 평가되고 있으나, 여전히 인프라 부족이 외국인 투자 유치에 큰 걸림돌로 작용하고 있음
  ○ 투자의 취약점으로 가장 많이 지적되고 있는 인프라의 부족을 개선하기 위해 브라질 행정부는 수송물류 인프라 구축에 정책 역점을 둘 것으로 전망됨

☐ 한국기업을 대상으로 한 FDI 관련 설문9)에 따르면, 브라질은 기업 활동의 경쟁력을 저하시키는 사회적 부대비용(Brazil Cost)이 투자 장애 요인으로 지적됨
  ○ 시장 진출시 느끼는 가장 큰 애로 사항으로 복잡한 조세제도와 세관 및 통관정책, 비효율적인 행정적 관행, 고용 및 노무관리, 환율 불안이 꼽혔음
  ○ 판매활동을 할 때 느끼는 가장 큰 애로 사항은 복잡한 세금제도와 고관세로 인한 비용 증가이며, 이밖에 대금회수 어려움, 가격조건 불리, 물류 및 A/S 고비용 등을 꼽은 기업도 있었음
  ○ 그 밖에 브라질의 복잡한 행정체계에 따른 불편과 브라질 시장에 대한 정보 부족도 투자시 고려사항이었음

☐ 우리나라의 대(對)브라질 투자(1968년~2010년)총액은 약 30억달러(신고기준)이며,

---

9) 브라질 투자기업 경영실태 분석, KOTRA 상파울루 KBC 사무소가 지난 2006년 12월에 브라질 진출 한국기업 37개사를 대상으로 실시함

주로 제조업과 광업 분야에 투자가 이뤄지고 있음
- ○ 최근 자동차와 제강업계가 브라질 현지 공장 설립을 확정하면서, 향후 투자가 더 활기를 띨 것으로 예상함

□ 브라질의 대(對)한국투자(1994년~2010년)는 4,200만달러(누계기준)로 상대적으로 미미하며, 업종별로는 서비스 분야가 97%(금액기준)로 대부분을 차지함

〈표 Ⅰ-9〉 한-브라질 연도별 투자 현황(신고기준)

(단위: 천달러, 건)

구 분		2005	2006	2007	2008	2009	2010	누계
對한 투자	금액	900	158	321	-	222	30,139	42,458
	건수	2	2	2	-	4	4	34
對브 투자	금액	248,799	207,716	214,418	739,840	114,486	757,777	2,998,676
	건수	29	22	35	37	30	57	313

주: 투자금액 누계기간은 對한국 투자(1994년-2010년), 대(對)브라질 투자(1968년-2010년)
자료: 한국수출입은행

3. 우리나라와 브라질의 교역 관계

□ 2010년 우리나라와 브라질의 총교역액은 약 125억달러를 기록, 교역규모는 전년 대비 37.7% 증가하였음
- ○ 수출은 77억 5,200만달러, 수입은 47억 1,200만달러로 집계됨
- ○ 2010년 대(對)브라질 전년 대비 수출·수입 증가율은 각 46%, 25.9%를 기록함

□ 한국의 총수출액 중 브라질로의 수출이 차지하는 비중은 전체의 1.66%를 차지하며, 최근 5년 사이 한국과 브라질 간 교역량은 약 2.5배 신장하였음
- ○ 브라질은 한국의 13위 수출국이며, 중남미 중 멕시코에 이어 제2대 교역국임
- ○ 최근 들어, 멕시코와의 수출 격차가 해마다 줄고 있어, 향후 중남미 제1위 시장으

로 부상할 것으로 전망됨

☐ 브라질 총수출액 중 한국으로 수출하는 비중은 전체의 1.86%로 전년 1.74% 대비 소폭 증가한 수치임
  ○ 우리나라에 대한 수출 증가율 41.5%는 브라질 전체 수출증가율 32%보다 높은 실적을 보임
  ○ 이에 따라, 우리나라는 2009년 브라질의 16위 수출국이었으나, 2010년 13위 수출국으로 올라섰음

☐ 우리나라에 대한 2010년 수입실적은 84.2억달러로 전년 대비 74.8% 증가하였으며, 동 증가율은 브라질 전체 수입증가율 42.2%보다 훨씬 높음
  ○ 브라질 총 수입액 중 한국이 차지하는 비중은 2009년 3.77%에서 2010년 4.64%로 증가하였음
  ○ 한국은 2009년 6위 수입국에서 2010년 5위 수입국으로 순위가 상승하였음
  ○ 우리나라로부터의 수입 증가율 74.8%는 30대 수입국가 중 인도(93.6%, 제10위 수입국)를 제외하고는 가장 높은 수치임

〈표 Ⅰ-10〉 최근 대(對)브라질 교역량 및 무역수지

(단위: 백만달러, %)

구분	2006	2007	2008	2009	2010
수출 (전년 대비 증감률)	3,063 (27.08)	3,487 (13.84)	5,926 (69.92)	5,311 (-10.37)	7,753 (45.97)
수입 (전년 대비 증감률)	2,707 (8.24)	2,794 (3.21)	4,380 (56.80)	3,744 (-14.54)	4,712 (25.87)
무역수지	357	693	1,545	1,567	3,040

자료: 한국수출입은행

☐ 교역품목에 있어서 2010년 MTI 3단위 기준 수출은 자동차가 27%, 수입은 철강이 전체의 38%로 각 가장 큰 비중을 차지함
  ○ 브라질의 자동차 초과수요로 인해 2010년 자동차 판매시장에서 차지하는 수입차

비중은 약 20%이며, 그 중 한국 자동차에 대한 인기가 높아 수입차 4대 중 1대가 한국산일 정도임
○ 브라질은 총 69종의 광물을 생산하고 있으며 2008년 광물 세계매장량 1위를 기록한 바 있음

〈표 Ⅰ-11〉 최근 대(對)브라질 10대 수출 품목

(단위: 천달러, %)

순위	2010년			2011년(1월~10월)		
	품목명	금액	전년 대비 증가율	품목명	금액	전년 대비 증가율
	총 계	7,752,579	46.0	총 계	10,395,826	61.2
1	자동차	2,113,976	65.5	선박해양구조물 및 부품	2,218,579	2,171.8
2	무선통신기기	977,067	-7.4	자동차	1,902,868	15.2
3	평판디스플레이 및 센서	497,342	84.0	석유제품	1,117,194	257.5
4	철강판	469,888	140.6	무선통신기기	1,000,082	14.7
5	영상기기	467,435	61.6	자동차부품	496,457	156.7
6	석유제품	312,760	-30.2	평판디스플레이 및 센서	475,218	9.2
7	자동차부품	283,585	427.3	영상기기	327,731	-20.9
8	건설광산기계	272,309	165.0	합성수지	272,477	38.4
9	컴퓨터	249,701	16.9	건설광산기계	255,943	14.3
10	합성수지	228,461	77.0	철강판	245,108	-41.2

주: MTI 3단위 기준
자료: 한국무역협회 무역통계

<표 Ⅰ-12> 최근 대(對)브라질 10대 수입 품목

(단위: 천달러, %)

순위	2010년			2011년(1월-10월)		
	품목명	금액	전년 대비 증가율	품목명	금액	전년 대비 증가율
	총 계	4,712,085	25.9	총 계	5,092,942	46.3
1	철광	1,801,037	67.0	철광	2,450,036	101.3
2	강반제품 및 기타철강제품	734,968	53.5	강반제품 및 기타철강제품	548,660	5.5
3	식물성물질	376,793	-33.1	기호식품	317,693	45.7
4	제지원료	315,442	123.8	식물성물질	252,977	-11.1
5	기호식품	287,842	20.2	합금철선철 및 고철	221,752	62.1
6	곡실류	233,167	-17.1	곡실류	220,603	11.4
7	기타농산물	186,586	23.3	기타농산물	182,466	34.4
8	합금철선철 및 고철	185,831	-19.2	동광	168,198	71.3
9	동광	98,209	10.4	제지원료	162,745	-41.6
10	육류	83,211	35.1	기타금속광물	90,433	204.5

주: MTI 3단위 기준
자료: 한국무역협회 무역통계

☐ 2010년 10대 수출 품목에 없었던 선박해양구조물 및 부품이 2011년 수출 품목 1위로 급부상하였고, 2010년 수출 품목 9위인 컴퓨터가 2011년 10위권에서 탈락함
  ○ 선박해양구조물 및 부품은 전년 대비 2,171.8% 급증하였고, 컴퓨터, 영상기기, 철강판의 수출비중은 감소함

☐ 대(對)브라질 주요 수입 품목은 철광, 강반제품 및 기타 철강 제품으로 2011년 기준 전체 수입 품목의 48%를 차지하며 전년 대비 46%의 증가율을 보임
  ○ 2011년에는 육류가 10대 수입 품목에서 탈락하는 대신, 기타금속광물이 새로이 10대 순위권에 진입함

4. 브라질의 자유무역협정(FTA, Free Trade Agreement) 현황 및 동향

□ 현 브라질 정부의 대외정책은 남미공동시장(Mercado Comun del Sur, 이하 MERCOSUR)[10]의 양적, 질적 성장과 남남협력의 강화에 초점을 두고 있음
  ○ 2011년 취임한 지우마(Dilma) 대통령은 중남미 통합이라는 목표를 향한 역내 지도력 강화에 주력할 것으로 예상됨
  ○ 중남미와 아프리카, 인도, 중국 등의 신규시장을 개척하기 위한 강력한 수출 드라이브 정책을 펼칠 것으로 예상됨

□ 브라질은 중남미 최대의 경제통합체인 MERCOSUR의 역내기능 강화에 무역정책의 초점을 두고 이에 대한 노력을 기울이고 있음
  ○ 중남미 전체 면적의 71%, 인구는 3억 6,500만명으로 중남미 전체인구의 절반가량, 경제규모는 4조달러에 달하는 매우 큰 시장임
  ○ MERCOSUR는 1985년 브라질과 아르헨티나 간의 경제협력 강화를 위한 이과수(Iguaçu) 선언으로부터 출발하여, 파라과이와 우루과이가 참여(1991)한 가운데 FTA로 출범함
  ○ 1994년 12월 무관세 거래에 합의(일부품목 제외), 1995년 1월 MERCOSUR 관세동맹으로 출범하였음. 이후 칠레(1996), 볼리비아(1997), 페루(2003)가 준회원국으로 가입함

□ 브라질은 MERCOSUR 이외에도 중남미 국가 중 멕시코, 안데스 공동체(CAN)[11]와 FTA를 체결함
  ○ 브라질-멕시코 양국 정부는 공동 성명(2010)에서, 멕시코와 800개 품목에 달하는 특혜관세협정을 체결하였으며, 관세 외에도 서비스, 투자, 정부 조달, 지적 소유권

---
10) 1995년 1월부로 아르헨티나, 우루과이, 파라과이와 MERCOSUR 관세동맹을 공식 출범시킴. 이후 베네수엘라(2007), 볼리비아(2008)도 회원국으로 받아들임
11) Comunidad Andiana로 콜롬비아, 에콰도르, 볼리비아, 페루 등 아메리카 4개국의 경제 협력체로 본부는 페루 리마에 있음

을 모두 포함할 것이라 밝힘
- ○ 브라질이 남미무역지대(South American Free Trade Area, SAFTA) 창설을 주창하면서 시발된 MERCOSUR와 CAN의 연합은 FTA(2008) 체결이라는 결과를 낳음

□ 미주자유무역지대(FTAA), MERCOSUR-EU 자유무역 재협정[12], 이스라엘과의 FTA(2010.4 발효) 등 타 경제블록과의 교역도 더욱 활발해질 전망임
- ○ 미주 자유무역지대(Free Trade Area of Americas, FTAA)는 쿠바를 제외한 아메리카 대륙의 모든 나라간의 자유무역협정을 맺기 위해 제안된 협정임
- ○ 2005년 아르헨티나 정상회의 이후 중단된 상태였으나, 최근 관세혜택 등 실효성으로 인한 재협정 논의가 진행중임
- ○ 브라질-EU FTA 체결을 위해, 브라질측은 농산물 시장 개방을 요구하고 있으며, EU측은 자동차 산업과 통신 등 서비스 시장 개방을 요구하고 있음
- ○ MERCOSUR 국가들의 對이스라엘 무역량은 전체 무역량의 1% 밖에 차지하지 않으나, 이스라엘과의 FTA는 MERCOSUR가 중남미 역외 국가와 최초로 체결한다는 점에서 의미가 있음

□ 인도-남아공 관세동맹(SACU) 및 걸프 협력협의회(GCC)와도 FTA 체결을 서두를 것으로 예상됨
- ○ 인도, 남아공, 브라질 3개국을 하나로 묶는 통상, 투자, 과학기술, 에너지 등 분야의 IBSA 포럼을 개최함
- ○ MERCOSUR 회원국과 남아공, 보츠나와, 레소토, 나미비아, 스와질란드 등 남아프리카 관세동맹, 인도 등이 참여하는 거대한 자유무역 지대가 탄생할 것으로 전망됨

□ 2010년 12월, 개발도상국간 특혜무역제도에 관한 협정(Global System of Trade Preferences Among Developing countries, 이하 GSTP)을 체결함
- ○ MERCOSUR 국가와 한국, 이집트, 인도네시아, 모로코, 말레이시아, 쿠바, 인도 등

---

[12] 1995년 말 MERCOSUR-EU 간 FTA체결 노력이 시도되었으며 수차례 협상실패 끝에 2005년부터 협상이 재개됐으며 2006년 브라질에서 협상을 가짐

11개 국가가 포함됨
- ○ GSTP 주요내용은 브라질을 포함한 MERCOSUR회원국이 총 수입품목수의 70%에 달하는 6,367개 품목에 대해 수입관세를 20% 인하시킨다는 것임
- ○ 주요 수혜품목은 브라질의 현지 생산이 약하거나 수입 수요가 높은 전기·전자부품, 기계류, 정밀기기, 철강 및 철강제품, 플라스틱제품, 선박, 철도차량, 유기화학품, 의료용품 등임13)

□ GSTP는 개도국 간에 체결된 역사적인 협정이며, 세계 무역 확대에 기여할 것으로 평가되고 있음
- ○ 동 협정은 2011년 말 발효를 앞두고 있으며, 수입관세 인하 대상 품목에 대해 높은 경쟁력을 보유하고 있는 한국의 경우 브라질과의 수출여건이 대폭 개선될 것으로 전망되고 있음

□ 향후 브라질의 무역정책은 양자 간 무역협정의 비중을 높이는 방향으로 전개될 것으로 추측됨
- ○ 세계무역기구(WTO), 도하 개발 어젠다(DDA) 등 다자 협상이 점점 더 어려워지고 있는 상황에서 무역상대국과 각료회담 형식으로 통상 분야의 협력방안을 협의하는 것에 중점을 둘 것으로 보임

□ 우리나라는 브라질과 양자 FTA협약은 없으나, 한-MERCOSUR 간 무역·투자 증진을 위한 공동협의체 설립 양해각서(MOU)에 서명한 바 있음
- ○ 4차례에 걸친 공동연구14) 끝에, 2009년 7월 한-MERCOSUR 간 무역과 투자의 증진을 위한 공동협의체 설립 양해각서(MOU)에 서명함

---

13) 부록 참조
14) ○ 2004.11.대통령 남미순방시 브라질 및 아르헨티나 정상과 공동연구 개시 합
  ○ 2005.5.4-5한-MERCOSUR TA 공동연구 제1차 회의 (아순시온, 파라과이)
  ○ 2005.8.17-18한-MERCOSUR TA 공동연구 제2차 회의 (서울)
  ○ 2006.3.2-3한-MERCOSUR TA 공동연구 제3차 회의 (부에노스아이레스, 아르헨티나)
  ○ 2006.10.31-11.01한-MERCOSUR TA 공동연구 제4차 회의 (브라질리아, 브라질)

<표 I-13> 브라질의 무역협정 체결 현황

대상국	협상 타결일자	추진현황
자유무역협정(FTA)		
이스라엘	2007.12.18	기체결
페루	2005.12.30	기체결
CAN	2004.10.18	기체결
볼리비아	1996.12.17	플라스틱, 광물 등 주요 협상 분야
칠레	1996.6.25	다품목
특혜무역협정(Preferential Trade Agreements)		
인도	2004.1.25	특혜무역협정
SACU	2004.12.16	특혜무역협정
Mercosur 이집트, 인도, 쿠바, 한국, 모로코, 인도네시아, 말레이시아 등 11개국	2010.12.16	개발도상국 간 특혜 무역 협정(GSTP)
기본 협력협정(Framework Agreements)		
CAN	2002.12.06	기본협력협정(ECA 56)
멕시코	2002.9.27	자동차분야 협정(ECA 55)
멕시코	2002.6.5	기본협력협정(ECA 54)
모로코	2004.11.26	기본협력협정
대상국	협상 타결일자	추진현황
이집트	2004.07.07	기본협력협정
GCC	2005.05.10	기본협력협정
요르단	2008.06.30	기본협력협정
파키스탄	2006.07.20	기본협력협정
진행 중인 FTA 및 향후 예상되는 FTA		
FTAA	-	2005.12월 아르헨티나 Mar del Plata 정상회의 이후 중단됨
GCC	-	현재 협상 재개 준비중임
EU	-	2004년 10월 이후 DDA 협상과 연계되어 협상이 중단되다 2010년 하반기부터 협상 재개 예정임
SCU, 인도	-	2007년 10월 제 2차 인도-브라질-남아공 정상회의 시 룰라 대통령이 제안함
기타		
브라질-멕시코	2002.7.3	부문별 특혜협정(식품, 의류, 광물 등) (MERCOSUR 회원국은 제3국과의 FTA 협상을 추진할 수 없으나 ALADI 회원국과는 양자협정 체결 가능함)

주: 1) CAN: 볼리비아, 콜롬비아, 에콰도르, 페루 등 4개국
    2) SACU: 남아프리카공화국, 보츠와나, 레소토, 나미비아, 스와질란드 등 5개국
    3) GCC: 사우디아라비아, 쿠웨이트, 바레인, 오만, 아랍에미리트연합, 카타르 등 6개국
자료: 브라질 개발상공부

5. 브라질의 AEO 유사 제도(Blue Line 제도)

☐ 브라질 공식명칭은 Linha Azul(영어로 Blue Line)로 안보제고와 신속한 통관을 위한 성실기업 우대제도임15)
  ○ WCO의 SAFE Framework의 일환으로 미국의 C-TPAT, EU지역의 AEO와 유사한 제도임
  ○ 공인대상은 수입자와 수출자 모두를 지정하고 있으나, 수입자 위주의 제도로 법 규준수와 안전관리를 목적으로 한 제도임

☐ 2010년 11월 기준 39개 업체가 공인기준에 따른 심사를 통해 동 제도에 대한 공인(Consórcio)을 받았음
  ○ 공인기준16)에 따라, 24개월간 법인으로 국가에 등록되어 신청서를 제출하는 시점을 기준으로 12개월 이전에 1천달러 금액 이상 거래가 있어야 함
  ○ 또한 주요 경제활동이 제조업, 광업, 가공, 광물의 추출을 지원하는 활동은 제외되며 의무준수, 서류, 세금 및 관세의 원활한 이행을 보장하기 위한 내부통제 감사보고서를 제출해야 함

☐ Blue Line 제도의 혜택은 세관검사 축소, 검사 시 우선검사, 세관 통관 등록 시 즉각 채널 확정, 통관 전 세관 보세창고에 항공화물 저장 불필요 등을 들 수 있음
  ○ 수출입물품 장치기간이 감소되거나 화물검사 없이 바로 통관되어 통관에 하루밖에 소요되지 않는 Green Channel을 이용할 수 있음
  ○ 국가에서 운영하는 공항 내 보관료를 할인 받을 수 있음
  ○ 물품통관 후 세관서류를 정정할 수 있어 오류발생시 수정 가능함
  ○ 안전한 물품 확보를 위한 재고가 감소되어 회사의 비용이 절감됨

☐ 만약 공인획득 후, 법률을 위반하면 5일간 혜택을 정지하거나 혜택의 지정을 취소 또

---
15) 2008년 제도가 만들어 졌으며, 2011년 현재 시행중임
16) 국세청의 준수사항 및 법률 제9430항, 제4544항에 의거

는 벌금이 부과됨
○ 취소되면 취소일로부터 2년이 경과되어야 재신청이 가능함
○ 재신청 시 모든 신청자격 요건을 구비하여 재신청해야 함

Ⅱ. 외국의 통상환경 보고서

1. World Bank의 『Doing Business 2011』

□ 세계은행(The World Bank)은 2004년부터 매년 '사업하기 좋은 나라(Ease of doing business)' 순위를 다양한 부문에 걸쳐 조사하여 『Doing Business』라는 보고서 명으로 발표하고 있음
  ○ 2011년에 발간된 당해 보고서는 2010년 한 해 동안 183개국에 대하여 부문별로 조사·평가한 내용을 수록함
  ○ 『Doing Business 2011』 보고서상 순위를 결정짓기 위하여 조사된 분야는 사업 개시(Starting a business), 건설 허가(Dealing with construction permit), 재산권 등록(Registering property), 신용 취득(Getting credit), 투자자 보호(Protecting investors), 세금 납부(Paying taxes), 무역(Trading across borders), 계약 이행(Enforcing contract) 및 폐업(Closing a business) 등 9개의 지표임
  ○ 2011년 보고서에 따르면, 종합적인 '사업의 용이성(Ease of Doing Business)' 순위에 있어 싱가포르가 1위를 차지하였으며, 우리나라는 16위에 랭크되었음

□ 당해 보고서의 무역 분야 순위는 수출입에 필요한 서류의 개수와 수출입 소요 일수 및 소요 비용 등을 산출하여 순위를 정하고 있으며, 필요서류가 적고 수출입 소요 기일이 짧을수록 더욱 높은 순위에 오르는 형식임
  ○ 무역 분야에서 우리나라는 2010년 보고서에 이어 2011년 보고서에서도 8위를 기록하며 상위권을 유지하였음

□ 『Doing Business 2011』에서 브라질은 전반적인 사업의 용이성에 있어 전체 조사국인 183국 중 127위에 올랐으며 이는 작년대비 3계단 하락한 순위임

○ 브라질은 법인 설립에 평균 152일, 각종 인허가 취득에 평균 460일이 걸리는 것으로 나타남
○ 이는 관련 법규의 처리 속도가 느리고 복잡한 조세체계 문제 등이 개선되지 않고 있기 때문임

〈표 Ⅱ-1〉 브라질의 무역 분야 순위 비교

구분	브라질	East Asia & Pacific	OECD	인도	중국	한국
수출필요서류(개수)	8	6.4	4.4	8	7	3
수출소요시간(일)	13	22.7	10.9	17	21	8
수출소요비용(달러/컨테이너)	1,790	889.8	1,058.7	1,055	500	790
수입필요서류(개수)	7	6.9	4.9	9	5	9
수입소요시간(일)	17	24.1	11.4	20	24	7
수입소요비용(달러/컨테이너)	1,730	934.7	1,106.3	1,025	545	790
무역분야 순위	114	-	-	100	50	8

자료: The World Bank, 『Doing Business 2011』 RANK

□ 부문별 주요 지표 중 무역분야(Trading Across Borders)에서 브라질은 전체 183국 중 114위를 기록함
  ○ 브라질에서의 해상 수출 비용은 컨테이너 당 약 1,790달러의 금액이 소요되는 것으로 조사되었으며, 수출에 필요한 서류는 8가지, 서류 준비를 비롯하여 수출 통관 및 국내 운송, 항만에서의 업무를 포함, 수출에 총 13일이 소요되는 것으로 조사되었음
  ○ 해상 수입에 있어서 컨테이너 당 약 1,730달러의 금액이 소요되며, 수입에 필요한 서류는 8가지이고, 서류 준비를 포함한 수입통관 및 국내 운송, 항만 업무를 포함하여 총 17일이 소요됨

□ 브라질 무역분야 순위가 낮은 원인은 수출입소요비용이 타국대비 월등히 높기 때문임
  ○ 수출필요서류 및 시간은 경제규모 및 성장력이 유사한 신흥경제국과 큰 차이가

없으나 수출입 소요비용이 중국의 약 3배, 인도의 약 1.6배인 점을 감안하면 경쟁력이 떨어짐을 확인할 수 있음

〈표 Ⅱ-2〉 브라질 수출입 소요 기간 및 비용

구분	수출		수입	
	소요기간(日)	비용(달러)	소요기간(日)	비용(달러)
서류준비	6	490	8	330
세관통관	3	200	4	250
항만(터미널)	3	250	3	300
내륙운송	1	850	2	850
합계	13	1,790	17	1,730

자료: The World Bank, 『Doing Business 2011』, Brazil

☐ 최근에는 이러한 무역환경상의 애로사항을 개선하기 위해 정부차원의 노력이 예상되고 있음
  ○ 국제기구나 국제 경영 컨설팅 업체로부터 '브라질 코스트' 개선에 대한 주문이 이어지면서 정부부처 간 협력방안이 논의되고 있음

2. 미국 국별 무역장벽 보고서(National Trade Estimate Report on Foreign Trade Barriers: NTE 보고서)

☐ 국별 무역장벽보고서는 1974년 통상법(Trade Act of 1974) 제181조에 근거하여 미국 무역 대표부(USTR)가 작성, 매년 3월 말 의회에 제출하는 연례 보고서임
  ○ 이 보고서는 미국 업계의 의견과 해외 주재 미국 대사관의 보고서와 관련 정부 부처의 의견 등을 기초로 작성됨
  ○ 2011년 보고서는 미국의 62개 주요 교역국 및 경제권의 무역과 투자 장벽에 대해 포괄적으로 기술하고 있음[17]

가. 관세분야

☐ 브라질의 관세품목은 총 8자리 숫자에 대해 10,000여 개 품목으로 분류되어 있고 관세율은 0~35%까지 분포되어 있음
  ○ 모든 관세는 종가관세(ad valorem tariffs)이며, 일부 통신제품을 제외하고는 CIF 가격을 기준으로 부과됨

☐ 브라질의 평균관세는 11.6%(2010)로 과거에 비해서는 많이 낮아졌으나, 평균양허관세율은 31.4%로 상당히 높은 편임[18]
  ○ 1990년에 브라질 평균관세는 32%였으며, 다른 국가와 마찬가지로 원자재(8~9%)나 반가공품(11.9%)은 완성품(평균 15.8%)에 대해 더 낮은 관세율을 적용 하고 있음
  ○ 하지만 양허관세율과 적용세율의 큰 편차로, 불확실성이 증대됨
    − 만약 적용세율을 조절할 수 있는 권한을 가진 브라질 정부가 세수확대를 위해 적용세율을 높일 시 무역업자의 예기치 못한 피해가 우려됨
  ○ 실제로, 2007년 이후로 브라질 적용관세율은 평균 3%씩 오르고 있고 자동차, 기계부품, 전자제품, 화학품, 플라스틱류, 직물 및 의류 분야에 종사하는 업체에 악재로 작용하고 있음

☐ 브라질은 수입품에 대해 연방세와 주세를 이중으로 부과하며, 조세시스템이 복잡하므로 이로 인해 진출기업들이 어려움을 겪음
  ○ 조세시스템으로 인해, 브라질로 수입되는 제품의 경우 실제 지불되는 비용이 두 배가 되는 격으로 미국 회사들이 브라질에서 사업을 운영하는데 있어 겪는 큰 어려움 중 하나로 지목되고 있음

---

17) 2010년부터 SPS(동식물 위생 및 검역) 및 TBT(무역에 대한 기술 장벽) 관련 사안은 NTE 보고서와 별도로 발표하고 있음
18) 한국수출입은행 해외자료실, KOTRA 상파울루 무역관

□ 특송을 통해 개인에게 수입되는 대부분의 제조소매제품에는 60%의 수입비례세가 적용됨
  ○ 일반적으로 RTS(Simplified Tax Regime)라 불리는 단순화된 통관 절차를 통해 처리되나 3,000달러가 넘는 제품은 이 체계를 통해 수입될 수 없음에 유의해야 함

나. 수입허가 · 관세평가 · 무역조치

□ 수입허가서(Import Licensing) 취득을 위해 모든 수입업자는 대외무역국(SECEX)의 전산화된 무역자동화시스템19)(이하 SISCOMEX)에 접속하여 등록해야함
  ○ SISCOMEX 등록구비서류는 최소자본 준비 등을 포함해 요구사항이 많은 편임

□ 식품을 비롯하여 위생 및 건강과 관련된 제품은 위생관리국(Ministry of Health's Regulatory Agency, 이하 ANVISA)의 허가가 필요함
  ○ ANVISA는 의약품 안전 여부를 확인하고 판매허가서를 발행하는 기관임
  ○ 허가 취득 기간이 길고(6개월~2년) 절차 및 서류 구비가 까다로워 기업들이 브라질 현지 투자를 망설이게 하는 원인임
  ○ 특히 2007년 이후 의료용구를 등록하려는 기업들은 제품의 가격정보를 제공하도록 하여 수입규제 장치로서 작용하고 있음

□ 브라질 관세당국은 관세평가(Customs Valuation)에 있어 소매가보다 더 높은 과세가격(dutiable value)을 적용하는 사례 많음
  ○ 따라서 회사에서 인식하고 있는 거래가격(transaction value) 보다 책정되는 관세가 더 높음

□ 수입금지 품목은 중고품으로 중고차, 의류 등이며 국내 반입은 거의 불가능함

---

19) 1997년부터 운영되고 있으며, 개발상공부의 무역국(Secretaria de Comercio Exterior)에 등록해야지만 이용할 수 있음. 2007년에 시스템을 업그레이드하여 무역등록 절차 이행에 소요되는 기간을 단축하고 수입세, 공업제품세, SISCOMEX 사용료를 이 시스템을 통해 산정하도록 개선함

- ○ 수입 금지는 주로 해당 품목의 국내 생산을 장려하려는 목적으로 정부가 취하는 조치임
- ○ 마나우스 자유무역지대로 수입되는 중고 기계나 설비에 대해서는 자국산업 보호에 대한 타당성이 인정되므로 규제를 완화하고 있음

다. 수출 보조금

□ 브라질은 수출지원을 위해 수출보조금, 수출금융 및 조세감면을 시행하고 있음
- ○ 브라질경제사회개발은행(BNDES)은 브라질 기업에게 장기 저리의 금융을 제공하고 있음
- ○ 헤알화 강세로 타격받는 섬유, 가구, 장식용 석재, 목재, 가죽, 중장비, 의류 자동차 및 자동차부품을 취급하는 수출기업을 위한 조세감면 조치를 부활시킴[20]

□ 소프트웨어와 정보기술을 수출하는 브라질 기업의 경우 수출비중이 연간수입의 80% 이상을 차지하면 수입품에 대한 사회보장세를 감면받을 수 있음
- ○ 2005년 도입된 IT수출지원프로그램(REPES)에 의해서 시행됨

□ 영업기간 3년 이상 기업 중 수출비중이 총소득의 80% 이상을 상회하는 수출기업의 경우, 수입하는 기계류에 대한 사회보장세를 감면받음
- ○ 2005년 도입된 수출기업 자본재 지원 프로그램(RECAP)에 의해서 시행됨

라. 정부 조달

□ 브라질은 WTO 회원국이나, 정부조달 협정에는 가입하지 않아 외국기업이 동 시장에 참여하는 것은 사실상 어려움

□ 통신, 컴퓨터, 소프트웨어 등 IT 관련제품, 에너지 및 건설 분야에서 불투명한 가격 및

---

[20] 2007년 10월

기술산정 방식, 외국기업에 대한 자본참여 제한을 두고 있어 시장접근이 다소 힘듦

□ 최근 정부조달 사업의 무차별 정책 도입 확산으로 인해 정부조달 시장의 여건이 다소 개선되고 있음
  ○ 국제개발은행 차관과 관련된 구매입찰의 경우 브라질 내에 법인을 세우면 외국기업에게도 개방하여 입찰에 부치는 등 정부조달시장의 기회가 생겨나고 있음
  ○ 특히 주정부 차원에서 산업 활동 지원을 위한 인프라 관련 국제 입찰이 늘어나고 있음

〈표 Ⅱ-3〉 기타 브라질 비관세 장벽

유형	내용
기술장벽(6)	- 중고기계, 중고 자동차, 중고 의료장비 등의 수입을 엄격히 제한(예외 인정) - 전기 전자 및 IT 제품 통관시 브라질 지적재산권협의회에 등록할 것을 요구하고 등록과정에서 수입제품에 대한 정보공개 요구가 지나쳐 영업비밀 침해가 우려됨 - 브라질 도량형 및 품질 관리기관인 INMETRO를 통해 독자적인 자동차 타이어 인증제도를 적용함으로써 국제표준을 받은 자동차 타이어 업체 및 수입업체에게 부담을 줌 - 유사상품 존재시 수입승인을 못 받는 등 IT 제품에 대한 장벽 - 국제표준과 동떨어진 비합리적인 기준 적용, 자국만의 인증을 요구, 인증비용 과도 책정 등 불필요한 비용 유발 - 외국인 투자기업에 대해 자국산 원자재 사용을 강요함으로써 품질이 떨어지는 원자재를 사용해 전반적 품질 저하 초래(일정 비율 이상의 국산부품 이용법: PPB존재)
위생검역(3)	- 농산물, 식물, 과일류에 대한 수입검역 강화 - 포장용 나무상자를 이용한 선적품에 위생증명 요구 - 생명공학 이용 제품에 대한 생산, 판매, 유통 엄격 규제
투자장벽(3)	- 주재원 파견 및 지사 설립에 관한 제한 - 전략산업 분야에 대한 투자 규제 - 기타 투자 및 진입관련 비관세장벽 (부동산 취득 및 사용제한, 금융 및 외환 등)
기타(5)	- 과다한 수수료와 내국세 부과 - 수출보조금 지급으로 내국산업 보호 추진 - 정부구매 분야에 대한 규제 - 지적재산권 보호체계 미비 - 각종 서비스 분야 진입 장벽(통신, 영상, 보험, 금융 등)

자료: 외교통상부, 외국의 통상환경, 2010

Ⅲ. 브라질의 통관 환경[21]

1. 통관 행정 개요

가. 통관 행정 조직

□ 수입허가, 통관, 외환관리 등 수출입 업무는 국가통화위원회(CMN)[22]를 중심으로 개발상공부(MDIC)[23] 산하 대외무역국(SECEX)[24], 재무부(RF)[25] 산하 연방 세무국(RFB)[26], 중앙은행(BCB)[27]이 각각 나누어 관리하고 있음
  ○ 개발상공부는 대외무역에 관한 정부 주무부서가 되며 그 산하 대외무역국이 재화나 서비스의 대외거래를 총 관장하는 정책 실무를 담당함
  ○ 재무부 산하 연방세무국은 세금징수를 포함한 관세행정을 책임지고 있음
  ○ 중앙은행은 대외거래에 관한 모든 금융활동을 감독 및 통제하는 역할을 수행함

---

21) 브라질 국가통화위원회, 브라질 개발상공부, 브라질 재무부, 브라질 중앙은행, 브라질 통계청
22) National Monetary Council
23) Ministerio de Desenvolvimento, Industria e Comercio Exterior
24) Secretaria de Comercio Exterior
25) Ministerio da Fazenda
26) Receita Federal do Brasil
27) Banco Central do Brasil

[그림 Ⅲ-1] 통관 행정 조직

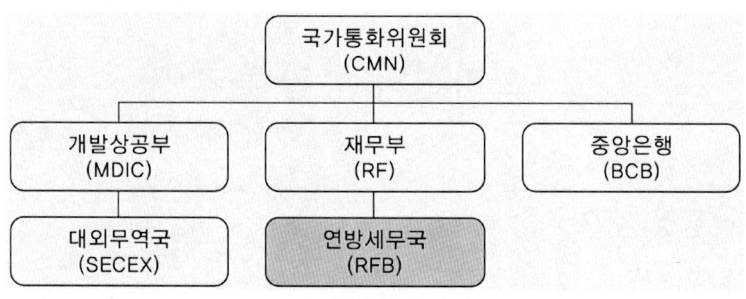

□ 우리나라의 관세청과 유사한 기능을 담당하는 기관은 재무부 산하 연방 세무국으로, 독립기관이며 관세와 내국세 문제를 담당함
   ○ 국경에서 수출입물품에 대해 관세 부과 및 징수
   ○ 법에 의한 벌금, 부과금 등의 부과, 안보를 위한 조치
   ○ 자국법에 따른 국제무역의 통제
   ○ 품목분류와 가격에 대한 심사
   ○ 밀수 및 부정무역 차단

□ 대외무역에 종사하는 모든 수입업체는 대외무역국이 주관하는 SISCOMEX에 무역업 등록을 하도록 되어 있음
   ○ 대외무역국에 의해 원산지증명을 발급받을 수 있음
   ○ 시스템에 등록을 하면 무역업자로 등록이 되며 이후 수출입절차를 전산화할 수 있음

[그림 Ⅲ-2] 브라질 연방세무국 조직도

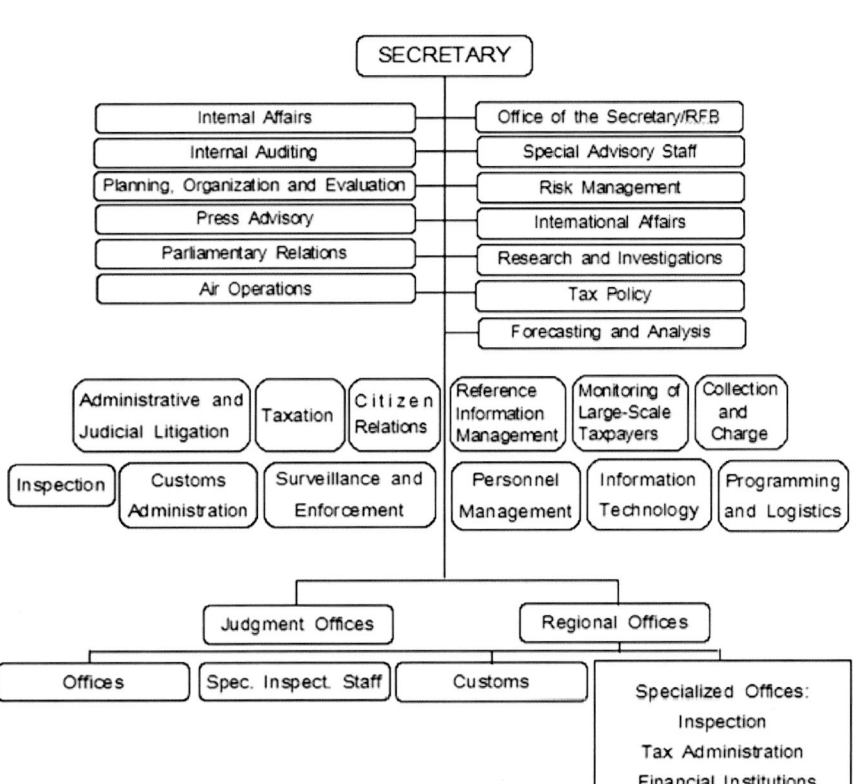

나. 관세[28]

□ 브라질은 MERCOSUR의 일원으로 회원국이 공동으로 사용하는 수입관세(II)[29], 공업제품세(IPI)[30], 유통세(ICMS)[31], 사회보장세(FIS/Cofins)[32]가 누진 적용됨

---

28) 부록 참조
29) Imposto de Importacao: II
30) Imposto sobre Produto Industrializado: IPI
31) Imposto sobre Circulação de Mercadorias e Serviços: ICMS

○ 수입관세는 CIF 가격을 기준으로 책정되며, MERCOSUR 형성 후 대외공동관세(Tarifa Externa Comun, 이하 TEC)를 사용함
○ 공업제품세, 유통세, 사회보장세는 부가가치세 원칙을 따름

□ 행정단위에 따라 수입관세, 공업제품세, 사회보장세는 연방세로 분류되어 연방법에 따라 과세되며, 유통세는 주(州)세로 주마다 세율이 달리 책정됨

1) 수입관세(II)

□ 연방 정부에서 관장하는 특별세로, TEC가 적용되며 수입관세 범위는 0~35%임
  ○ 2010년 기준 브라질의 평균 수입관세는 11%로 과거(1990년 32%)에 비해서 대폭 낮아짐
  ○ 다른 국가와 마찬가지로 원자재(평균 8~9%)나 반가공품(평균 11.9%)은 완성품(평균 15.8%)보다 더 낮은 관세율을 적용 하고 있음

2) 공업제품세(IPI)

□ 연방세이며, 대부분의 국내 생산품과 외국 수입품에 대해 적용되며, 일반적으로 수입관세가 높은 품목은 공업제품세도 높은 경향이 있음
  ○ 국내 생산품의 경우 제조업체의 판매시, 수입품의 경우 통관시에 적용됨

□ 공업제품세의 범위는 0~365.6%까지 다양하나, 평균적으로 0~20%임
  ○ 공업제품세는 제품의 종류에 따라 큰 차이가 있음
  ○ 담배나 향수 등 국민생활 필수품이 아닌 경우는 과세율이 높고 생필품은 과세율이 낮음
  ○ 예를 들어 운송수단은 35%, 주류는 60%, 담배는 330%가 적용됨

---

32) Programa de Integração Social: PIS - Importação/ Contribuição Social para o Financiamento da Seguridade Social: Cofins - Importação

□ 수입품을 판매할 경우 공업제품세 금액 공제 가능함
  ○ 수입품을 최종 소비자에게 판매할 때 공업제품세 금액만큼을 면제받게 되어, 결론적으로 수입업자가 부담하는 비용이 아님

□ 공업제품세는 행정부령 발표시 즉각 시행이 가능해, 정책이 빠르고 효과가 직접적이라는 면에서 연방정부의 조세정책에 자주 사용됨
  ○ 다른 조세와 달리 연방정부가 행정부령[33])을 통해 결정할 수 있기 때문에 연방의 회의 개입 여지가 없으며, 행정부령을 발표함과 동시에 바로 시행이 가능함

3) 유통세(ICMS)

□ 유통세는 수입품에 적용하는 주(州) 부가가치세로 주정부의 가장 큰 세수원임
  ○ 1965년 제정되어 연방의 각 주와 브라질리아 연방 특구가 징세 권한을 보유하고 있음
  ○ 제품 및 서비스가 판매될 때 부과되는 세금으로 세금수준이 주별로 상이하며 각 주의 최대 수입원임

□ 주 유통세는 일반적으로 주에 따라 7%, 12%, 또는 18% 가 부과됨
  ○ 공업제품세와 같이 수입품이 통관될 때 과세되며, 수입업자가 최종 소비자에게 판매할 때 공제할 수 있음
  ○ 상파울루 주의 경우 통상 18%가 부과되지만, 품목에 따라 감면 혜택을 받는 경우도 있음
    - 일부 기업들은 유통세가 낮은 주로 생산 및 판매거점을 옮기거나 유통세가 낮은 주로부터 제품을 구입하는 사례도 있음
  ○ 수입품 외에 상품의 유통, 서비스 제공, 주간(州間) 운송 시에 부과되며 수입품에 대해서도 마찬가지로 적용됨

---

33) Decreto Executivo; Executive Decree

4) 사회보장세(PIS/Cofins)

□ 사회보장세는 연방보완법34)에 의해 사회통합기여세(PIS)와 사회복지기여금 (COFINS)으로 나뉘며, 모든 법인에 대해 부과됨
  ○ PIS/COFINS는 2004년에 시행되었고, SIMPLES의 적용을 받는 영세 기업에 대해서는 면제 혜택을 줌35)
  ○ PIS는 1.65%로 일괄 적용되고 있고, COFINS 기준세율은 7.6%임

〈표 Ⅲ-1〉 브라질 수입시 과세되는 최종가격 도출 예

CIF 가격	100	달러
수입관세(I.I)	14	%
공업세(IPI)	15	%
유통세(ICMS)	18	%
사회 보장세(PIS/Cofins)	9.25	%
적용 시		
CIF 가격	100.00	달러
수입관세(I.I)	14.00	%
수입관세 산정가격	14.00	달러
공업세 산정기준(CIF+I.I)	114.00	달러
공업 제품세(IPI)	15.00	%
공업 제품세 산정가격	17.10	달러
유통세 산정기준(CIF+I.I+IPI)	131.10	달러
새로운 유통세 산정기준 [(CIF+I.I+IPI)*100]/(100-ICMS)	159.88	달러
유통세(ICMS)	18.00	%
유통세 산정가격	28.78	달러
사회 보장세 산정기준(CIF+I.I+IPI+ICMS)	188.66	달러
사회 보장세(PIS/Cofins)	9.25	%
사회 보장세 산정가격(수입자 부담)	17.45	달러
최종가격	177.33	달러

자료: KOTRA KBC 상파울루

---

34) Lei Complementar 07/1970
35) SIMPLES는 법률 제9317호(Lei 9317/96)로 제정된 영세기업을 위한 조세통합법임

다. 관세특혜제도

1) 환급/감면

☐ 수출용 원재료에 대한 관세, 부가세 및 내국세를 면세해 줌
   ○ 수입관세, 공업제품세, 주 유통세, 사회보장세 모두 해당됨
   ○ 주정부 관세특혜제도(FUMDAP)를 통해 환급 제도를 실시하고 있음

2) 마나우스(Manaus) 자유무역지대

☐ 1967년 아마존지역 종합개발 및 고용증대를 위해 설립된 자유무역지대로 브라질 북부 최대 공업지대임
   ○ 마나우스는 아마존(Amazon)강과 네그로(Negro)강 접점에 위치해 있는 Amazon 주의 수도임
   ○ 현재 약 600개가 넘는 외국인 투자기업이 진출해 있음

☐ 지역 내에서 소비 또는 제조되는 물품에 대해 수입관세, 공업제품세, 사회보장세가 면제되며, 브라질 타 지역에서 마나우스로 부품반입시 주유통세가 환급됨
   ○ 이 외에도 공단 입주업체에 대해 10년간 재산세, 환경세, 법인세 면제 또는 감면 혜택을 주고 있음
   ○ 주로 전자제품 업체들이 수입된 자재로 조립 및 가공하여 내수시장에 공급함
   ○ 마나우스 공단에 입주하기 위해서는 최소국내생산 요건의 만족과 SUFRAMA(마나우스 경제특구 관리청) 승인이 필요함

☐ 감세혜택 이외에도 사업비용 혜택 및 물류시설의 편의를 제공하고 있음
   ○ 별도의 입주비용 없고, 공장 설립시 약 1달러/m^2로 매우 저렴한 비용이 듬
   ○ 운송 및 물류에 있어 아마존강은 수심이 깊어 컨테이너선이 공단지역까지 들어올 수 있도록 바로 연결되어 있으며, 창고, 컨테이너 야적장 등이 갖춰져 있어 물류시

설도 충분한 편임

3) 보세창고(EADI)

☐ 세금 미납상태에서 보세창고에 물품 장치 및 수입신고 수리 후 반출 가능함
  ○ 물품이 도착하면 보세창고로 입고되는데, 이때 세금 미납상태에서도 보세창고에 물품을 장치 가능하며, 수입신고 수리 후 반출 가능함
  ○ 해상은 도착 전 48시간, 항공은 도착 후 24시간 이내에 보세운송 신고시 현도배정

2. 수입 통관 절차

[그림 Ⅲ-3] 브라질의 수입 통관 절차

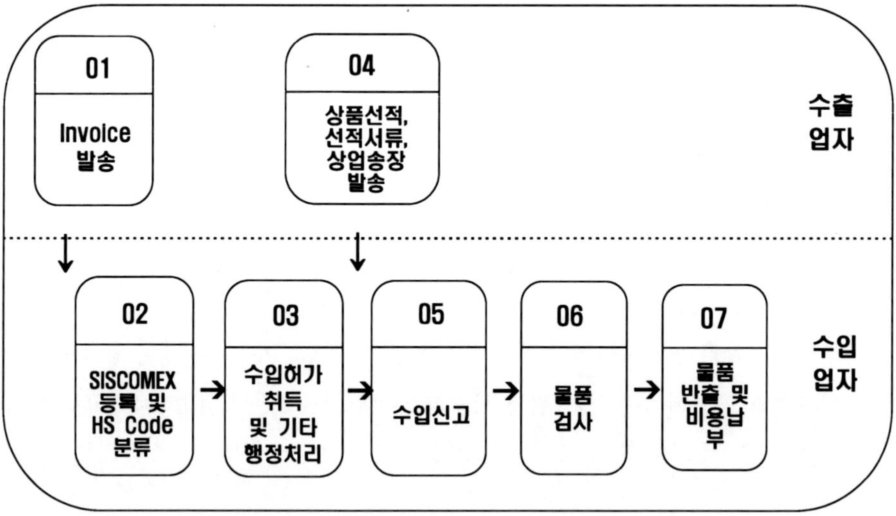

```
01          04                              수출
Invoice    상품선적,                         업자
발송        선적서류,
           상업송장
           발송
---------------------------------------------------
02         03         05      06        07         수입
SISCOMEX   수입허가    수입신고  물품     물품        업자
등록 및    취득                 검사     반출 및
HS Code   및 기타                        비용납
분류       행정처리                       부
```

☐ 브라질 수입통관 절차는 ① SISCOMEX 등록 및 HS Code(NCM) 분류 → ② 수입허가 취득 및 기타 행정처리 → ③ 수입신고 → ④ 물품검사 → ⑤ 물품 반출 및 비용납부 순서로 이루어지며, 통관은 통상적으로 2주 정도 소요됨

가. 수입허가

□ 수입물품의 통관은 ① 수입허가(Licença de Importação, 이하 LI)가 불필요하여 자동 수입신고 되는 경우와, ② 수입허가가 필요한 경우로 나눠서 진행됨
  ○ ① LI 자동 발급 품목의 경우, 수입허가는 수입신고시 자동으로 발급됨
  ○ ② LI 자동발급 불가품목의 경우, 수입신고 전에 수입허가서를 받아야 함

□ LI 필요 여부는 수입품의 종류나 성격에 따라 달라지며, 관련당국의 허가가 필요한 경우 승인절차를 거쳐 통관이 결정됨
  ○ LI 자동발급이 불가한 제품은 사전통제 및 수입제한 품목으로 인간 및 동·식물에 피해를 주는 제품, 환경문제를 야기할 수 있는 제품, 할당관세 적용 물품임

□ 관세환급, BEFIEX, CNPq, ZFM 제도를 통해 수입되는 제품도 사전 수입허가가 필요함[36]
  ○ SECEX의 특별관리를 받는 제품이나 다른 정부기관의 허가를 취득해야 하는 물품이 이에 해당함
  ○ 수입 자동 허가 제외 품목(선적 전 수입허가서 요망 품목)
    - 관세 환납 대상 품목
    - 관세 감면 혜택 대상 품목
    - 수입 쿼터 대상 품목(섬유, 자동차 등)
    - 수출용 자재로 수입되는 품목들에 대한 관세 감면 혜택 제도인 BEFIEX 프로그램을 적용 받고 있는 회사들이 수입하는 품목
    - 국가 과학 기술 위원회의 사전 허가가 요구되는 품목
    - 모든 중고 상품
    - 국내에서 제조되지 않는다는 사실의 입증이 필요한 품목(중고 기계 및 장비)
    - 이라크로부터 수입되는 품목
    - 브라질의 무역자유지대에 위치하고 있는 회사들로부터 수입되는 품목
    - 무가 상품(샘플, 기부품, 일시적 체류, 인체 및 동물 연구 용품, 정신질환 치료

---
[36] SISCOMEX 행정조치표에 열거

제, 군수품, 방사능물질, 원유, 원유가공품, 환경유해물질, 항공기 등)

□ 수입허가서가 불필요한 경우, 해당 관리국의 사전 검사가 불필요하며 자동수입신고 처리되어 통관 완료됨

□ 수입허가서가 필요한 경우, 즉 수입신고 이전에 수입을 위한 브라질 당국의 사전 허가가 필요한 경우에는 선적 전 수입허가서를 발급받아야 함
  ○ 수입허가서는 농림부, 보건부, 환경부 등 수입품에 따른 담당기관에서 발급되며, 위생과 안전에 관련한 허가를 포함해 기술 인증 등 상이한 내용을 포함함

[그림 Ⅲ-4] 자동발급(수입허가 불필요) 및 자동발급 불가(수입허가 필요)물품의 통관 절차

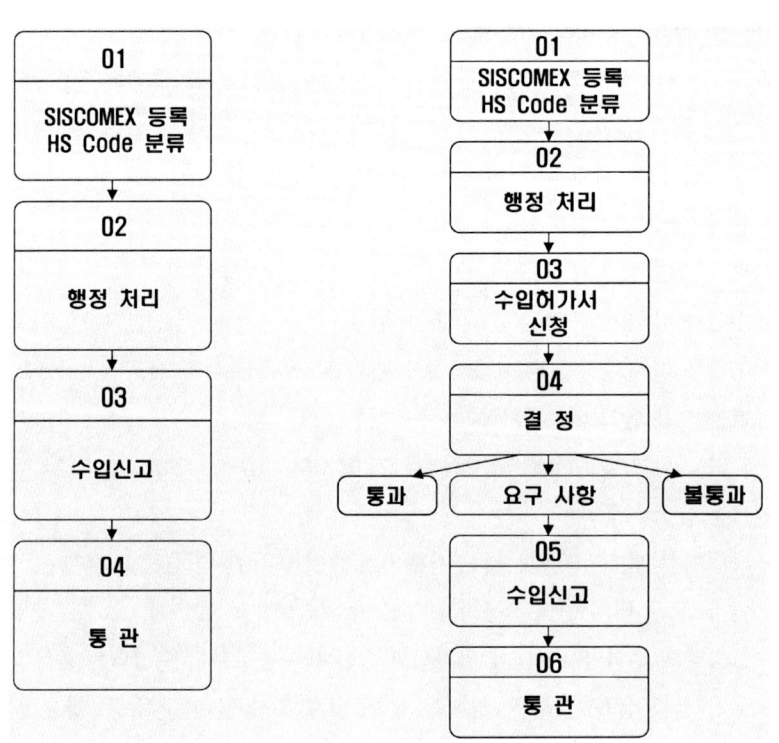

자료: KOTRA/OIS 브라질 통관(2009)

나. 수입신고

☐ 수입자는 화물도착 전까지 수입신고(Declaração de Importação, DI)의 절차를 밟아야 함
  ○ 수입신고란, 세관에 수입하고자 하는 의사를 표시하는 행위를 말함
  ○ 신고자란, 수입을 하기 위하여 그의 명의로 세관에 신고서를 제출하는 자이며 신고 시기는, 화물이 보세구역 또는 장치장소에 반입된 후임

☐ 수입신고에 필요한 기본서류는 수입허가증(L/I), 선하증권(B/L), 상업송장(C/I), 적하목록(P/L)이며 의약품, 농수산물 등 화물의 성격에 따라 기타 서류 및 인허가를 요하기도 함
  ○ 정확한 원산지와 가격이 기재된 상업송장이 통상 5부 필요함
  ○ 서류는 영어 혹은 포르투갈어로 작성해야 함
  ○ 상업송장이 통관서류와 일치하지 않는 등 서류미비로 인한 관세법 위반시 1~5% 내의 관세와 동일한 금액의 벌금을 부과함

다. 물품검사 후 화물 출고

☐ 수입신고를 완료하면 SISCOMEX는 자동적으로 세관반출을 위한 화물검사를 지시하며, 화물검사는 녹색, 황색, 적색, 회색 4가지 채널로 분류됨
  ○ 녹색 : 자동 통관
  ○ 황색 : 서류심사
  ○ 적색 : 서류심사 및 화물 검사
  ○ 회색 : 서류·화물의 정밀검사 및 수입회사 조사

☐ 자동통관인 녹색채널을 제외한 기타 세관검사는 통관대기 건수, 현물 수량, 세관 인력 상황 등에 따라 통관 소요시간이 결정됨
  ○ 최대 90일 통관 지연 시 압류 처리됨

○ 수입자가 연방 세무국에 직접 수입서류를 제출해야 함

[그림 Ⅲ-5] 수입신고 후 물품검사 과정

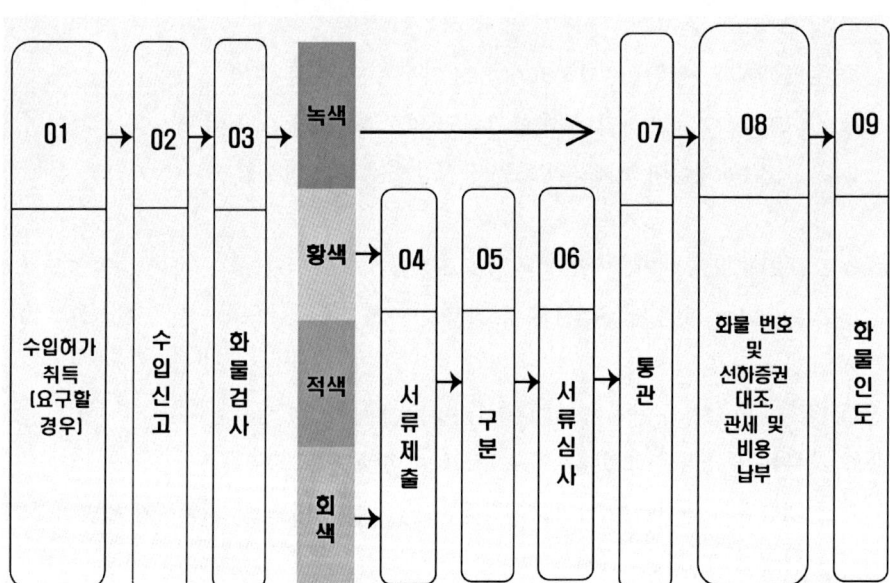

자료: KOTRA/OIS 브라질 통관, 2009

3. 수출 통관 절차

가. SISCOMEX 업체 등록 단계

□ 대외무역국(SECEX)의 무역자동화시스템(SISCOMEX)을 통해 업체 및 수출정보를 등록함
  ○ 판매 등록(Sale Registration): 수출등록 전에 이뤄져야 하는 수출품의 기본적인 물품거래 판매정보를 등록하는 단계임(Secex 법령 36/07번 참조)
  ○ 신용 등록(Credit Registration): 수출물품의 자금정보를 등록하는 단계로, 지불기간이 180일 이상으로 정해져 있을 때, 동일기간 혹은 더 짧은 기간에 이자가 발생

했을 때 의무 등록
- ○ 수출 등록(Export Registration): 상업, 자금, 재정에 관한 전반적인 정보를 등록하는 단계로 반드시 수출신고 전에 이뤄져야 함. SISCOMEX상의 정보기재 표를 작성하면 대외무역국 및 관련부처의 심사에 따라 등록유효, 등록유효연기로 분류됨

나. 수출신고 단계

- □ SISCOMEX를 통해 수출신고절차를 완료함
  - ○ 수출신고 필요서류는 상업송장, 선하증권, 적하목록, 필요시 각종 허가·등록증 등 임

다. 물품검사·심사 단계 후 통관 완료

- □ 수출신고가 접수되면 물품은 3가지 채널로 분류되어 검사 및 심사의 단계를 거치게 됨
  - ○ 녹색 : 자동수리됨
  - ○ 황색 : 관련서류 제출 후 수리됨
  - ○ 적색 : 관련서류 제출 및 물품검사 후 수리됨
  - ○ 회색 : 서류·화물의 정밀검사 및 수입회사 조사

- □ 모든 심사가 끝나면, 통관이 완료되며 물품을 선적하여 수출함

Ⅳ. 통관 절차별 고려 사항

〈표 Ⅳ-1〉 브라질 통관 절차별 유의사항

단계	유의 사항
1. SISCOMEX 등록 및 NCM 분류	○ SISCOMEX에 수입자 등록을 해야만, 수입허가 자동발급 가능여부, 수입신고, 비용납부 등의 통관을 진행할 수 있으므로 등록이 의무적 ○ HS Code에 부합하는 정확한 NCM을 기재
2. 수입허가 취득 및 기타 행정처리	○ 세관별 상이한 업무 방식으로 인해 동일 제품에 대해 다른 관세율을 적용 받는 등의 문제 발생 ○ 선적서류 작성 시 제품의 기술설명과 같은 item description 필요 ○ 사전승인이 필요한 물품의 경우 반드시 선적 전에 브라질 당국의 승인 필요
3. 수입신고	○ 수입신고 시 필요한 기본서류(C/I, P/L)의 요구사항을 명확히 확인해야 하고, 물품 정보와 동일하게 기재 ○ 일부 서류에 대해서는 포르투갈어 서류만 허가하므로 유의
4. 물품 검사	○ 현물 검색 시 물품포장 별로 Packing List나 내용물에 대한 표시가 없을 경우 전수 검사를 시행하므로 주의 ○ 저가신고(Under Invoicing)에 대한 단속강화로 물품가격 기입 시 주의 요망 ○ 법률위반 의혹에 따른 통관지연(90일 이상)시 압류 처리
5. 물품반출 및 비용 납부	○ 물가인상으로 인한 창고료, SISCOMEX사용료 등 통관비용이 상승하여 예전가격과 혼동이 있을 수 있으므로 사전 비용 탐색 필요 ○ 관세 환급은 현금이 아닌 Credit으로 받는 형식이 대부분으로, 물품 판매 및 구매 시 공제받는 방법

1. SISCOMEX 등록 및 NCM 분류 단계

가. 통관 절차상 특이사항

☐ 서류작업을 통한 수입절차가 아닌, SISCOMEX에 수입업자 등록을 해야 통관업무 및 비용납부가 가능함
  ○ 등록양식에는 무역업체의 법적 대표자 정보, 대표활동(수출, 수입, 예금자/공탁자, 수송자), 시스템접속유형 등의 정보를 기재하도록 되어 있음

☐ 브라질은 메르코수르 관세코드인 NCM을 사용하고 있음
  ○ HS Code에 해당되며 8자리로 구성되어 있고, 1995년부터 시행되었음

나. 애로 사례 및 업무상 유의점

☐ 고비용 대비 효율성이 적은 SISCOMEX 시스템을 설치해서 수입허가를 받아야 하므로 시스템 미설치 시 수입업무 자체가 진행이 불가한 등 진입 장벽이 생김
  ○ 2011년 기준 SISCOMEX 사용료는 250헤알로, 2006년 대비 5배 인상됨
  ○ 수입규제 규정이 SISCOMEX에 등록된 수입업체만 열람 가능하도록 되어있어, 수입허가 단계에서 정보의 폐쇄성으로 인한 통관지연이 발생함

☐ 수입허가 자동발급 불가 품목에 대해 정부기관이 요구하는 위생요건, 품질요건, 안전요건 등의 승인취득을 통한 행정규제가 많은 편으로, 선적 및 통관이 지연됨
  ○ 자동수입허가품목을 확대하고 있으나 아직도 자동수입허가 불가 품목이 더 많아서 이러한 지연문제는 지속될 것으로 보임

□ NCM Code 기재 오류로 인해서 통관이 보류되거나 관세가 오납되는 경우가 발생하고 있음
  ○ 정확한 분류를 위해 전문적인 지식이 필요하므로 제품 엔지니어를 통해 NCM 분류하는 것이 정확도를 높일 수 있음

□ 우리나라에서 브라질로 물품 수출 전, 해당 품목이 덤핑방지관세 부과 등 규제 대상 품목인지 여부를 확인할 필요가 있음. 덤핑방지관세 등이 부과되는 경우 수입자는 통관을 위해 예상치 못했던 많은 세금을 내야하거나, 현지 수입상이 수입을 거절할 경우 물품이 한국으로 반송되는 경우도 발생할 수 있으므로 규제 사항을 사전에 확인해 두는 것이 좋음
  ○ 한국무역협회 통상·수입규제 홈페이지(http://antidumping.kita.net)에서는 세계 각국의 통상 현안을 비롯하여 국가별 반덤핑 및 상계관세 부과 정보 등 다양한 관련 정보를 제공하고 있음
    - 한국무역협회 기본 홈페이지(www.kita.net)에서는 우측 하단 '자주 찾는 서비스' 메뉴 중 '통상수입규제'로 접속 가능함
  ○ 현재 브라질이 반덤핑관세 등의 규제를 가하는 품목 확인을 위해서는 'KITA 통상·수입규제' 홈페이지 상단 메뉴 중 '수입규제현황' → '주요국제소 및 규제내역' → '중남미'에서 브라질의 내용을 점검할 수 있음
    - 또한 '수입규제현황' → '국가별 현황'에서는 필요 정보 지정 후 검색 기능을 통해 영문 품명과 정확한 HS 코드 등 보다 세밀한 정보를 확인할 수 있음
  ○ 그 외에 WTO에서 반기별로 공개하는 국가별 규제 동향도 살펴 볼 수 있는데, 이는 '통상·수입규제' 사이트 상단 메뉴 중 '각국규제동향'에서 확인 가능함
    - 단, 본 자료는 한국무역협회 웹페이지 무료 회원가입 후 로그인하여 열람 가능함

<표 Ⅳ-2> 브라질 제소 및 규제내역

제소 년도	품목명	제소근거 (규제근거)	조사결과			11년 09월
			규제확정 및 형태	조사종결	조사중	
99	나일론 스텐레스강관	반덤핑 반덤핑	AD(01.6)	무혐의		규제종료
01	PVC	반덤핑		무혐의		
02	합성장섬유직물	긴급수입제한	Quota(03.1)			규제종료
03	PE테레프탈레이트 레진	반덤핑		무혐의		
07	PVC	반덤핑	AD(08.09.29)			규제중
10	합성고무(SBR) 강판 NBR 합성고무	반덤핑 반덤핑 반덤핑	AD(11.6)		O O O	규제중 조사중 조사중
11	열연강판	반덤핑			O	조사중

자료 : 한국무역협회

2. 수입허가 취득 및 행정처리 단계

가. 통관 절차상 특이사항

□ 수입자는 SISCOMEX 수입자 등록 후 수입허가 자동 발급대상 여부를 확인하게 되며, 이때 자신의 수입 물품이 사전 수입허가가 필요한 물품인지, 만약 필요하다면 어떤 종류의 허가가 필요한 지를 확인해야 함

  ○ 수입품목의 사양, HS 코드, 수량, 가격, 운송료 등 SISCOMEX가 요구하는 정보를

입력해야 함
- ○ 특별허가 요망 품목
  - 농림부 허가 : 육류, 해산물, 식품, 우유, 낙농가공품, 달걀, 꿀, 과일, 야채 등
  - 환경부 허가 : 천연 고무나 인조 고무
  - 위생감시국 허가 : 비료, 화장품, 약품, 향수

□ 수입허가를 자동 발급할 수 없는 품목들은 시기상으로 반드시 선적 전에 수입허가서를 받아야 함
- ○ 선적 전 선적서류 copy 송부 → 수입허가 승인(물품에 따라 Lead Time 상이) → 수입자 선적 지시 → 선적의 순서임
- ○ 수입허가가 승인되지 않을 경우에는 수입신고, 보세운송이 불가함

□ 브라질 수입관세율 중 수입세의 조회를 통해 비용발생에 대해 비교적 정확한 예측을 할 수 있음
- ○ www.desenvolvimento.gov.br을 접속 → 위의 목록중에 comercio exterior를 클릭 → 왼쪽에 있는 tarifa externo comon을 클릭 → 아래에 있는 arquivo de download를 클릭한 뒤 다운로드 함

□ 브라질의 도량형·산업 품질 관리기구(INMETRO) 인증제도를 취득하기 위해서는 www.inmetro.gov.br에 접속 → 수입물품이 강제인증(certificacao compulsoria)과 자율인증(certificacao voluntaria) 중 어떤 품목이 해당되는지 판별 → 강제인증에 해당되는 물품인 경우 인증서 제품 인증기관(OCP)을 접촉해서 기관에 따라 인증서 취득 신청[37]

나. 애로 사례 및 업무상 유의점

□ 만약 선적한 후에 수입허가가 승인된 경우 벌금이 부과 되는데, 그 금액은 CIF 금액

---

[37] 부록 참조

의 30% 또는 최소 500헤알 ~ 최대 5,000헤알 정도임

□ 위생감시국(ANVISA)의 제품 등록을 위한 기간이 길어 통관에 장애를 줌
  ○ 건강용품, 의약품, 음료 등은 보건부 위생감시국에 제품등록을 해야 수입 또는 판매가 가능한데, 등록을 위한 자격 심사 기간이 필요 이상으로 지연되는 경우가 많아 큰 불편을 겪고 있음
  ○ 허가 취득기간의 경우, 제품에 따라 6개월~1년 정도 소요된다고 하지만 실제로는 2~3년 이상 걸리는 경우도 많아 브라질 시장 진출을 저해하는 비관세 장벽 중 하나로 인식되고 있음

□ 일부 공무원 파업이 발생하는 사례가 있어, 업무 과정에서의 시간적 및 물리적 비용이 발생하는 경우도 있음
  ○ 일부 세관, 연방경찰 등 공무원들의 파업 사례로 예상치 못한 업무 차질이 다소 발생함
  ○ 관료주의 관행이 있는 곳도 존재할 수 있음으로, 이로 인해 인프라 부문에 대한 투자가 지연되는 결과를 가져오고 있음
    - 브라질은 전체 수출 가운데 92%가 항만을 통해 이루어지고 있으나 인프라 투자 부족으로 항만 시설 현대화 작업이 늦어지는 등 인프라 건설 사업이 국제 수준보다 최소한 5~6개월 이상씩 늦어지고 있는 것으로 나타남

□ 1998년 10월부터 수입허가 품목에 대하여는 추가적으로 위생검역, 정부관련 부처로부터의 품질 및 안전승인 의무화 조치를 취하고 있음

3. 수입신고 단계

가. 통관 절차상 특이사항

☐ 수입 허가된 물품의 수입신고는 SISCOMEX를 통해 자동 처리되나, 사전에 수입허가가 필요한 물품은 구비서류를 가지고 직접 세관에 신고해야 함
  ○ 상업송장, 적하목록 내용이 물품과 일치하도록 유념하여 작성해야 문제발생의 소지가 적음

☐ 브라질에서 통관 대행업체들이 모든 통관 절차와 세금 납부 처리를 대행하는 것이 일반적인 관례임
  ○ 수입상이 직접 통관 업무를 할 수 있으나 절차의 복잡성으로 인해 공인통관사를 지정하여 통관을 의뢰하는 것이 통상적임

나. 애로 사례 및 업무상 유의점

☐ 선적서류 및 수입신고 내용 관련 사소한 오류에 대해 벌금을 부과하는 등 기준이 엄격하고 Item Description에 대한 명확한 가이드라인이 없음
  ○ 실제 중량과 선적서류상 기재 중량이 일치하지 않으면 현지 통관 시 문제가 발생할 확률이 높으며, 바이어도 이 과정에서 벌금 이외에 적기 제품 공급 등에 문제가 생겨 큰 불편을 겪게 됨
  ○ 벌금액수는 세관원의 자의적인 판단에 따라서 가변적이므로 비용부담이 발생하더라도 바이어 요청대로 수출면장과 B/L을 수정하여 재발송해야 함

□ 수입신고 시 정보오류가 발견될 경우 수입허가 수정이 필요하고 벌금이 부과됨
  ○ 브라질 도착 후 수입신고 수정이 이루어졌을 경우 황색채널로 배정되어 서류심사를 받게 됨
  ○ 수입허가 정보 수정에 시간이 소요되므로 벌금 및 통관지연으로 인한 비용이 증가함

□ 통관 전반에 있어 일관된 외국인 대외무역법이 없고, 있다 하더라도 이해하기 어려운 법제도로 외국인의 무역행위 자체가 어렵다는 문제가 있음
  ○ 브라질 세관은 통관 절차가 복잡하고 주(州)에 따라 이중통관제도를 하는 경우가 발생하고 있음
  ○ 법규 및 세제의 빈번한 개정으로 조세부담률의 크며 세무관리비용이 높다는 문제도 지적됨

□ 외국인 투자와 관련된 규정이 WTO 기준에 미달되거나, 내외국인 간에 차별 대우가 존재함
  ○ 지적재산권 관련 선진국 기준에 미달하여 간혹 선진국과 마찰이 있기도 하며, 정부구매 시 모든 조건이 동등하다면 브라질 국내 기업 들을 우대하는 경향이 있음

4. 물품검사 단계

가. 통관 절차상 특이사항

□ 최소가격제 등의 비관세장벽을 공지 없이 불시에 설치하는 등 강력한 수입규제 정책

을 실시하는 품목이 많아, 세이프가드나 반덤핑조치의 위험이 따름

☐ 물품검사 4채널(녹, 황, 적, 회) 중 검사 강도가 가장 큰 회색채널에 대해 세관은 물품검사 뿐 아니라 수입회사에 대한 조사 권한도 가짐
  ○ 선적 서류와 물품의 일치 여부를 항상 확인해야 하며, 수입물품의 포장 단위별로 상세 물품정보가 기입되어야 강도 높은 검사의 시행을 면할 수 있음

☐ 브라질 세관은 많은 수입품에 저가 신고(Under Invoicing)가 이루어지는 것으로 보고, 이 경우 검사 시 물품가격 증명 및 재평가 등 통제를 강화하고 있음
  ○ 세관원이 수입제품의 가격에 이상이 있다고 판단할 때에는 8일 기간 내에 새로운 관세가격을 책정할 수 있음
  ○ 수입자가 이에 이의가 있을 때에는 30일 이내에 관련 입증서류를 제출하여 재심을 요청할 수 있음
  ○ 만약 양측 모두 이의제기 시 통관에 기본 38일이 소요됨

나. 애로 사례 및 업무상 유의점

☐ 동아시아 지역으로부터 수입되는 제품의 경우, 저가신고 물품적발 건수가 늘어나고 있어 전수검사 실시하는 경우가 많아짐
  ○ 수입이 빈번한 제품(직물류)에 대해서는 통관 시 엄격한 가이드라인을 적용하고 있음

☐ 일방적 무역제재조치의 경우 무역 분규 발생 소지가 높은 점을 감안하여 통관검사의 강화를 통해 사실상 수입을 억제하는 관행이 많음
  ○ 최근 브라질 세관에서는 특송 화물에 대한 통관 규정을 엄격히 적용하여 검사하고 있으며, 규정에 부합되지 않는 다수 화물의 통관 지연이 발생하고 있음

5. 물품반출 및 환급 단계

가. 통관 절차상 특이사항

□ 모든 세금 및 비용 납부가 완료되고 화물검사 및 화주 확인이 끝나면 연방 세무국은 SISCOMEX를 통해 수입면장을 발급하며, 이것으로 서류상 통관이 완료됨
  ○ 수입 통관 비용으로 관세와 내국세(공업제품세, 주유통세, 사회보장세)를 포함해 창고세, 터미널 사용세, 상해운세, 세관사용인조합 기여금, SISCOMEX 사용료, 화물운송비, 통관수수료를 지불해야 함

나. 애로 사례 및 업무상 유의점

□ Tax ID 가 부정확하거나 누락되었을 겨우 통관 지연이 발생하게 됨
  ○ 브라질로 반입되는 모든 Dutiable Shipment (WPX) 화물의 통관을 위해서는 수취인의 Tax ID(기업용: CNPJ38) – / 개인용: CPF –)가 필요함
  ○ AWB 및 Invoice에 반드시 Tax ID를 기재하여야 하며, Data Entry시에도 입력해야함
  ○ 통관 시 수취인과 원활히 연락할 수 있도록 반드시 AWB 및 Invoice에 수취인의 정확한 전화번호를 기재해야 함

---

38) National Directory of Legal Entities

참고문헌

외교통상부,『2010 외국의 통상환경 브라질』, 2011
한국수출입은행,『브라질: 국가현황 및 진출방안』, 2009
한국은행,『브라질 경제의 주요 현안과 전망』, 2011
KOTRA,『브라질 투자핵심가이드』, 2008
The World Bamk Group,『Doing Business 2011』, 2011
USTR,『National Trade Estimate Report on Foreign Trade Barriers』, 2011

대한민국 관세청, www.customs.go.kr
대한무역투자진흥공사 국가정보〉브라질, www.kotra.or.kr
대한상공회의소, www.korcham.net
세계무역기구, www.wto.org
양자협약사무국, www.bilaterals.org
해외진출정보시스템, www.ois.go.kr
브라질주재 대한민국대사관, www.bra-brasilia.mofat.go.kr
브라질 개발상공부, www.mdic.gov.br
브라질 연방세무국, www.receita.fazenda.gob.br
브라질 대외무역국, www.secex.gob.br
브라질 중앙은행, www.bcb.gob.br
사회경제개발은행, www.bndes.gob.br
국립산업재산권연구소, www.inpi.gob.br
브라질 과학기술연구기관, www.serpro.gob.br
해외진출 정보시스템 국가정보, www.ois.go.kr

부록 Ⅰ. 비즈니스 팁

□ 현지법인 설립을 위한 영주 비자 취득에 어려움이 있음
  ○ 브라질에서 지사를 설치하기 위해서는 대통령의 허가를 받아야 하는데, 지사승인 사례가 거의 없음
  ○ 따라서 현지사업을 위해서는 현지법인을 설치해야 하는데 법인설립을 해서는 영주비자를 받아야 현지경영이 가능함
  ○ 영주비자를 받기 위해서는 본사 파견 직원 1인당 20만달러를 투자해야 하는 법안이 있었으나, 이는 5만달러로 인하됨 그러나 2년 내에 10명의 일자리를 창출해야 하므로 여전히 어려움은 산재해 있음

□ 현지 직원 고용 의무가 있음
  ○ 브라질 노동법상 외국기업이 현지직원 고용 시, 임금의 총합 또는 직원 총합의 2/3를 브라질인으로 고용해야 하고 나머지 1/3은 외국인으로 고용해야 하는 2/3 조항을 준수해야 함
  ○ 즉 1명의 본사직원(외국인) 파견 시 2/3에 해당하는 2명의 현지 직원을 고용해야 하며 현지 직원이 많이 필요한 기업의 경우 부담이 없으나, 현지직원을 필요로 하지 않는 경우 부담이 될 수 있음

□ 고용주에 불리한 노동법으로 노무관리가 매우 어려움
  ○ 직원을 고용함에 따른 부가 비용이 매우 큼
    - 직원 1명을 고용하게 되면 급여 외에도 각종 사회보장세, 연금, 소득세, 상여금, 휴가 비, 정기 급여 인상 등 부대 비용이 많이 발생함
  ○ 해고 시에도 퇴직벌금 및 퇴직부대비용이 발생하며 늘 소송에 걸릴 위험에 노출되어 있음

○ 브라질은 노동법 자체가 노동자와 약자 위주로 되어 있어, 소송에 걸릴 경우 노동자가 거의 대부분 승소하게끔 되어 있음
  - 소송비용(인지대 등)을 패소한 측에서 상대방 비용까지 내는 게 원칙이나 노동법에는 해당이 안 돼 패소할 경우 노동자가 불리하게 될 사항이 전혀 없음이에 따라 노동법 전문 변호사들은 해고된 노동자에게 소송을 부추기는 경우도 매우 흔함
○ 노동 계약상에서도 당사자 간의 자치주의(합의) 원칙이 제한되어 있어, 외국 기업들은 이를 이해하기가 매우 어려움

□ 치안이 불안함
  ○ 상파울루 및 리우 등 대도시 치안이 불안하여 주재원들이 강도 또는 납치를 당하는 사례가 자주 발생하여 현지경영 및 투자에 애로사항으로 작용하고 있음. 외국 기업 또는 주택가만이라도 치안 인력을 확충하는 노력이 필요함

□ 브라질이 시장개방을 한 후 발생하고 있는 부족한 인프라 문제와 이에 따른 엄청난 물류 비용, 낙후된 부품산업에 기인하는 안정된 부품조달의 문제와 일관성이 없는 정부의 수출입정책 등도 또 다른 애로 사항으로 꼽히고 있음

□ 브라질의 경기지수가 너무 단기적이고 불규칙한 사이클을 형성하기 때문에 기업의 입장에서 장기투자의 불확실성이 크다는 지적임
  ○ 불규칙한 경기 사이클을 예측하기 힘들고 판매망이나 A/S망의 확보 및 기업의 입맛에 맞는 현지 전문 인력을 키우고 현지상황에 적응하는 데 시간이 걸리기 때문에 2~3년의 단기투자로는 성공적인 정착을 하는 것이 어려움

□ 복장
  ○ 일반적으로 자수성가한 기업인이나 가족기업의 기업인들은 비교적 느슨하고 격식을 차리지 않고 편한 복장을 선호하나, 비즈니스맨은 대부분 복장에 세심한 신경을 씀

□ 인사
- ○ 브라질 사람과 비즈니스 만남 시에는 악수를 하는 것이 정석이며 평소에는 여성과 인사 시 양 볼에 키스를 하고 안면이 있는 남성끼리는 어깨나 등을 툭툭 치거나 반포옹을 함. 또한 처음 본 사람을 낯설어 하는 경우가 없고 어느 정도 대화를 하다보면 금세 친근감을 표시하기 때문에 남미 사람들은 한국인들이 처음 만남 사람과 낯을 가리고 거리를 두는 모습을 보고 서로 싫어하는 것으로 오해를 하는 경우가 있음
- ○ 회의석상에서 서로 인사를 나눌 때 참석한 사람들에게 일일이 악수하고 인사를 나누어야 하고, 회의가 끝날 때에서 반드시 모든 사람에게 인사를 나누고 헤어져야 함
- ○ 보통, 점심이나 저녁 시간 전에 회의가 끝나는 경우는 브라질 측에서 먼저 식사약속을 하게 되는데, 만일 이러한 약속 없이 회의를 한 경우라 하더라도 분위기에 따라 식사초대를 하는 경우가 종종 있음. 따라서 회의 종료 후 먼저 회의장을 나서지 말고 상대방의 태도를 관망하는 것이 좋음. 저녁식사의 초대는 상담이 잘 되고 있다는 신호이며 식사를 하면서 개인적인 친분을 쌓을 수 있음

□ 선물
- ○ 첫 만남에 선물을 주는 경우는 없으며 대신 점심이나 저녁을 초대하는 것은 아주 좋음. 일반적으로 점심은 예의를 의미하고 저녁은 어느 정도 비즈니스가 진전되고 있음을 의미함
- ○ 회사 로고가 찍힌 선물은 비즈니스 상담 기념으로 아주 좋으나, 턱없이 비싼 선물은 오해를 사기 때문에 금해야 함

□ 약속
- ○ 브라질 사람들은 약속시간 엄수에 철저하지 않은 편이며, 특히 비공식적인 자리일 경우 30분 이상 늦게 도착하는 것에 별로 미안해하지 않는 편임. 그러나 이것을 브라질리언 타임으로 생각하고 한국 측에서도 습관적으로 늦는다면 좋지 않은 인상을 줄 수도 있음

- ○ 브라질 사람과 약속을 잡기 위해서는 전화를 통해 구두약속을 한 후 가능하면 이메일 등으로 다시 한 번 확인하는 것이 좋음
- ○ 적어도 1~2주 전 미리 날짜를 약속하는 것이 좋고, 특히 정부 기관과의 면담일 경우 1~2개월 전에 미리 면담 가능성을 알아보는 것이 현명함

□ 식사 에티켓
- ○ 저녁 식사 시간이 9시나 10시 이후인 경우가 많아 식사에 초대할 경우에는 너무 이른 시간에 초대하는 것은 바람직하지 않음
- ○ 식사 중에는 입에 음식을 가득 담은 채 이야기하지 말아야 하며, 최대한 소리를 내지 않고 먹는 것이 예의임
- ○ 술을 즐겨 마시나 많이 마시지는 않는 편임. 까이삐리냐(Caipirinha)는 사탕수수로 만든 브라질 사람들이 가장 즐겨 마시는 전통주임
- ○ 술 한잔 시켜놓고 한 두 시간 대화를 즐기는 브라질 사람들에게 한국식 폭음은 이해하기 어려운 문화이므로 술을 강권하면 상대방이 곤욕스러워 할 수 있음

□ 문화적 금기사항
- ○ 엄지와 검지를 동그랗게 모으고 나머지 세 손가락을 피는 동작은 한국에서는 OK 표시지만, 브라질에서는 상대방을 비난하는 표시로 이해됨
- ○ 엄지 손가락을 둘째와 셋째 사이에 넣어 주먹을 쥐는 행동은 한국에서는 욕으로 간주되나 브라질에서 Figa라고 불리는 이러한 동작은 '행운을 빈다'는 의미가 담겨 있음
- ○ 중남미 국가 중 선두 국가로서의 자긍심이 강하고 미국과도 대등하게 생각하는 등 자존심 강한 민족이기 때문에 브라질 비하식의 발언 또는 타국과의 비교는 삼가는 게 좋고 Brazil을 일컬을 때 영어식으로 발음하기 보다는 포르투갈어식으로 Brasil(브라지우)라고 하면 매우 좋아함

□ 이민국가라는 점을 잊지 말 것
- ○ 상파울루에서 상권은 주로 이탈리아계, 독일계, 중동계, 유대계, 스페인계가 주로

장악하고 있고 우리가 상대하는 기업인들도 대부분 이들로 봐도 무방함
- ㅇ 따라서 중동계 바이어와 상담을 하면서 이스라엘을 편든다거나 이탈리아계 바이어와 만나면서 이탈리아인들의 단점을 얘기하지 말아야 함

☐ 외상거래 비중이 높음
- ㅇ 브라질은 세계에서 이자율이 가장 높은 국가 중 하나이고 관행적으로 외상거래가 일반화되어 있어 외상거래를 선호함
- ㅇ 상담 시, 융통성 있는 상담자세가 필요하며 만일의 사태에 대비해 신용상태 파악이나 수출보험에 가입하는 것이 필요함

☐ 주요제품 물가 현황 (2011년 9월 기준)

(단위: 헤알)

구분	항목	가격
식품류	쌀 1kg	5.16
	계란 12개	5
	쇠고기 등심 1kg	33.79
	돼지고기 등심 1kg	10.09
	우유 400ml	6.05
	식용유 1병(900ml기준)	7
	생수 1.5L	2.24
	맥주(하이네켄 355ml)	3
	담배 1갑(말보로 라이트)	4.5
	햄버거(맥도날드 빅맥)	8.75
	김치찌개 1인분	30.00
의료비	의료보험료(4인가족, 치과제외 Full Cover, 1년)	16,000.00
	병원진료비(의료보험 X, 몸살감기 내과초진)	150.00
	병원진료비(의료보험, 몸살감기 내과조진)	0
차량관련	중형승용차(2000cc 신차, 오토, 에어컨포함 기본사양)	70,000.00
	무연휘발유 1L	2.79
	자동차 등록비(2000cc 신차 기준)	1,700.00
	자동차보험료 의무(2000cc신차, 운전경력10년, 대인/대물커버, 1년)	2,500.00
교통비	도심 1시간 주차료	13.00
	지하철 기본요금(1구간)	2.79

통신	시내버스 기본요금	3.00
	택시 기본요금	4.10
	시내전화 요금(1분, 250분 패키지)	0.11
	국제전화 요금(1분, 한국으로 걸 때)	2.89
	휴대전화 요금(월표준 1분)	1.10
	인터넷 월사용료(ADSL 기준) (12메가 NET 기준)	219.90
주택	아파트 월 임차료(150sm, semi-furnished, 시내, 중상급)	6,000.00
교육	외국인학교 초등 1년 수업료(중상급)	33,000.00
	외국인학교 중등 1년 수업료(중상급)	44,000.00
	외국인학교 고등 1년 수업료(중상급)	50,000.00
숙박	특급호텔(5성급) 1박 정상요금(싱글)	600.00
	중급호텔(3성급) 1박 정상요금(싱글)	200.00
임금/노무	대졸 초임(중상급 대졸, 영어구사, 외국인회사 초임 월급여)	3,500.00
	생산직 초임(학력무관 월급여 초임)	700.00
	매니저급 급여(인사담당 5년 경력 과장급 월급여)	9,000.00
	주당 법정근무시간	44
	출산휴가일 수	30
	연간 국경일 수	10
	주5일 근무 여부	Y
기타	드라이크리닝(정장 1벌 기준)	30.00

주: 상파울루 기준(2011년 9월) 환율: 1달러 = 1.66헤알
자료: 상파울루 무역관

부록 Ⅱ. 주요 유관 기관 정보

■ 주 브라질 대한민국 대사관

웹페이지	http://bra-brasilia.mofat.go.kr
주소	SEN-Avenida Das Nacoes Lote 14, 70436-900, Brasilia-DF, Brasil
전화번호	(55-61) 3321-2500 *휴무비상전화 (55-61) 9962-8197 또는 9962-9993
팩스번호	(55-61) 3321-2508

■ 주 상파울루 총영사관

웹페이지	http://bra-saopaulo.mofat.go.kr
주소	Av. Paulista 37, 9 andar cj. 91 - Bela Vista, Sao Paulo - SP Brasil 01311-902
전화번호	(55-11) 3141-1278
팩스번호	(55-11) 3141-1279
이메일	cscorcia@mofat.go.kr

■ KOTRA 상파울루 무역관(KBC)

웹페이지	www.kotra.or.kr - 해외무역관 - 상파울루 무역관
주소	Alameda Santos 700, CONJ 81,82, Ed.Trianon Corporate, CEP 01418-100 Cerqeira Cesar, Sao Paulo, SP, Brazil
전화번호	TEL.55-11-3175-3030
팩스번호	FAX.55-11-3175-3031
이메일	saopaulo@kotra.com.br

■ 브라질 재무부(Ministério da Fazenda)

웹페이지	http://www.fazenda.gov.br
주소	Esplanada dos Ministérios, Bloco P, 70048-900, Brasília-DF
전화번호	(55-61) 3412-2000/3000

■ 브라질 경제사회 개발은행(BNDES, Brazilian develop bank)

주소	Rio de Janeiro - RJ - Brasil - 20031-917
전화번호	(55-21) 2172-7447

■ 상파울로주 경제인 연맹

웹페이지	http://www.fiesp.com.br
주소	Av. Paulista, 1313, São Paulo/SP - CEP: 01311-923
전화번호	(55-11) 3549-4499
이메일	relacionamento@fiesp.org.br

■ 한국수출보험공사 상파울루지사

주소	Alameda Santos, 880, 5°Andar Conj. 52/53 CEP:01418-100-Cerqueira Cesar, Sao Paulo SP, Brasil
전화번호	(55-11)3284-1105, 3285-1951
팩스번호	(55-11)3284-4081
이메일	E-Mail Address : keicsp@hotmail.com

■ 한인 상공회의소

웹페이지	www.kocham.com.br
주소	R.Tres Rios,263, Bom Retiro Sao Paulo, SP01123-000
전화번호	(55-11) 3326-9562

■ 한국산업은행(KDB) 브라질

주소	Av. Brigadeiro Faria Lima, 3400 Ed. Faria Lima Financial Center 15° and. Conj.152 CEP:04538-132, Itaim Bibi, Sao Paulo-SP-Brasil
전화번호	(55-11) 2138-0000
팩스번호	(55-11) 2138-0150

■ 브라질 한인회

웹페이지	www.haninbrasil.com.br
주소	R.dos Parecis,107, Cambuci Sao Paulo, SP 01527-030
전화번호	(55-11) 3209-9042, (5511)3399-2768
팩스번호	(55-11) 3208-6860
이메일	haninbrazil@hanmail.net webmaster@haninbrazil.com.br

■ 브라질 개발통상 상공부(Ministério do Desenvolvimento, Indústria e Comércio Exterior)

웹페이지	http://www.mdic.gov.br
주소	Esplanada dos Ministérios, Bloco "J" Brasília, DF, 70053-900
전화번호	(55-61) 2027-7000
팩스번호	(55-61) 2027-7445
이메일	decom@mdic.gov.br

■ 브라질 한인닷컴

웹페이지	www.hanin.com.br(한인업소 및 각종 생활 정보)

부록 Ⅲ. 법령 정보

□ 선적서류 관련 법령
  ○ Article 557. The commercial invoice must include the following:
    Ⅰ. name and address, complete the exporter;
    Ⅱ. name and address, complete the importer and, where applicable, the purchaser or encomendante , p p , pp , p predetermined;
    Ⅲ. Specification of goods in Portuguese or official language of the General Agreement on Tariffs and Trade, or, if in another language, a translation in English, at the discretion of the customs authority, containing the individual and commercial names, indicating the elements essential to its unambiguous identification;
    Ⅳ. marks, numbers and, if any, reference number of the packages;
    Ⅴ. Number and kind of packages;
    Ⅵ. gross weight of packages, it being understood, as such, the goods with all their containers, packaging and other packaging;
    Ⅶ. Net weight, considered the merchandise free of any and all packaging;
    Ⅷ. country of origin, which means, there is one where the merchandise was produced or where it underwent its last substantial transformation;
    Ⅸ. the country of purchase, considered as one from which the goods were purchased to be exported to Brazil, regardless of country of origin of goods or its components;
    Ⅹ. country of origin, so that where he was considered a commodity at the time of its acquisition;
    Ⅺ. unit price and total for each type of goods, and if the amount and nature of

discounts and rebates;

XII. cost of transport referred to in Item I of art. 77 and other expenses relating to the goods specified in the invoice;

XIII. Terms and currency of payment;

X IV. a term of condition of sale (INCOTERM).

- Article 558. Items covered by a single invoice will have a single brand and will be numbered, sealed the repetition of numbers.
- Article 558. Items covered by a single invoice will have a single brand and will be numbered, sealed the repetition of numbers.

  § It is first admitted the use of numerals in the title tag, long as they are within a geometric figure, keeping with the standards prescribed in § 2 on the numbering of volumes.

  § The second number in each volume will be placed next to the brand or geometric figure that contains it.

  § 3 Numbering is not required:

  I . in the case of goods normally imported in bulk and shipped loose or in bundles, since it is not packaged, and

  II . in the case of batches of the same commodity, fifty or more volumes, since the whole batch consists of uniform volumes, with the same y, y , , weight and measure.

- Article 559. The first copy of the invoice will always be original and may be issued, as well as other means, by any means.
- Article 560. Parallels the commercial invoice, for all practical purposes, knowledge of cargo by air, since it included the signs of quantity, type and value of the goods relating thereto (Decree Law No. 37 of 1966, art. 46, § first, with the wording amended by Decree-Law No 2472, 1988, art. 2nd).
- Article 561. Can be established by the regulations of the Internal Revenue Service of Brazil, the sight of the request of the Foreign Trade Chamber, the requirement

of a visa on commercial invoice (Decree-Law No. 37 of 1966, art. 46, § 2, with the wording amended by Decree-Law No 2472, 1988, art. 2nd).

o Article 562. The Internal Revenue Service of Brazil might have in relation to the commercial invoice, to:

I . cases of non-requirement;

II . cases of waiver submission for purposes of customs clearance, in which case the importer must keep the document in his possession, the statutory limitation period, the disposal of the customs control;

III. Number of lanes that must be issued and their disposal;

IV. Other items to be given, other than those specified in Art. 557.

□ 수입금지 · 제한 및 수입허가 관련 법령

	Prohibitions		
Wines	Prohibited if transported in bottles of more than 5 litres		Article 26 of Law No. 7,678 of 8 November 1988
Grapes and grape juice	Foreign grapes or grape juice may not be used in the production of wine and its derivative products		Article 57 of Decree No. 99,066 of 8 march 1990
Toys that replicate firearms	Prohibited in all circumstances (domestic production is also prohibited)		Article 26 of Law No. 10,826 of 22 December 2003
Weapons and ammunitions	Private importation prohibited if the goods are intended for exclusive use of the army		Decree No. 2,998 of 23 March 1999
Endangered animals and plants	Animals and plants listed as endangered by CITES		Decree No. 3,607 of 21 September 2001
Used tyres	Granting of non-automatic licences prohibited, including if the tyres are for use as raw material; imports of retreaded tyres from other MERCOSUR member countries are allowed		Article 41 of Portaria SECEX No.36of22November2007
Used consumer goods	Granting of non-automatic licences prohibited, except for imports by the State or educational and scientific institutions		Article 27 of Portaria SECEX No. 235of7December2006
	Licensing requirements		
Imports under drawback scheme	Automatic licence		Portaria SECEX No. 36 of 22November2007
Used goods	Non-automatic licence required for imports of all used goods, with the exception of packaging material used in temporary importation or re-importation		Portaria SECEX No. 36 of 22 November 2007
Weapons and products made for warlike purposes	Non-automatic licence		Decree No. 3,665 of 20 November 2000
Goods restricted by a UN resolution	Non-automatic licence required for specific goods whose trade is restricted by a UN resolution		Portaria SECEX No. 36 of 22November2007
Scheduled chemicals controlled under the Chemical Weapons Convention	Non-automatic licence		Decree No. 2,977 of 1March1999.

☐ 지식재산보호 법률(2008기준)

Patents			
Industrial Property Law No. 9,279 of 14 May 1996; Law No. 10,196 of 2001. Decree No. 4,830/2003			
Any invention that is new and involves an inventive step, that is capable of industrial application	20 years from the date of filing	Substances, matter, mixtures, and processes for their modification, biological processes and natural living material; compulsory licenses may be granted in cases of national emergency or in the public interest	Protection for IPRs, taking into account the country's social interest and technological and economic development; LawNo.10,196of2001: prior approval from the National Sanitary Surveillance Agency (ANVISA) for the granting of patents for medicines and its processes; DecreeNo.4,830/2003a mendsDecreeNo.3,201 of6October1999,which providesforthegrantofc ompulsorylicencesinca sesofnationalemergenc yorinthepublicinterest
Industrial designs			
Industrial Property Law, Normative Act No. 129 of 1997 Resolution No. 076 of 2000. Normative Act No. 161 of 2002			
New ornamental form of an object or new ornamental arrangement of lines or colours whose visual configuration is capable of industrial application	10 years from date of filing; which can be extended for 3 successive 5-year periods	Not registrable when contrary to morals and good customs or when it is an ordinary shape of an object determined essentially by technical or functional considerations	Resolution No. 076/2000 provides for the adoption of the international classification system
Utility models			
Industrial Property Law No. 9,279 of 14 May 1996.			
New invention in a new shape or	15 years from date of filing	Substances, matter, mixtures, and	

arrangement, capable of industrial application		processes for their modification, biological processes and natural living material	
Trade marks			
Industrial Property Law, Normative Acts No. 83, 159 and 160 of 2001. Normative Act No. 110 of 2004			
Visually perceptible sign that distinguishes or certifies a good or service	10 years renewable for equal successive periods	Crests, armorial bearings, emblems, flags, national and international monuments	Normative Act 83/2001 provides for registration forms in accordance with the goods and services international classification system; Normative Act No. 110 of 2004 establishes rules for the recognition of famous marks
Geographic indications			
Industrial Property Law, Normative Act No. 075 of 2000			
Name of a country or region used to designate a service or good whose characteristics or reputation are derived from the country or region.	Undetermined		Normative Act No. 075 of 2000 establishes conditions for the registration of geographic indications
Copyright and related rights			
Law No. 9,610 of 19February1998; Law No. 10,695 of July 2003			
Text of literary, scientific or artistic works; musical compositions, audiovisual works, drawings, paintings, photographic works. No registration necessary	Life of the author plus 70 years as the general term of protection; term varies according to the type or nature of the work	No authorization required where the name of the author is cited in the reproduction of current affairs, or the copier uses for educational purposes without intent for financial gain.	Protects the work of the author and of foreigners resident outside Brazil; Law No. 10,695 amends the Criminal Code to include stiffer sanctions for copyright violations and to improve criminal procedures

부록 IV. 조세 체계

In Brazil, the major tax guidelines are defined by the Federal Constitution, which sets down general principles, the limits of taxing authority, jurisdictions and the question of sharing of tax revenues.

Consequently, our National Tax System was instituted by the Constitution itself, which determines that the Union, States, Federal District and Municipalities can institute taxes, considering the power to tax as one of the inherent qualities of the State. Political-administrative autonomy, considered an essential characteristic of our federative system, grants each level of government the right to institute taxes, fees (corresponding to utilization of public services and police power) and contributions targeted at improvements (resulting from public works).

According to the 1988 Constitution (with the alterations introduced by Constitutional Amendment no. 3, dated 03/17/93), the taxes under the specific jurisdiction of the Union, States and Federal District and Municipalities are as follows, classified by their nature:

TAXES	JURISDICTION
Foreign Trade Taxes	
- Import Tax - II	Union
- Export Tax - IE	Union
Taxes on Assets and Income	
- Income Tax - IR	Union
- Rural Land Tax - ITR	Union
- Tax on Automotive Vehicles - IPVA	States
- Tax on Property Transmission Causa Mortis - ITCD	States

- Urban Building and Land Tax – IPTU	Municipalities
- Transmission Tax Inter Vivos - ITBI	Municipalities
Taxes on Production and Circulation:	
- Industrialized Products Tax - IPI	Union
- Tax on Credit Operations, Exchange and Insurance – IOF	Union
- Tax on the Circulation of Merchandise and Interstate and Intermunicipal Transportation Services and Communications – ICMS	States
- Tax on Services of Any Nature - ISS	Municipalities

Aside from the taxes listed above, the Federal Constitution reserves exclusive authority to the Union to institute social contributions, contributions on intervention in the economic domain and those of interest to professional or economic categories. In the case of social contributions, one should stress that the States, Federal District and Municipalities may levy contributions on their civil servants in order to cover the costs of their Social Security and social assistance systems targeted to those workers.

Among social contributions, the following deserve mention:
- Contribution to Social Security Financing – COFINS
- Contribution to the Social Integration Program and Civil Service Asset Formation Program – PIS/PASEP
- Social Contribution on Net Corporate Profits – CSLL
- Provisional Contribution on Financial Operations – CPMF; and
- Social Security Contribution on payroll(employee/employer) and the self-employed.

Tax Table - 2007					
Tax (Acronym)	Income Tax - IR				
	IRPF	IRPJ	IRF		
			Labor	Capital	Outros
Type / Nature	Income	Income	Income	Income	Income
Calculation Base	Wages and earnings	Profits	Wages and earnings	Difference between purchase and sale value	Awards and lotteries; earnings on profissional services
Subject Liable	Individuals	Corporate entities	Individuals	Individuals or corporate entities	Individuals or corporate entities
Rates	Zero, 15% to 27.5%	15% and 25%	15% and 27.5%	10%, 15% and 20%	30% and 1.5%
Taxing Authority	Union	Union	Union	Union	Union

Tax Table - 2007					
Tax (Acronym)	COFINS	PIS	PASEP	IPI	FGTS
Type / Nature	Production	Produção	Produção	Produção	Produção
Calculation base	Gross Revenues (including financial)	Gross Revenues (including financial)	Gross revenues	Industrialized products sold (aggregate value)	Payroll
Subject Liable	Corporate entity	Corporate entity	Corporate entity governed by public law	Corporate entity	Corporate entity: or individual (domestic employer doméstico)
Rates	3% 7.6	0.65% 1.65	1%	From 0% to 365.63%, according to TIPI	8%
Taxing Authority	Union	Union	Union	Union	Union

Tax Table - 2007					
Taxes (acronym)	CSLL	ITR	IE	II	CPMF
Type / Nature	Income	Assets	Production	Production / Consumption	Production / Consumption
Calculation Base	profits	Value of rural real estate	Value of exported product or service	Value of imported product or service	Debited to bank accounts
Subject Liable	Corporate entity	Individual or corporate entity	Corporate entity	Individual or corporate entity	Individual or corporate entity
Rates	8%	0.03% to 20%	from 0% to 150%	from 0% to 35%, according to the TEC	0.38%
Taxing Authority	Union	Union	Union	Union	Union

Tax Table - 2007					
Tax (Acronym)	Contribution to Social Security (INSS)			Contribution to Civil Service Social Security	
	Self-employed	Employee	Employer	Union	States and Municipalities
Type / Nature	Income	Income	Production	Income	Income
Calculation Base	Earnings	Wages	Payroll	Earnings	Earnings
Subject Liable	Individual	Individual	Corporate entity; or individual (domestic employer)	individual (federal civil servant)	Individual (state or municipal civil servant)
Rates	20%	from 8% to 11%	15%, 17.5%, 20% and 22.5%; or 12% (empr.dom.)	11%	Varies by State or Municipality
Taxing capital Authority	Union	Union	Union	Union	States and Municipalities

Tax Table – 2007						
Tax (Acronym)	ICMS	IPVA	ITCD	ISS	IPTU	ITBI
Type / Nature	Production / Consumption	Assets	Assets	Production / Consumption	Patrimônio	Patrimônio
Generating Fact	Circulation of merchandise	Proprietor-ship	Donations or transmission of properties – causa mortis	Services rendered	Proprietorship or possession	Donations or transmission of goods – inter vivos
Calculation Base	Value of Merchandise and Services Sold (aggregate value)	Value of automotive vehicle	Value of good, movable or not, donated or transmitted	Value of the Service Rendered	Value of Urban Real Estate	Value of Real Estate Sold
Subject Liable	Corporate Entity	Individual or corporate entity	Individual	Corporate entity; or individual (self-employed service provider)	Individual or corporate entity	Individual or corporate entity
Rates*	4%, 7%, 12%, 17%, 18%, 21% and 25% (levied within price)	from 1% to 4%	4%	from 0.5% to 10%	from 0.3% to 3%	2%
Taxing Authority	States	States	States	Municipalities	Municipalities	Municipalities

* The rates of those taxes for which States and Municipalities are responsible are based on those in effect in the Federal District (which includes Brasilia, the Capital of Brazil).

부록 V. Names and Acronyms

Unit	Acronym
SECRETARIAT OF THE FEDERAL REVENUE OF BRAZIL	RFB
SECRETARY OFFICE	Gabin
SPECIAL ASSISTANCE OFFICE	Asesp
INTERNAL AFFAIRS	Coger
GENERAL COORDINATION OF INTERNAL AUDITING	Audit
GENERAL COORDINATION OF INSTITUTIONAL PLANNING, ORGANIZATION AND EVALUATION	Copav
GENERAL COORDINATION OF RISK MANAGEMENT	Cgris
COMMUNICATION COORDINATION	Ascom
INTERNATIONAL TAX AFFAIRS COORDINATION	Asain
SPECIAL COORDINATION OF PARLIAMENTARY ACTIVITIES	Copar
GENERAL COORDINATION OF RESEARCH AND INVESTIGATION	Copei
SPECIAL COORDINATION OF AIR OPERATIONS	Ceoar
GENERAL COORDINATION OF TAX POLICY	Copat
GENERAL COORDINATION OF FORECAST AND ANALYSIS	Copan
GENERAL COORDINATION OF ADMINISTRATIVE AND LEGAL DISPUTES	Cocaj
GENERAL COORDINATION OF TAXATION	Cosit
SPECIAL COORDINATION OF RECORDS MANAGEMENT	Cocad
GENERAL COORDINATION OF RELATIONS WITH CITIZENS	Coint
SPECIAL COORDINATION OF LARGE TAXPAYERS MONITORING	Comac
GENERAL COORDINATION OF TAX COLLECTION	Codac
GENERAL COORDINATION OF TAX INSPECTION	Cofis
GENERAL COORDINATION OF CUSTOMS ADMINISTRATION	Coana
SPECIAL COORDINATION OF CUSTOMS ENFORCEMENT	Corep
GENERAL COORDINATION OF PERSONNEL MANAGEMENT	Cogep
GENERAL COORDINATION OF INFORMATION TECHNOLOGY	Cotec
GENERAL COORDINATION OF PROGRAMMING AND LOGISTICS	Copol
REGIONAL SUPERVISORY OFFICES OF THE FEDERAL REVENUE OF BRAZIL	SRRF
JUDGMENT OFFICES OF THE FEDERAL REVENUE OF BRAZIL	DRJ
OFFICES OF THE FEDERAL REVENUE OF BRAZIL	DRF
SOCIAL SECURITY OFFICES OF THE FEDERAL REVENUE OF BRAZIL	DRP
TAX ADMINISTRATION OFFICES OF THE FEDERAL REVENUE OF BRAZIL	Derat
TAX INSPECTION OFFICES OF THE FEDERAL REVENUE OF BRAZIL	Defis
FINANCIAL INSTITUTIONS SPECIALIZED OFFICES	Deinf
INTERNATIONAL AFFAIRS SPECIALIZED OFFICE	Dean
BRANCHES OF THE FEDERAL REVENUE OF BRAZIL	ARF
INSPECTORATE OFFICES OF THE FEDERAL REVENUE OF BRAZIL	IRF
CUSTOMS OFFICES OF THE FEDERAL REVENUE OF BRAZIL	ALF

부록 Ⅵ. 인증 주관 기관 및 시험기관

☐ INMETRO (Instituto Nacional de Metrologia de Normalização e Qualidade Industrial) : 도량형 및 품질 관리국
  ○ 동 기관은 통상산업개발부 소속으로 본부는 리우 데 자네이루 시에 위치
  ○ 각종 제품의 품질검사를 주관하며, 기준에 합당한 제품에 한해서 품질인증서를 발행함
  ○ 동 기관의 주요 업무는 다음과 같음
    - 각종 제품의 물리 화학적 도량형을 연구, 표준 도량형을 규정
    - 각 업체에게 제품 관련 표준규정을 통보, 업체로 하여금 항상 규정에 부합하는 제품을 생산 할 수 있도록 유도
    - 전문 인증기관으로 활동하기 희망하는 업체를 대상으로 각종 테스트를 거친 후 공인된 인증기관 자격을 부여하며 인증 관련 기술 및 인프라를 지속적으로 제공함
    - 품질 인증 : INMETRO의 규정에 따른 품질 인증업체가 자체적으로 실시한 검수 시험 결과 검토 및 품질 인정 공인된 기관을 통해 품질을 인정받은 제품에게 품질보증 실(Seal) 부착
    - 본부 주소 : Rua Santa Alexandrina, 416- 5º andar, Rio Comprido - Rio de Janeiro - RJ, CEP: 20261-232, Brazil
    - 전화: 0800- 285-1818 FAX: (21) 2563-2970
    - E-Mail: homepage@inmetro.com.br
    - Site: www.inmetro.gov.br

☐ IPEM (Istituto de Pesos e Medidas) : 도량형, 품질관리국
  ○ 주정부 소속 기관으로 INMETRO와 공조 관계를 유지하고 있음

○ INMETRO와 더불어 각종 제품 및 서비스의 품질, 규격 등을 검사, 관리하는 기관으로 각 주별로 별도의 기관이 있음

○ 상파울루 주의 경우 IPEM-SP (IPEM 상파울루 지국)이 있음
- IPEM- SP 주소: Rua Santa Cruz, nº 1.922 - 7º andar - Vila, Cep 04122-002 Gumercindo, São Paulo, SP, Brazil
- Fone/Fax: (55-11) 5085.2602 / 5085.2603
- E-mail: gabinete-ipem@ipem.sp.gov.br
- Site: www.ipem.sp.gov.br

☐ INMETRO로부터 허가를 취득한 국내 외 전문 인증기관
○ OCS (Organismo de Certificação de Sistema de Qualidade)
- 특징: 시스템의 품질 인증
- 적용 규정: ABNT, ISO9001
- 기관 수: 브라질(29), 아르헨티나(1), 베네수엘라(1), 우루과이(2), 미국(1)
○ OCP (Organismo de Certificação de de Produto)
- 특징: 제품 품질 인증
- 적용 규성: 제품에 따라 각종 국내 및 해외 규정을 적용
- 기관 수: 브라질(50), 아르헨티나(3), 코스타리카(1), 베네수엘라(1)
○ OCA (Organismo de Certificação de Sistema de Gestão Ambiental)
- 특징 : 환경관리 시스템 인증
- 적용 규정: NBR ISO 14001
- 기관 수: 브라질(17), 아르헨티나(1), 미국(1), 우루과이(1)
○ OHC (Organismos de Certificação de Sistema de Gestão da Análise de Perigos e Pontos Críticos de Controle)
- 특징: 식품안전 관련 인증
- 적용 규정: ABNT NBR 14900
- 기관 수: 브라질(1)
○ OPC (Organismo de Certificação de Pessoas)

- 특징: 인력품질 인증
- 적용 규정: SBAC
- 기관 수: 브라질 (7)

○ OCF (Organismo de Certificação de Manejo de Florestas)
- 특징: 삼림관리 관련 인증
- 적용 규정: NBR 14789
- 기관 수: 브라질 (2)

○ OCE (Organismo de Certificação de Sistemsas de Gestão da Qualidade NBR 15100)
- 특징: 우주공학 관련 프로젝트, 건축물, 서비스 등의 품질인증
- 적용 규정: NBR 15100
- 기관 수: 브라질 (3)

○ OCQ (Organismo de Certificação de Sistemas de Gestão da Qualidade QS9000)
- 특징: QS 9000 관련 인증
- 적용 규정: QS 9000
- 기관 수: 브라질 (11), 아르헨티나(1)

○ OCO (Organismo de Certificação de Sistemas de Gestão da Qualidade de Empresas de Serviços e Obras na Construção Civil (SiAC/PBQP-H))
- 특징: 건축공사 관련 품질인증
- 적용 규정: PBQP-H
- 기관 수: 브라질 (9)

☐ ANATEL (Agencia Nacional de Telecomunicações) : 국가정보통신국
○ 정보통신부 소속 기관으로 통신 기기 관련 각종 법률 및 규정을 제정함
○ 통신기기 업자들은 동 기관이 인정하는 인증기관 및 시험 기관을 통해 품질인증 및 등록 절차를 마쳐야 브라질 시장 내 유통이 가능함
- Anatel - 본부 주소: SAUS Quadra 06 Blocos C, E, F e H,CEP 70.070-940 - Brasília - DF, Brazil

- 전화 : (55 61) 2312-2000, Fax: (55 61) 2312-2264
- Anatel - 상파울루 지국 주소 : Rua Vergueiro, 3073, Vila Mariana - CEP 04101-300 São Paulo/SP 전화: (55 11) 2104-8800, FAX: (55 11) 2104-8815

부록 Ⅶ. GSTP 혜택 품목

HS CODE	Description of Product	Base Rate-MFN Applied Rate of Duty(%)	GSTP Margin of Preference (%)
0106903020	Yarn earth worms	8	20
0209002000	Poultry fat	3	20
0301999094	Grass carp	10	20
0303799040	Thorny head	10	20
0502100000	Pigs', hogs' or boars' bristles and hair and waste thereof	3	20
0502909000	Other	3	20
0506100000	Ossein and bones treated with acid	3	20
0506901010	Of tigers	3	20
0507902020	Whalebone and whale	8	20
0508002030	Oyster shells	8	20
0508002040	Snail shells	8	20
0508002050	Trocus shells	8	20
0508002060	Agaya shells	8	20
0508002070	Fresh water shells (Megalonaiasnervosa, Amblemaplicata, Quadrula quadrula spp.)	8	20
0511911090	Other	8	20
0511996000	Natural sponges of animal origin	8	20
1204000000	Linseed, whether or not broken.	3	20
1207910000	Poppy seeds	3	20
1212910000	Sugar beet	3	20
1302311000	Agar-agar in stripe form	8	20
1501002000	Poultry fat	3	20
1503002000	Lard-oil	3	20
1503009000	Other	3	20
1504301000	Whale oil and its fractions	3	20
1504309000	Other	3	20
1521901000	Spermaceti	8	20
2501001010	Rock salt	1	20
2501001020	Sea salt made by the heat of the sun	1	20
2501009010	Edible salt	8	20
2501009020	Pure sodium chloride	8	20

2501009090	Other	8	20
2502000000	Unroasted iron pyrites.	2	20
2503000000	Sulphur of all kinds, other than sublimed sulphur, precipitated sulphur and colloidal sulphur.	2	20
2504101000	Natural graphite, crystalline	3	20
2504102000	Natural graphite, amorphous	3	20
2504109000	Other	3	20
2504901000	Natural graphite, crystalline	3	20
2504902000	Natural graphite, amorphous	3	20
2504909000	Other	3	20
2505100000	Silica sands and quartz sands	3	20
2505901010	Clayey sand	3	20
2505901020	Felspathic sand	3	20
2505901090	Other	3	20
2505909000	Other	3	20
2506101000	Containing less than 0.06 % of impurities	3	20
2506102000	Containing not less than 0.06 % but not more than 0.1 % of impurities	3	20
2506103000	Containing more than 0.1 % of impurities	3	20
2506201000	Crude or roughly trimmed	3	20
2506209000	Other	3	20
2507001010	Not calcined	3	20
2507001090	Other	3	20
2507002010	Gairome	3	20
2507002020	Kibushi	3	20
2507002090	Other	3	20
2507009000	Other	3	20
2508100000	Bentonite	3	20
2508300000	Fire-clay	3	20
2508401000	Acid clay	3	20
2508402000	Decolourising earths and fuller's earth	3	20
2508409000	Other	3	20
2508501000	Andalusite	3	20
2508502000	Kyanite	3	20
2508503000	Sillimanite	3	20
2508600000	Mullite	3	20
2508701000	Shamotte	3	20
2508702000	Dinas earth	3	20
2509000000	Chalk.	3	20
2510102000	Natural aluminium calcium phosphates	1	20
2510109000	Other	1	20
2510201000	Natural calcium phosphates	3	20
2510202000	Natural aluminium calcium phosphates	3	20
2510209000	Other	3	20
2511100000	Natural barium sulphate (barytes)	3	20

2511200000	Natural barium carbonate (witherite)	3	20
2512000000	Siliceous fossil meals (for example, kieselguhr, tripolite and diatomite) and similar siliceous earths, whether or not calcined, of an apparent specific gravity of 1 or less.	3	20
2513101000	Crude or in irregular pieces, including crushed pumice ("bimskies")	3	20
2513109000	Other	3	20
2513201010	Emery	3	20
2513201020	Natural corundum	3	20
2513201030	Natural garnet	3	20
2513201090	Other	3	20
2513202010	Emery	3	20
2513202020	Natural corundum	3	20
2513202030	Natural garnet	3	20
2513202090	Other	3	20
2515111000	Marble	3	20
2515112000	Travertine	3	20
2515121000	Marble	3	20
2515122000	Travertine	3	20
2515200000	Ecaussine and other calcareous monumental or building stone; alabaster	3	20
2517101000	Pebbles	3	20
2517102000	Broken or crushed stone	3	20
2517109000	Other	3	20
2517200000	Macadam of slag, dross or similar industrial waste, whether or not incorporating the materials cited in subheading 2517.10	3	20
2517300000	Tarred macadam	3	20
2517410000	Of marble	3	20
2518100000	Dolomite, not calcined or sintered	3	20
2518200000	Calcined or sintered dolomite	3	20
2518300000	Dolomite ramming mix	3	20
2519100000	Natural magnesium carbonate (magnesite)	3	20
2519901000	Fused and dead-burned magnesia	3	20
2519902000	Natural magnesium oxide	3	20
2519909000	Other	3	20
2520101000	Gypsum	5	20
2520102000	Anhydrite	5	20
2521001000	Limestone	3	20
2521009000	Other	3	20
2522100000	Quicklime	3	20
2522200000	Slaked lime	3	20
2522300000	Hydraulic lime	3	20
2524100000	Crocidolite	5	20
2524901000	Amosite	5	20

2524902000	Chrysotile	5	20
2524909000	Other	5	20
2525100000	Crude mica and mica rifted into sheets or splittings	3	20
2525200000	Mica powder	3	20
2525300000	Mica waste	3	20
2526101000	Whether or not roughly trimmed or merely cut, by sawing or otherwise, into blocks or slabs of a rectangular shape (including square)	3	20
2526109000	Other	3	20
2526200000	Crushed or powdered	5	20
2528100000	Natural sodium borates and concentrates thereof (whether or not calcined)	3	20
2528901000	Calcium borates	3	20
2528902000	Magnesium chloroborate	3	20
2528903000	Natural boric acid	3	20
2528909000	Other	3	20
2529100000	Feldspar	3	20
2529211000	Powder	2	20
2529219000	Other	2	20
2529221000	Powder	2	20
2529229000	Other	2	20
2529301000	Leucite	2	20
2529302000	Nepheline	2	20
2529303000	Nepheline syenite	2	20
2530101000	Vermiculite	3	20
2530102000	Perlites and chlorites	3	20
2530200000	Kieserite, epsomite (natural magnesium sulphates)	3	20
2530901000	Natural arsenic sulfides	3	20
2530902000	Pyrolusite (manganese ore) suitable for manufacturing dry batteries	3	20
2530903000	Strontianite	3	20
2530904000	Cinnabar	3	20
2530905000	Pyrophyllite	3	20
2530906000	Zeolites	3	20
2530907000	Alunites	3	20
2530908000	Wollastonites	3	20
2530909020	Sericites	3	20
2530909030	Earth colours	8	20
2530909040	Natural micaceous iron oxides	8	20
2530909050	Natural cryolite and natural chiolite	3	20
2530909091	Natural calcium carbonate	3	20
2530909099	Other	3	20
2601200000	Roasted iron pyrites	1	20
2618000000	Granulated slag (slag sand) from the manufacture of iron or steel.	2	20

2619001010	Blast furnace slag	2	20
2619001090	Other	2	20
2619002000	Dross	2	20
2619003000	Scalings	2	20
2619009000	Other	2	20
2620110000	Hard zinc spelter	2	20
2620210000	Leaded gasoline sludges and leaded anti-knock compound sludges	2	20
2620290000	Other	2	20
2620300000	Containing mainly copper	2	20
2620400000	Containing mainly aluminium	2	20
2620600000	Containing arsenic, mercury, thallium or their mixtures, of a kind used for the extraction of arsenic or those metals or for the manufacture of their chemical compounds	2	20
2620910000	Containing antimony, beryllium, cadmium, chromium or their mixtures	2	20
2620990000	Other	2	20
2621100000	Ash and residues from the incineration of municipal waste	2	20
2621900000	Other	2	20
2701201000	Briquettes	1	20
2701202000	Ovoids	1	20
2701209000	Other	1	20
2702100000	Lignite, whether or not pulverised, but not agglomerated	1	20
2702200000	Agglomerated lignite	1	20
2703001000	Not agglomerated	1	20
2703002000	Agglomerated	1	20
2704001010	Of coal	3	20
2704001090	Other	3	20
2704002000	Semi-coke	3	20
2704003000	Retort carbon	3	20
2705000000	Coal gas, water gas, producer gas and similar gases, other than petroleum gases and other gaseous hydrocarbons.	5	20
2706001000	Coal tars	5	20
2706002000	Tars from lignit or peat	5	20
2706009000	Other	5	20
2707100000	Benzol (benzene)	3	20
2707200000	Toluol (toluene)	3	20
2707300000	Xylol (xylenes)	3	20
2707400000	Naphthalene	5	20
2707910000	Creosote oils	5	20
2707991000	Solvent naphtha	5	20
2707992000	Anthracene	5	20
2707993000	Phenols	8	20
2707999000	Other	5	20
2708100000	Pitch	5	20

2708200000	Pitch coke	5	20
2710911010	Of motor spirit, aviation spirit and jet fuel	5	20
2710911090	Other	5	20
2710912010	Of kerosene and jet fuel	5	20
2710912090	Other	5	20
2710913000	Of gas oils	5	20
2710914010	Of light fuel oil (bunker A), fuel oil (bunker B) and bunker C	5	20
2710914090	Other	5	20
2710915000	Of raw oils, lubricating oil (other than extender oil) and lubricating base oil	7	20
2710919000	Other	8	20
2710991010	Of motor spirit, aviation spirit and jet fuel	5	20
2710991090	Other	5	20
2710992010	Of kerosene and jet fuel	5	20
2710992090	Other	5	20
2710993000	Of gas oils	5	20
2710994010	Of light fuel oil (bunker A), fuel oil (bunker B) and bunker C	5	20
2710994090	Other	5	20
2710995000	Of raw oils, lubricating oil (other than extender oil) and lubricating base oil	7	20
2710999000	Other	8	20
2712101000	Vaseline	8	20
2712109000	Other	8	20
2712200000	Paraffin wax containing by weight less than 0.75 % of oil	8	20
2712901010	Slack wax and scale wax	8	20
2712901020	Microcrystalline wax	8	20
2712901090	Other	8	20
2712909010	Montan wax	8	20
2712909020	Peat wax	8	20
2712909030	Ceresin wax	8	20
2712909040	Synthetic paraffin wax	8	20
2712909090	Other	8	20
2713110000	Not calcined	5	20
2713120000	Calcined	5	20
2713200000	Petroleum bitumen	5	20
2713900000	Other residues of petroleum oils or of oils obtained from bituminous minerals	5	20
2714100000	Bituminous or oil shale and tar sands	5	20
2714901000	Bitumen and asphalt, natural	5	20
2714902000	Asphaltites	5	20
2714903000	Asphaltic rock	5	20
2715001000	Cut-backs	5	20
2715002000	Emulsions or stable suspensions of asphalt, bitumen, pitch	5	20

	or tar		
2715003000	Mastics	5	20
2715009000	Other	5	20
2716000000	Electrical energy.	5	20
2801100000	Chlorine	5.5	20
2801200000	Iodine	5.5	20
2801301000	Fluorine	5.5	20
2801302000	Bromine	5.5	20
2802001000	Sulphur, sublimed	5	20
2802002000	Sulphur, precipitated	5	20
2802003000	Colloidal sulfur	5	20
2803001000	Acetylene black	5.5	20
2803009010	Carbon blacks	5.5	20
2803009090	Other	5.5	20
2804100000	Hydrogen	5.5	20
2804210000	Argon	5.5	20
2804291000	Helium	5.5	20
2804292000	Neon	5.5	20
2804293000	Krypton	5.5	20
2804294000	Xenon	5.5	20
2804299000	Other	5.5	20
2804300000	Nitrogen	5.5	20
2804400000	Oxygen	5.5	20
2804501000	Boron	5.5	20
2804502000	Tellurium	5.5	20
2804610000	Containing by weight not less than 99.99 % of silicon	3	20
2804690000	Other	5.5	20
2804701000	Yellow phosphorous	5	20
2804709000	Other	5.5	20
2804800000	Arsenic	5.5	20
2804900000	Selenium	5.5	20
2805110000	Sodium	5.5	20
2805120000	Calcium	5.5	20
2805190000	Other	5.5	20
2805301000	Cerium group	5.5	20
2805302000	Terbium group	5.5	20
2805303000	Erbium group	5.5	20
2805304000	Yttrium	5.5	20
2805305000	Scandium	5.5	20
2805309000	Other	5.5	20
2805400000	Mercury	5.5	20
2806100000	Hydrogen chloride (hydrochloric acid)	5.5	20
2806200000	Chlorosulphuric acid	5.5	20
2807001010	For making semiconductor	5.5	20
2807001090	Other	5.5	20

2807002000	Oleum	5.5	20
2808001010	For making semiconductor	5.5	20
2808001090	Other	5.5	20
2808002000	Sulphonitric acids	5.5	20
2809100000	Diphosphorus pentaoxide	5.5	20
2809201010	For making semiconductor	5.5	20
2809201090	Other	5.5	20
2809202010	Metaphosphoric acid	5.5	20
2809202020	Pyrophosphoric acid	5.5	20
2809202090	Other	5.5	20
2810001010	Diboron trioxide	5.5	20
2810001090	Other	5.5	20
2810002000	Ortho boric acid	5.5	20
2810003000	Meta boric acid	5.5	20
2810009000	Other	5.5	20
2811111000	For making semiconductor	5.5	20
2811119000	Other	5.5	20
2811191000	Hydrogensulphide	5.5	20
2811192000	Hydrobromic acid	5.5	20
2811193000	Sulphamic acid	5.5	20
2811194000	Perchloric acid	5.5	20
2811195000	Chloric acid	5.5	20
2811196000	Hypophosphorous acid	5.5	20
2811197000	Phosphorous acid	5.5	20
2811198000	Arsenic acid	5.5	20
2811199010	Hydrogen cyanide	5.5	20
2811199090	Other	5.5	20
2811210000	Carbon dioxide	5.5	20
2811221000	White carbon	5.5	20
2811229090	Other	5.5	20
2811291000	Carbon monoxide	5.5	20
2811292000	Nitrous oxide	5.5	20
2811293000	Nitrogen dioxide	5.5	20
2811294000	Arsenic trioxide	5.5	20
2811295000	Arsenic pentoxide	5.5	20
2811299000	Other	5.5	20
2812101010	Iodine trichloride	5	20
2812101020	Phosphorous trichloride	5	20
2812101030	Phosphorous pentachloride	5	20
2812101040	Arsenic trichloride	5	20
2812101050	Sulphur monochloride	5	20
2812101060	Sulphur dichloride	5	20
2812101090	Other	5	20
2812102010	Thionyl chloride	5	20
2812102020	Carbonyl dichloride (phosgene)	5	20

2812102030	Phosphorous oxychloride	5	20
2812102090	Other	5	20
2812901000	Boron trifluoride	5.5	20
2812902000	Sulphur hexafluoride	5.5	20
2812909000	Other	5.5	20
2813100000	Carbon disulphide	5.5	20
2813901020	Phosphorous pentasulphide	5.5	20
2813901090	Other	5.5	20
2813902010	Diarsenic pentasulphide	5.5	20
2813902090	Other	5.5	20
2813903000	Silicon sulphide	5.5	20
2813909000	Other	5.5	20
2814100000	Anhydrous ammonia	1	20
2814200000	Ammonia in aqueous solution	2	20
2815110000	Solid	5.5	20
2815120000	In aqueous solution (soda lye or liquid soda)	8	20
2815200000	Potassium hydroxide (caustic potash)	5.5	20
2815301000	Sodium peroxide	5.5	20
2815302000	Potassium peroxide	5.5	20
2816101000	Magnesium hydroxide	5.5	20
2816102000	Magnesium peroxide	5.5	20
2816400000	Oxides, hydroxides and peroxides, of strontium or barium	5.5	20
2817001000	Zinc oxide	5.5	20
2817002000	Zinc peroxide	5.5	20
2818109000	Other	3	20
2818200000	Aluminium oxide, other than artificial corundum	1	20
2818301000	Alumina gel	5.5	20
2819100000	Chromium trioxide	5.5	20
2819901010	Chromic oxides	5.5	20
2819901090	Other	5.5	20
2819902000	Chromium hydroxides	5.5	20
2820100000	Manganese dioxide	5.5	20
2820901000	Manganese oxide	5.5	20
2820902000	Manganic oxide	5.5	20
2820909000	Other	5.5	20
2821101000	Iron oxides	5.5	20
2821102000	Iron hydroxides	5.5	20
2821200000	Earth colours	5.5	20
2822001010	Cobaltic oxide	5.5	20
2822001091	For manufacturing secondary battery	4	20
2822001099	Other	5.5	20
2822002010	Cobaltous hydroxide	5.5	20
2822002090	Other	5.5	20
2823001000	Anatase type	5.5	20
2823009000	Other	5.5	20

2824100000	Lead monoxide (litharge, massicot)	5.5	20
2824901000	Red lead and orange lead	5.5	20
2824909000	Other	5.5	20
2825101000	Hydrazine hydrate	5.5	20
2825109010	Hydrazine	5.5	20
2825109020	Inorganic salts of hydrazine	5.5	20
2825109030	Hydroxylamine	5.5	20
2825109041	Hydroxyl ammonium chloride (hydroxylamine hydrochloride)	5.5	20
2825109049	Other	5.5	20
2825201000	Lithium oxide	5.5	20
2825202000	Lithium hydroxide	5.5	20
2825301000	Vanadic pentoxide	2	20
2825309000	Other	3	20
2825401000	Nickel oxides	5.5	20
2825402000	Nickel hydroxides	5.5	20
2825501000	Copper oxides	5.5	20
2825502010	Material for manufacturing agricultural chemicals (registered material under the Agricultural Chemicals Management Act)	2	20
2825502090	Other	5.5	20
2825601000	Germanium oxides	5.5	20
2825602000	Zirconium dioxide	5.5	20
2825701000	Molybdenum oxides	3	20
2825702000	Molybdenum hydroxide	5.5	20
2825800000	Antimony oxides	5.5	20
2825901010	Calcium oxide	5.5	20
2825901020	Tungsten oxides	1	20
2825901030	Tin oxides	5.5	20
2825901090	Other	5.5	20
2825902010	Calcium hydroxide	5.5	20
2825902020	Manganes hydroxides	5.5	20
2825902030	Tungsten hydroxides	5.5	20
2825902040	Tin hydroxides	5.5	20
2825902090	Other	5.5	20
2825903010	Nickel peroxides	5.5	20
2825903090	Other	5.5	20
2825909000	Other	5.5	20
2826120000	Of aluminium	5.5	20
2826191000	Calcium fluoride	5.5	20
2826193010	Potassium hydrogen fouoride	5.5	20
2826193090	Other	5.5	20
2826194000	Ammonium or sodium fluoride	5.5	20
2826195000	Tungsten Hexafluoride(WF6)	5.5	20
2826199000	Other	5.5	20

2826300000	Sodium hexafluoroaluminate (synthetic cryolite)	5.5	20
2826901000	Artificial chiolite	5.5	20
2826902000	Calcium fluorosilicate	5.5	20
2826903000	Fluoroborates	5.5	20
2826904000	Fluorophosphates	5.5	20
2826905000	Fluorosulphates	5.5	20
2826906000	Fluorosilicates of sodium or of potassium	5.5	20
2826909000	Other	5.5	20
2827100000	Ammonium chloride	5.5	20
2827200000	Calcium chloride	5.5	20
2827310000	Of magnesium	5.5	20
2827320000	Of aluminium	5.5	20
2827350000	Of nickel	5.5	20
2827391000	Of copper	5.5	20
2827399000	Other	5.5	20
2827411000	Copper chloride oxides	5.5	20
2827412010	Material for manufacturing agricultural chemicals (registered material under the Agricultural Chemicals Management Act)	2	20
2827412090	Other	5.5	20
2827491000	Chloride oxides	5.5	20
2827492000	Chloride hydroxides	5.5	20
2827511000	Sodium bromide	5.5	20
2827512000	Potassium bromide	5.5	20
2827591000	Calcium bromide	5.5	20
2827599000	Other	5.5	20
2827601000	Iodide oxides	5.5	20
2827609010	Potassium iodide	5.5	20
2827609090	Other	5.5	20
2828100000	Commercial calcium hypochlorite and other calcium hypochlorites	5.5	20
2828901010	Sodium hypochlorite	5.5	20
2828901020	Potassium hypochlorite	5.5	20
2828901090	Other	5.5	20
2828902010	Sodium chlorite	5.5	20
2828902020	Aluminium chlorite	5.5	20
2828902090	Other	5.5	20
2828903000	Hypobromites	5.5	20
2829110000	Of sodium	5.5	20
2829191000	Potassium chlorate	5.5	20
2829192000	Barium chlorate	5.5	20
2829199000	Other	5.5	20
2829901010	Sodium perchlorate	5.5	20
2829901020	Ammonium perchlorate	5.5	20
2829901090	Other	5.5	20

2829902010	Bromates	5.5	20
2829902020	Perbromates	5.5	20
2829902030	Iodates	5.5	20
2829902040	Periodates	5.5	20
2830101000	Sodium hydrogen sulphide	5.5	20
2830109000	Other	5.5	20
2830901000	Sulphides	5.5	20
2830902000	Polysulphides	5.5	20
2831101000	Sodium dithionite	5.5	20
2831102000	Sodium sulphoxy late (sodium form aldehyde sulphoxylate)	5.5	20
2831901000	Dithionites	5.5	20
2831902000	Sulphoxylates	5.5	20
2832101000	Sodium bisulphite	5.5	20
2832109000	Other	5.5	20
2832201000	Ammonium sulphite	5.5	20
2832202000	Potassium sulphites	5.5	20
2832203000	Calcium sulphites	5.5	20
2832209000	Other	5.5	20
2832301000	Ammonium thiosulphate	5.5	20
2832302000	Sodium thiosulphate	5.5	20
2832303000	Potassium thiosulphate	5.5	20
2832309000	Other	5.5	20
2833110000	Disodium sulphate	5.5	20
2833191000	Sodium hydrogen sulphate	5.5	20
2833192000	Disodium disulphate	5.5	20
2833199000	Other	5.5	20
2833210000	Of magnesium	5.5	20
2833220000	Of aluminium	5.5	20
2833240000	Of nickel	5.5	20
2833251000	Material for manufacturing agricultural chemicals (registered material under the Agricultural Chemicals Management Act)	2	20
2833259000	Other	5.5	20
2833270000	Of barium	5.5	20
2833299000	Other	5.5	20
2833300000	Alums	5.5	20
2833401000	Diammonium peroxodisulphate	5.5	20
2833402000	Disodium peroxodisulphate	5.5	20
2833403000	Calcium peroxodisulphate	5.5	20
2833409000	Other	5.5	20
2834101000	Sodium nitrite	5.5	20
2834109000	Other	5.5	20
2834210000	Of potassium	5.5	20
2834291000	Barium nitrate	5.5	20
2834299000	Other	5.5	20

2835101010	Sodium hypophosphite	5.5	20
2835101020	Calcium hypophosphite	5.5	20
2835101090	Other	5.5	20
2835102000	Phosphites	5.5	20
2835221000	Of mono-sodium	5.5	20
2835222000	Of disodium	5.5	20
2835240000	Of potassium	5.5	20
2835250000	Calcium hydrogenorthophosphate ("dicalcium phosphate")	5.5	20
2835260000	Other phosphates of calcium	5.5	20
2835291000	Aluminium phosphate	5.5	20
2835299000	Other polyphosphates	5.5	20
2835310000	Sodium triphosphate (sodium tripolyphosphate)	5.5	20
2835399000	Other	5.5	20
2836200000	Disodium carbonate	4	20
2836300000	Sodium hydrogencarbonate (sodium bicarbonate)	5.5	20
2836400000	Potassium carbonates	5.5	20
2836600000	Barium carbonate	5.5	20
2836910000	Lithium carbonates	5.5	20
2836920000	Strontium carbonate	5.5	20
2836991010	Magnesium carbonate	5.5	20
2836991020	Commercial ammonium carbonate and other ammonium carbonates	5.5	20
2836991090	Other	5.5	20
2836992000	Peroxocarbonates (percarbonates)	5.5	20
2837111000	Sodium cyanides	5.5	20
2837112000	Sodium cyanide oxides	5.5	20
2837191010	Potassium cyanide	5.5	20
2837191020	Copper cyanides	5.5	20
2837191030	Zinc cyanide	5.5	20
2837191090	Other	5.5	20
2837192000	Cyanide oxides	5.5	20
2837201000	Ferrocyanides	5.5	20
2837202000	Ferricyanides	5.5	20
2837209000	Other	5.5	20
2839110000	Sodium metasilicates	5.5	20
2839190000	Other	5.5	20
2839901000	Zirconium silicates	5.5	20
2839902000	Barium silicates	5.5	20
2839909000	Other	5.5	20
2840110000	Anhydrous	5	20
2840190000	Other	5	20
2840200000	Other borates	5	20
2840300000	Peroxoborates (perborates)	5	20
2841300000	Sodium dichromate	5.5	20
2841501000	Potassium chromate	5.5	20

2841509000	Other	5.5	20
2841610000	Potassium permanganate	5.5	20
2841691000	Manganites	5.5	20
2841692000	Manganates	5.5	20
2841693000	Permanganates	5.5	20
2841700000	Molybdates	5.5	20
2841800000	Tungstates (wolframates)	5	20
2841901000	Stannates	5.5	20
2841902010	Barium titannate	5.5	20
2841902020	Strontium titannate	5.5	20
2841902030	Lead titannate	5.5	20
2841902090	Other	5.5	20
2841903000	Antimonates	5.5	20
2841904000	Ferrates and ferrites	5.5	20
2841905000	Vanadates	5.5	20
2841906000	Bismuthates	5.5	20
2841909000	Other	5.5	20
2842101000	Aluminosilicates	6.5	20
2842109000	Other	5.5	20
2842901000	Salts of selenium acids	5.5	20
2842903000	Double or complex salts containing sulphur	5.5	20
2842905000	Double or complex salts of selenium	5.5	20
2842909000	Other	5.5	20
2843101000	Colloidal silver	5.5	20
2843102000	Colloidal gold	5.5	20
2843103000	Colloidal platinum	5.5	20
2843109000	Other	5.5	20
2843211000	For making semiconductor	5.5	20
2843219000	Other	5.5	20
2843291000	For making semiconductor	5.5	20
2843299000	Other	5.5	20
2843301000	Potassium gold cyanide for making semiconductor	5.5	20
2843309000	Other	5.5	20
2843901000	Amalgams	5.5	20
2843909010	Platinum compounds	5.5	20
2843909090	Other	5.5	20
2846100000	Cerium compounds	5	20
2846901000	Yttrium oxide	5	20
2846909000	Other	5	20
2847002000	For making semiconductor	5.5	20
2847009000	Other	5.5	20
2848001000	Of copper (phosphor copper), containing more than 15 % by weight of phosphorus	5.5	20
2848002000	Aluminium phosphide	5.5	20
2848009000	Other	5.5	20

2849100000	Of calcium	5.5	20
2849901000	Complex carbides	5.5	20
2849909010	Tungsten carbides	5.5	20
2849909090	Other	5.5	20
2850001000	Hydrides	5.5	20
2850002000	Nitrides	5.5	20
2850003000	Azides	5.5	20
2850004000	Silicides	5.5	20
2850005000	Borides	5.5	20
2852001000	Of subheading 2825.90, 2827.39, 2827.49, 2827.60, 2830.90, 2833.29, 2834.29, 2835.39, 2837.19, 2837.20, 2841.50, 2842.10, 2842.90, 2843.90, 2848.00, 2849.90, 2850.00 or 2853.00	5.5	20
2852002000	Of subheading 2918.11, 2931.00, 2932.99, 2934.99.9090, 3201.920000, 3201.90.4000, 3206.50, 3707.90, 3822.00.1091 or 3822.020091	6.5	20
2852003000	Of subheading 2934.99.2000, 3822.00.1092 or 3822.020092	6.5	20
2852004000	Of subheading 3502.90 or 3504.00	8	20
2853001000	Distilled or conductivity water and water of similar purity	5.5	20
2853002000	Compressed air	5.5	20
2853003000	Amalgam	5.5	20
2853004010	Cyanogen chloride	5.5	20
2853004090	Other	5.5	20
2853005000	Alkali amides	5.5	20
2853009000	Other	5.5	20
2902110000	Cyclohexane	5	20
2902191000	Ethylidene Norbornene	5	20
2902199000	Other	5	20
2902410000	o-xylene	5	20
2902420000	m-xylene	5	20
2902440000	Mixed xylene isomers	3	20
2902600000	Ethylbenzene	5	20
2902700000	Cumene	3	20
2903111000	Chloromethane (methyl chloride)	5.5	20
2903112000	Chloroethane (ethyl chloride)	5.5	20
2903120000	Dichloromethane (methylene chloride)	5.5	20
2903130000	Chloroform (trichloromethane)	5.5	20
2903140000	Carbon tetrachloride	5.5	20
2903191000	1,1,1-trichloroethane (methyl chloroform)	5.5	20
2903199000	Other	5.5	20
2903210000	Vinyl chloride (chloroethylene)	5.5	20
2903220000	Trichloroethylene	5.5	20
2903230000	Tetrachloroethylene (perchloroethylene)	5.5	20
2903290000	Other	5.5	20
2903310000	Ethylene dibromide (ISO) (1,2-dibromoethane)	5.5	20

2903391000	Bromomethane (methyl bromide)	5.5	20
2903392000	Bromoethane, excluding 1,2-dibromoethane	5.5	20
2903393000	Iodomethane	5.5	20
2903394000	Hexafluoroethane (CFC-116)	5.5	20
2903395000	1,1-difluoro ethane (HFC-152a)	5.5	20
2903396000	1,1,1,2-tetra fluoro ethane (HFC-134a)	5.5	20
2903397000	1,1,3,3,3-penta fluoro-2-(trifluoromethyl)pro-1-pene	5.5	20
2903399000	Other	5.5	20
2903410000	Trichlorofluormethane	5.5	20
2903420000	Dichlorodifluoromethane	5.5	20
2903430000	Trichlorotrifluoroethanes	5.5	20
2903441000	Dichlorotetrafluoroethanes (CFC-114)	5.5	20
2903442000	Chloropentafluoroethane (CFC-115)	5.5	20
2903451010	Chlorotrifluoromethane (CFC-13)	5.5	20
2903451090	Other	5.5	20
2903452010	Pentachlorofluoroethane (CFC-111)	5.5	20
2903452020	Tetrachlorodifluoroethane (CFC-112)	5.5	20
2903452090	Other	5.5	20
2903453010	Heptachlorofluoropropane (CFC-211)	5.5	20
2903453020	Hexachlorodifluoropropane (CFC-212)	5.5	20
2903453030	Pentachlorotrifluoropropane (CFC-213)	5.5	20
2903453040	Tetrachlorotetrafluoropropane (CFC-214)	5.5	20
2903453050	Trichloropentafluoropropane (CFC-215)	5.5	20
2903453060	Dichlorohexafluoropropane (CFC-216)	5.5	20
2903453070	Chloroheptafluoropropane (CFC-217)	5.5	20
2903453090	Other	5.5	20
2903461000	Bromochlorodifluoromethane (Halon-1211)	5.5	20
2903462000	Bromotrifluoromethane (Halon-1301)	5.5	20
2903463000	Dibromotetrafluoroethane (Halon-2402)	5.5	20
2903471000	Hydrobromofluorocarbon	5.5	20
2903479000	Other	5.5	20
2903491110	Dichlorofluoromethane (HCFC-21)	5.5	20
2903491120	Chlorodifluoromethane (HCFC-22)	5.5	20
2903491130	Chlorofluoromethane (HCFC-31)	5.5	20
2903491190	Other	5.5	20
2903491210	Dichlorotrifluoroethane (HCFC-123)	5.5	20
2903491220	Chlorotetrafluoroethane (HCFC-124)	5.5	20
2903491230	Dichlorofluoroethane (HCFC-141)	5.5	20
2903491240	Chlorodifluoroethane (HCFC-142)	5.5	20
2903491290	Other	5.5	20
2903491310	Dichloropentafluoropropane (HCFC-225)	5.5	20
2903491390	Other	5.5	20
2903492000	Derivatives of methane, ethane or propane, halogenated only with fluorine and bromine	5.5	20
2903499000	Other	5.5	20

2903510000	1,2,3,4,5,6-Hexachlorocyclohexane (HCH (ISO)), including lindane (ISO, INN)	5.5	20
2903520000	Aldrin (ISO), chlordane (ISO) and heptachlor (ISO)	5.5	20
2903590000	Other	5.5	20
2903611000	Chlorobenzene	5.5	20
2903619000	Other	5.5	20
2903621000	Hexachlorobenzene (ISO)	5.5	20
2903622000	DDT (ISO) (clofenotane (INN), 1,1,1-trichloro-2, 2-bis(p-chlorophenyl)ethane)	5.5	20
2903691000	Benzyl chloride	5.5	20
2903692010	1,2,4-Trichlorobenzene	5.5	20
2903692090	Other	5.5	20
2903693000	Benzotrichloride	5.5	20
2903699000	Other	5.5	20
2904101000	Benzene sulphonic acid	5.5	20
2904201000	Nitrotoluene	5.5	20
2904209010	Nitrobenzene	5.5	20
2904209020	4-Nitrobiphenyl and its salts	5.5	20
2904209090	Other	5.5	20
2904901000	2,4-dinitrochlorobenzene	5.5	20
2904902000	p-nitrochlorobenzene	5.5	20
2904903000	Trichloronitromethane (chloropicrin)	5.5	20
2904909000	Other	5.5	20
2905110000	Methanol (methyl alcohol)	2	20
2905121000	Propan-1-ol (propyl alcohol)	5.5	20
2905122010	For making semiconductor	5.5	20
2905122090	Other	5.5	20
2905130000	Butan-1-ol (n-butyl alcohol)	5	20
2905169000	Other	5.5	20
2905171000	Dodecan-1-ol (lauryl alcohol)	5.5	20
2905172000	Hexadecan-1-ol (cetyl alcohol)	5.5	20
2905173000	Octadecan-1-ol (stearyl alcohol)	5.5	20
2905191000	Heptyl alcohols	5.5	20
2905192000	Nonyl acohol	5.5	20
2905193000	Isononyl alcohol	3	20
2905194000	Pentanol (amyl alcohol) and isomers thereof	5.5	20
2905199010	3,3-dimethyl butan-2-ol (pinacolyl alcohol)	5	20
2905199020	2-Propyl heptyl alcohol	5	20
2905199030	Isodecyl alcohol	3	20
2905199090	Other	5	20
2905221000	Geraniol, citronellol, linalool, rhodinol and nerol	5	20
2905229000	Other	5	20
2905290000	Other	5	20
2905391000	1,4-Butanediol	5.5	20
2905392000	Neopentyl glycol	5.5	20

2905399000	Other	5.5	20
2905410000	2-Ethyl-2-(hydroxymethyl)propane-1,3-diol (trimethylolpropane)	5.5	20
2905420000	Pentaerythritol	5.5	20
2905490000	Other	5.5	20
2905510000	Ethchlorvynol (INN)	5.5	20
2906120000	Cyclohexanol, methylcyclohexanols and dimethylcyclohexanols	5.5	20
2906131000	Sterols	5.5	20
2906132000	Inositols	5.5	20
2906191000	Borneol	5.5	20
2906192000	Terpineols	5.5	20
2906199000	Other	5.5	20
2906210000	Benzyl alcohol	5.5	20
2906291000	Phenylethyl alcohol	5.5	20
2906292000	Phenylpropyl alcohol	5.5	20
2906293000	Cinnamyl alcohol	5.5	20
2906299000	Other	5.5	20
2907112000	Salts of phenol	5.5	20
2907121000	Cresols	5.5	20
2907122000	Salts of cresols	5.5	20
2907131000	Octylphenol	5.5	20
2907132000	Nonylphenol	5	20
2907139000	Other	5.5	20
2907151000	Naphthols	5.5	20
2907152000	Salts of naphthols	5.5	20
2907191000	Thymol	5.5	20
2907192000	Xylenols and their salts	5.5	20
2907199000	Other	5.5	20
2907211000	Resorcinol	5.5	20
2907212000	Salts of resorcinol	5.5	20
2907221000	Hydroquinone	5.5	20
2907222000	Salts of hydroquinone	5.5	20
2907232000	Salts of 4,4'-isopropylidenediphenol (bisphenol A)	5.5	20
2907291000	Catechol	5.5	20
2907299000	Other	5.5	20
2908110000	Pentachlorophenol (ISO)	5	20
2908191000	Chlorophenols, excluding pentachlorophenol	5	20
2908192000	Tetra bromo bisphenol-A	5	20
2908193000	Tribromophenol	5	20
2908910000	Dinoseb (ISO) and its salts	5.5	20
2908991000	Naphthol sulphonic acids and their salts	5.5	20
2908992000	Phenol sulphonic acids	5.5	20
2908993000	Nitrated derivatives and their salts	5.5	20
2908994000	Nitrosated derivatives and their salts	5.5	20

2908999000	Other	5.5	20
2909110000	Diethyl ether	5.5	20
2909191000	Bis (chloromethyl) ether	5.5	20
2909192000	Methyl tertiary butyl ether	5.5	20
2909201000	Cineole	5.5	20
2909209000	Other	5.5	20
2909301000	Anisole	5.5	20
2909302000	Anethole	5.5	20
2909303000	Diphenylether	5.5	20
2909304000	Ambrette musk	5.5	20
2909305000	Decabromodiphenyl oxide	5.5	20
2909309010	Material for manufacturing agricultural chemicals (registered material under the Agricultural Chemicals Management Act)	2	20
2909309090	Other	5.5	20
2909410000	2,2'-Oxydiethanol (diethylene glycol, digol)	5.5	20
2909449000	Other	5.5	20
2909491000	Triethylene glycol	5.5	20
2909501000	Eugenol	5.5	20
2909502000	Isoeugenol	5.5	20
2909503000	Ether-alcohol-phenols	5.5	20
2909601000	Alcohol peroxides	5.5	20
2909603000	Methyl ethyl ketone peroxide	5.5	20
2909609000	Other	5.5	20
2910100000	Oxirane (ethylene oxide)	5	20
2910200000	Methyloxirane (propylene oxide)	5.5	20
2910300000	1-Chloro-2,3-epoxypropane (epichlorohydrin)	5.5	20
2910400000	Dieldrin (ISO, INN)	5.5	20
2910900000	Other	5.5	20
2911001010	Acetals	5.5	20
2911001020	Hemiacetals	5.5	20
2911009000	Other	5.5	20
2912110000	Methanal (formaldehyde)	5.5	20
2912120000	Ethanal (acetaldehyde)	5.5	20
2912191000	Citronellaldehyde	5.5	20
2912192000	Citral	5.5	20
2912193000	Butanal (butyraldehyde, normal isomer)	5.5	20
2912199000	Other	5.5	20
2912292000	Phenylacetaldehyde	5.5	20
2912293000	Cinnamaldehyde	5.5	20
2912294000	Alpha-amylcinnamaldehyde	5.5	20
2912295000	Cyclamen aldehyde	5.5	20
2912301000	Hydroxycitronell aldehyde	5.5	20
2912309000	Other	5.5	20
2912410000	Vanillin (4-hydroxy-3-methoxybenzaldehyde)	5	20

2912420000	Ethylvanillin (3-ethoxy-4-hydroxybenzaldehyde)	5.5	20
2912491000	3,4,5-trimethoxybenz-aldehyde	5.5	20
2912501000	Trioxan	5.5	20
2912502000	Paraldehyde	5.5	20
2912503000	Metaldehyde	5.5	20
2912600000	Paraformaldehyde	5.5	20
2913000000	Halogenated, sulphonated, nitrated or nitrosated derivatives of products of heading 29.12.	5.5	20
2914110000	Acetone	5.5	20
2914130000	4-Methylpentan-2-one (methyl isobutyl ketone)	5.5	20
2914191000	3,3-dimethyl-2-butanone (pinacolone)	5.5	20
2914199000	Other	5.5	20
2914210000	Camphor	5	20
2914221000	Cyclohexanone	5	20
2914222000	Methylcyclohexanones	5	20
2914231000	Ionones	5	20
2914232000	Methylionones	5	20
2914291000	Jasmone	5	20
2914299000	Other	5	20
2914310000	Phenylacetone (phenylpropan-2-one)	5.5	20
2914390000	Other	5.5	20
2914401000	Diacetone alcohol(4-Hydroxy-4-methylpentane-2-one)	5.5	20
2914409000	Other	5.5	20
2914501000	Ketone-phenols	5.5	20
2914509000	Other	5.5	20
2914610000	Anthraquinone	5.5	20
2914691000	Derivatives of anthraquinone	5.5	20
2914699010	Qunione-alcohols, quinonephenols, and quinone-aldehydes	5.5	20
2914701000	Ketone musk	5	20
2914709010	Material for manufacturing agricultural chemicals (registered material under the Agricultural Chemicals Management Act)	2	20
2914709090	Other	5	20
2915110000	Formic acid	5.5	20
2915121000	Calcium formate	5.5	20
2915122000	Ammonium formate	5.5	20
2915129000	Other	5.5	20
2915131000	Methyl formate	5.5	20
2915132000	2-ethylhexylchloroformate	5.5	20
2915139000	Other	5.5	20
2915240000	Acetic anhydride	5.5	20
2915291000	Calcium acetate	5.5	20
2915292000	Sodium acetate	5.5	20
2915293000	Cobalt acetate	5.5	20

2915299000	Other	5.5	20
2915310000	Ethyl acetate	5.5	20
2915331000	For making semiconductor	5.5	20
2915339000	Other	5.5	20
2915360000	Dinoseb (ISO) acetate	5.5	20
2915391000	Amyl acetate	5.5	20
2915392000	Isoamyl acetate	5.5	20
2915393000	Methyl acetate	5.5	20
2915394000	Isobutyl acetate	5.5	20
2915395000	2-Ethoxyethyl acetate	5.5	20
2915399000	Other	5.5	20
2915401000	Monochloroacetic acid	5.5	20
2915409000	Other	5.5	20
2915600000	Butanoic acids, pentanoic acids, their salts and esters	5.5	20
2915701000	Palmitic acid, its salts and esters	5.5	20
2915702030	Lead stearate	5.5	20
2915702040	Zinc stearate	5.5	20
2915702050	Barium stearate	5.5	20
2915702060	Cadmium stearate	5.5	20
2915702090	Other	5.5	20
2915901000	Neodecanoilchloride and pivaloylchloride	5.5	20
2915909010	2-ethyl hexoic acid	5.5	20
2916121000	Ethyl acrylate	6.5	20
2916129000	Other	6.5	20
2916131000	Methacrylic acid	6.5	20
2916139000	Other	6.5	20
2916152000	Linoleic acid, its salts and esters	6.5	20
2916153000	Linolenic acid, its salts and esters	6.5	20
2916201000	Cyclohexane carboxylic acid	6.5	20
2916202000	Cyclopentenyl acetic acid	6.5	20
2916209010	Material for manufacturing agricultural chemicals (registered material under the Agricultural Chemicals Management Act)	2	20
2916311000	Benzoic acid	6.5	20
2916312000	Sodium benzoate	6.5	20
2916313000	Benzyl benzoates	6.5	20
2916319010	Material for manufacturing agricultural chemicals (registered material under the Agricultural Chemicals Management Act)	2	20
2916321000	Benzoyl peroxide	6.5	20
2916322000	Benzoyl chloride	6.5	20
2916341000	Phenylacetic acid	6.5	20
2916342000	Salts of phenylacetic acid	6.5	20
2916351000	Ethyl phenyl acetate	6.5	20
2916352000	Isobutyl phenyl acetate	6.5	20

2916353000	Isoamyl phenyl acetate	6.5	20
2916359000	Other	6.5	20
2916360000	Binapacryl (ISO)	6.5	20
2916391000	Cinnamic acid	6.5	20
2916399010	Material for manufacturing agricultural chemicals (registered material under the Agricultural Chemicals Management Act)	2	20
2917111000	Oxalic acid	6.5	20
2917112000	Salts of oxalic acid	6.5	20
2917113000	Esters of oxalic acid	6.5	20
2917121000	Adipic acid	6.5	20
2917122000	Salts of adipic acid	6.5	20
2917123010	Dioctyl adipate	6.5	20
2917123090	Other	6.5	20
2917131000	Azelaic acid, its salts and esters	6.5	20
2917132000	Sebacic acid, its salts and esters	6.5	20
2917140000	Maleic anhydride	6.5	20
2917191000	Maleic acid	6.5	20
2917192000	Succinic acid	6.5	20
2917193000	Sodium succinate	6.5	20
2917194000	Diethyl malonate	6.5	20
2917195000	Diisopropyl malonate	6.5	20
2917199000	Other	6.5	20
2917200000	Cyclanic, cyclenic or cycloterpenic polycarboxylic acids, their anhydrides, halides, peroxides, peroxyacids and their derivatives	6.5	20
2917321000	Di-2-ethyl hexyl orthophthalate	6.5	20
2917329000	Other	6.5	20
2917331000	Dinonyl orthophthalate	6.5	20
2917332000	Didecyl orthophthalates	6.5	20
2917341000	Diheptyl orthophthalate	6.5	20
2917342000	Diisodecyl orthophthalate	6.5	20
2917343000	Dibutyl orthophthalates	6.5	20
2917349000	Other	6.5	20
2917350000	Phthalic anhydride	6.5	20
2917361000	Terephthalic acid	3	20
2917369000	Other	6.5	20
2917370000	Dimethyl terephthalate	6.5	20
2917391000	Isophthalic acid	6.5	20
2917392000	Trioctyltrimellitate (T.O.T.M)	6.5	20
2917393000	Trimellitic anhydrate	6.5	20
2917399000	Other	6.5	20
2918111000	Lactic acid	6.5	20
2918112000	Salts of lactic acid	6.5	20
2918113000	Esters of lactic acid	6.5	20

2918131000	Salts of tartaric acid	6.5	20
2918132000	Esters of tartaric acid	6.5	20
2918140000	Citric acid	6.5	20
2918151010	Calcium citrate	6.5	20
2918152000	Esters of citric acid	6.5	20
2918161000	Gluconic acid	6.5	20
2918162000	Salts of gluconic acid	6.5	20
2918180000	Chlorobenzilate (ISO)	6.5	20
2918191010	Malic acid	6.5	20
2918191090	Other	6.5	20
2918192010	Salts of malic acid	6.5	20
2918192090	Other	6.5	20
2918193010	Esters of malic acid	6.5	20
2918193020	Methyl benzilate	6.5	20
2918193090	Other	6.5	20
2918194000	2,2-diphenyl-2-hydroxyacetic acid (benzilic acid)	6.5	20
2918211000	Salicylic acid	6.5	20
2918212010	Sodium salicylate	6.5	20
2918212090	Other	6.5	20
2918221000	O-acetylsalicylic acid	6.5	20
2918222000	Salts of o-acetylsalicylic acid	6.5	20
2918223000	Esters of o-acetylsalicylic acid	6.5	20
2918231010	Methyl salicylate	6.5	20
2918231020	Ethyl salicylate	6.5	20
2918231090	Other	6.5	20
2918232000	Salts of other esters of salicylic acid	6.5	20
2918291000	β-oxynaphthoic acid and its salts	6.5	20
2918299010	Gallic acid	6.5	20
2918299020	Parahydroxynaphthoic acid	6.5	20
2918299030	Parahydroxybenzoic acid	6.5	20
2918299040	Salts and esters of gallic acid	6.5	20
2918299090	Other	6.5	20
2918301000	Material for manufacturing agricultural chemicals (registered material under the Agricultural Chemicals Management Act)	2	20
2918309000	Other	6.5	20
2918910000	2,4,5-T (ISO) (2,4,5-trichlorophenoxyacetic acid), its salts and esters	6.5	20
2918991000	Material for manufacturing agricultural chemicals (registered material under the Agricultural Chemicals Management Act)	2	20
2919901011	Material for manufacturing agricultural chemicals (registered material under the Agricultural Chemicals Management Act)	2	20
2919901019	Other	6.5	20

2919901020	Glycerophosphoric acid	6.5	20
2919901090	Other	6.5	20
2919902000	Salts of phosphoric esters	6.5	20
2919909000	Other	6.5	20
2920111000	Material for manufacturing agricultural chemicals (registered material under the Agricultural Chemicals Management Act)	2	20
2920119000	Other	6.5	20
2920191000	Material for manufacturing agricultural chemicals (registered material under the Agricultural Chemicals Management Act)	2	20
2920199010	0,0-dimethyl-0-(3-methyl-4-nitrophenyl) thiophosphate	6.5	20
2920199090	Other	6.5	20
2920901010	Dimethyl sulfate	6.5	20
2920901020	Diethyl sulfate	6.5	20
2920901090	Other	6.5	20
2920902000	Of nitrous and nitric esters	6.5	20
2920903000	Of carbonic esters	6.5	20
2920904010	Dimethyl phosphite	6.5	20
2920904020	Diethyl phosphite	6.5	20
2920904030	Trimethyl phosphite	6.5	20
2920904040	Triethyl phosphite	6.5	20
2920909010	Material for manufacturing agricultural chemicals (registered material under the Agricultural Chemicals Management Act)	2	20
2920909090	Other	6.5	20
2921111010	Methylamine	6.5	20
2921111020	Salts of methylamine	6.5	20
2921112010	Dimethylamine	6.5	20
2921112020	Salts of dimethylamine	6.5	20
2921113010	Trimethylamine	6.5	20
2921191000	Dimethylaminoethyl chloride hydrochloride	6.5	20
2921192000	Diethylamine and its salts	6.5	20
2921199010	Dimethyl laurylamine	6.5	20
2921199020	Chlormethine (INN) (bis(2-chloroethyl)methylamine)	6.5	20
2921199030	Bis (2-chloroethyl) ethylamine	6.5	20
2921199040	Trichlormethine (INN) (tris(2-chloroethyl)amine)	6.5	20
2921199050	Di-isopropylamine	6.5	20
2921199060	N,N-diisopropyl-β -aminoethylchloride	6.5	20
2921199070	N,N-Dialkyl(methyl, ethyl, n-propyl or isopropyl) 2-chloroethylamines and their protonated salts	6.5	20
2921211000	Ethylenediamine	6.5	20
2921212000	Salts of ethylenediamine	6.5	20
2921221000	Hexamethylenediamine	6.5	20
2921222000	Hexamethylenediamine adipate	6.5	20

2921229000	Other	6.5	20
2921291000	Diethylenetriamine	5	20
2921292000	Triethylene tetramine	5	20
2921299000	Other	5	20
2921301000	Cyclohexylamine	6.5	20
2921309000	Other	6.5	20
2921411000	Aniline	6.5	20
2921412000	Salts of aniline	6.5	20
2921421000	Nitrohalogenated derivatives of aniline	6.5	20
2921422000	2,4,5-trichloroaniline	6.5	20
2921429010	Material for manufacturing agricultural chemicals (registered material under the Agricultural Chemicals Management Act)	2	20
2921429090	Other	6.5	20
2921431000	Para-toluidine-m-sulfonic acid and its salts	6.5	20
2921432000	2-chloro-para-toluidine-5-sulfonic acid and its salts	6.5	20
2921433000	3-amino-6-chlorotoluene-4-sulfonic acid and its salts	6.5	20
2921439010	Toluidines	6.5	20
2921439091	Material for manufacturing agricultural chemicals (registered material under the Agricultural Chemicals Management Act)	2	20
2921439099	Other	6.5	20
2921441000	Diphenylamine	6.5	20
2921449000	Other	6.5	20
2921451000	1-naphthylamine-4-sulfonic acid and its salts	6.5	20
2921459010	1-Naphthylamine (alpha-naphthylamine) and its salts	6.5	20
2921459020	2-Naphthylamine (beta-naphthylamine) and its salts	6.5	20
2921459030	2-naphthylamine-3,6,8-trisulfonic acid and its salts	5	20
2921459090	Other	6.5	20
2921460000	Amfetamine (INN), benzfetamine (INN), dexamfetamine (INN), etilamfetamine (INN), fencamfamin (INN), lefetamine (lNN), levamfetamine (INN), mefenorex (INN) and phentermine (INN); salts thereof	6.5	20
2921511000	n-phenyl-n-isopropyl para-phenylenediamine	6.5	20
2921512000	N-(1,3-Dimethyl butyl)-N-phenyl-para-phenylene-diamine	6.5	20
2921519010	o-phenylene diamine	6.5	20
2921519020	m-phenylene diamine	6.5	20
2921519030	p-phenylene diamine	6.5	20
2921519040	Diaminotoluenes	6.5	20
2921591000	3,3-Dichloro benzidine sulfonic acid salts	6.5	20
2921599010	Benzidine	6.5	20
2921599020	Benzidine dihydrochloride	6.5	20
2921599030	4,4'diaminostilbene-2,2'-disulfonic acid and its salts	6.5	20
2921599040	Benzidine's salts other than benzidine dihydrochloride	6.5	20

2921599050	o-Tolidine and its salts	6.5	20
2921599090	Other	6.5	20
2922111000	Monoethanolamine	6.5	20
2922112000	Salts of monoethanolamine	6.5	20
2922121000	Diethanolamine	6.5	20
2922122000	Salts of diethanolamine	6.5	20
2922131000	Triethanolamine	3	20
2922132000	Salts of triethanolamine	6.5	20
2922140000	Dextropropoxyphene (INN) and its salts	6.5	20
2922191000	Arylethanolamines	6.5	20
2922193010	N,N-Dimethyl-2 aminoethanol and its protonated salts	6.5	20
2922193020	N,N-Diethyl-2-aminoethanol and its protonated salts	6.5	20
2922193090	Other	6.5	20
2922194000	Ethyldiethanolamine	6.5	20
2922195000	Methyldiethanolamine	6.5	20
2922196000	Diethylaminoethanol	6.5	20
2922199000	Other	6.5	20
2922211000	7-amino-1-naphthol-3-sulphonic acid (gamma acid) and its salts	6.5	20
2922212000	8-amino-1-naphthol-3, 6-disulphonic acid (H acid) and its salts	3	20
2922213000	2-amino-5-naphthol-7-disulphonic acid (J acid) and its salts	6.5	20
2922219000	Other	6.5	20
2922291000	Para-aminophenol	6.5	20
2922299010	Meta-aminophenol	6.5	20
2922299020	Ortho-aminophenol	6.5	20
2922299030	Amino cresols	6.5	20
2922299040	Phenetidines and their salts	6.5	20
2922299090	Other	6.5	20
2922310000	Amfepramone (INN), methadone (INN) and normethadone (INN); salts thereof	6.5	20
2922392000	Amino anthraquinons and their salts	6.5	20
2922393000	Amino anthraquinons of derivatives	6.5	20
2922399000	Other	6.5	20
2922411000	Lysine	6.5	20
2922421000	Glutamic acid	5	20
2922422000	Sodium glutamate	6.5	20
2922423000	Other salts of glutamic acid	6.5	20
2922431000	Anthranilic acid	6.5	20
2922439000	Salts of anthranilic acid	6.5	20
2922440000	Tilidine (INN) and its salts	6.5	20
2922492000	Alanine	6.5	20
2922493000	Leucine	6.5	20
2922494000	Valine	6.5	20
2922495000	Aspartic acid	6.5	20

2922497000	Ethyl para amino benzoate	6.5	20
2922501000	Serine	6.5	20
2922502000	Para-amino salicylic acid and its salts	6.5	20
2922503000	1-p-nitrophenol-2-amino-1,3-propane diol	6.5	20
2922504000	Dialphahydroxyphenylglycine	6.5	20
2922509010	Material for manufacturing agricultural chemicals (registered material under the Agricultural Chemicals Management Act)	2	20
2923201000	Lecithins	6.5	20
2923202000	Other phosphoaminolipids	6.5	20
2923900000	Other	6.5	20
2924110000	Meprobamate (INN)	6.5	20
2924121000	Fluoroacetamide (ISO)	6.5	20
2924122000	Monocrotophos (ISO)	6.5	20
2924191000	Dimethylformamide	6.5	20
2924192000	Dimethylacetamide	6.5	20
2924211000	Material for manufacturing agricultural chemicals (registered material under the Agricultural Chemicals Management Act)	2	20
2924230000	2-Acetamidobenzoic acid (N-acetylanthranilic acid) and its salts	6.5	20
2924240000	Ethinamate (INN)	6.5	20
2924291010	Aminoacetanilide and its derivatives	6.5	20
2924292000	Aceto acetanilide and its derivatives	5	20
2924299010	Lidocaine hydrochloride	6.5	20
2925111000	Saccharin	6.5	20
2925112000	Salts of saccharin	6.5	20
2925120000	Glutethimide (INN)	6.5	20
2925191000	Phthalimide	6.5	20
2925199010	Material for manufacturing agricultural chemicals (registered material under the Agricultural Chemicals Management Act)	2	20
2925199090	Other	6.5	20
2925210000	Chlordimeform (ISO)	6.5	20
2925291000	Diphenyl guanidine	6.5	20
2925299010	Material for manufacturing agricultural chemicals (registered material under the Agricultural Chemicals Management Act)	2	20
2926200000	1-Cyanoguanidine (dicyandiamide)	6.5	20
2926300000	Fenproporex (INN) and its salts; methadone (INN) intermediate (4 - cyano - 2 - dimethylamino - 4, 4 - diphenylbutane)	6.5	20
2926901000	Acetonitrile	6.5	20
2926902000	1,4-diamino-2,3-dicyanoanthraquinon	6.5	20
2926909010	Malono nitrile	6.5	20

2927001100	6-nitro-1-diazo-2-naphthol-4-sulfonic acid	6.5	20
2927001900	Other	6.5	20
2927002910	Azoisobutyronitrile	6.5	20
2927002990	Other	6.5	20
2927003000	Azoxy-compounds	6.5	20
2928001000	Phenylhydrazine	6.5	20
2928009010	Perillartine	6.5	20
2928009020	Methylethyl ketoxime	6.5	20
2928009091	Material for manufacturing agricultural chemicals (registered material under the Agricultural Chemicals Management Act)	2	20
2929101000	Toluene diisocyanate	6.5	20
2929102000	Diphenyl methane diisocyanate	6.5	20
2929109000	Other	6.5	20
2929901000	Isocyanides	6.5	20
2929903000	Dialkyl (methyl, ethyl, n-propyl or isopropyl) N,N-dialkyl (methyl, ethyl, n-propyl or isopropyl) phosphoramidates	6.5	20
2929904000	Diethyl-n,n-dimethylphosphoramidates	6.5	20
2929905000	o-ethyl-2-diisopropylaminoethyl methylphosphonite	6.5	20
2929906000	N,N-Dialkyl (methyl, ethyl, n-propyl or isopropyl) phosphoramidic dihalides	6.5	20
2929909000	Other	6.5	20
2930201010	Material for manufacturing agricultural chemicals (registered material under the Agricultural Chemicals Management Act)	2	20
2930201090	Other	6.5	20
2930202010	Material for manufacturing agricultural chemicals (registered material under the Agricultural Chemicals Management Act)	2	20
2930202090	Other	6.5	20
2930301000	Thiuram mono-sulphides	6.5	20
2930302000	Thiuram di-sulphides	6.5	20
2930303000	Thiuram tetra-sulphides	6.5	20
2930400000	Methionine	6.5	20
2930501000	Captafol (ISO)	6.5	20
2930502000	Methamidophos (ISO)	6.5	20
2930901000	Sodium-2-amino-4-methylthicbutylate	6.5	20
2930902010	Thiourea	6.5	20
2930902020	Thiocarbanilide	6.5	20
2930903010	Thioalcohols	6.5	20
2930903020	Thiophenols	6.5	20
2930903030	N,N-Diisoprophyl-β-aminoethanthiol	6.5	20
2930903040	N,N-Dialkyl (methyl, ethyl, n-propyl or isopropyl) aminoethane-2-thiols and their protonated salts	6.5	20
2930904010	Thiodiglycol (INN) (bis(2-hydroxyethyl)sulphide)	6.5	20

2930904020	Thioaniline	6.5	20
2930904090	Other	6.5	20
2930905010	2-Chloroethylchloromethylsulphide	6.5	20
2930905020	Bis (2-chloroethyl) sulphide	6.5	20
2930905030	Bis (2-chloroethylthio) methane	6.5	20
2930905040	1,2-Bis (2-chloroethylthio) ethane	6.5	20
2930905050	1,3-Bis (2-chloroethylthio)-n-propane	6.5	20
2930905060	1,4-Bis (2-chloroethylthio)-n-butane	6.5	20
2930905070	1,5-Bis (2-chloroethylthio)-n-pentane	6.5	20
2930905081	Bis(2-chloroethylthiomethyl)ether	6.5	20
2930905082	Bis(2-chloroethylthioethyl)ether	6.5	20
2930905090	Other	6.5	20
2930906000	[S-2-(dialkyl (methyl, ethyl, n-propyl or isopropyl)amino) ethyl] hydrogen alkyl (methyl, ethyl, n-propyl or isopropyl)phosphonothioates and their O-alkyl ($\leq$C10, including cycloalkyl) esters; alkylated or protonated salts thereof	6.5	20
2930907000	O,O-Diethyl s-[2-(diethylamino) ethyl] phosphorothioate and its alkylated or protonated salts	6.5	20
2930908000	O-Ehtyl, S-phenyl ethylphosphonothiolothionate (fonofos)	6.5	20
2930909010	Thioacids	6.5	20
2930909020	Isothiocyanates	6.5	20
2930909030	Cysteine	6.5	20
2930909060	8-Chloro-6-tosylotinic acid ethyl ester	6.5	20
2930909070	Containing a phosphorus atom to which is bonded one methyl, ethyl, n-propyl or isopropyl group but not further carbon atoms	6.5	20
2930909080	Dithiocarbonates (xanthates)	6.5	20
2931002010	2-Chlorovinyldichloroarsine	6.5	20
2931002020	Bis (2-chlorovinyl) chloroarsine	6.5	20
2931002030	Tris (2-chlorovinyl) arsine	6.5	20
2931002091	Material for manufacturing agricultural chemicals (registered material under the Agricultural Chemicals Management Act)	2	20
2931002099	Other	6.5	20
2931003100	[O-2-(dialkyl(methyl, ethyl, n-propyl or isopropyl) amino) ethyl]hydrogen alkyl (methyl,ethyl, n-propyl or isopropyl) phosphonites and their O-alkyl ($\leq$C10, including cycloalkyl)esters; alkylated or protonated salts thereof	6.5	20
2931003300	O-Isopropyl methylphosphonochloridate	6.5	20
2931003400	O-Pinacolyl methylphosphonochloridate	6.5	20
2931003500	O-Alkyl ($\leq$C10,including cycloalkyl) alkyl (methyl, ethyl, n-propyl or isopropyl) phosphonofluoridates	6.5	20
2931003700	O-Alkyl (<c10,including cycloalkyl) N,N-dialkyl (methyl, ethyl, n-propyl or isopropyl) phosphoramidocyanidates	6.5	20

2931003911	Dimethyl methylphosphonate	6.5	20
2931003912	Diethyl ethylphosphonate	6.5	20
2931003913	Diethyl methylphosphonate	6.5	20
2931003914	Dimethyl ethylphosphonate	6.5	20
2931003915	Material for manufacturing agricultural chemicals (registered material under the Agricultural Chemicals Management Act)	2	20
2931003919	Others	6.5	20
2931004010	Alkyl (methyl, ethyl, n-propyl or isopropyl)phosphonyl difluorides	6.5	20
2931004090	Other	6.5	20
2931005010	Methyl phosphonyl dichloride	6.5	20
2931005020	Methyl phosphinyl dichloride	6.5	20
2931005030	Ethyl phosphinyl dichloride	6.5	20
2931005040	Ethyl phosphinyl dichloride	6.5	20
2931005090	Other	6.5	20
2931009010	Dibutyl tin oxide	6.5	20
2931009020	Diethyl aluminium chloride	6.5	20
2931009091	Material for manufacturing agricultural chemicals (registered material under the Agricultural Chemicals Management Act)	2	20
2931009099	Other	6.5	20
2932110000	Tetrahydrofuran	6.5	20
2932120000	2-Furaldehyde (furfuraldehyde)	6.5	20
2932131000	Furfurylalcohol	6.5	20
2932132000	Tetrahydrofurfuryl alcohol	6.5	20
2932191000	Material for manufacturing agricultural chemicals (registered material under the Agricultural Chemicals Management Act)	2	20
2932199000	Other	6.5	20
2932211000	Coumarin	5	20
2932212000	Methylcoumarins	5	20
2932213000	Ethylcoumarins	5	20
2932291000	Nonalactone	5	20
2932292000	Undecalactone	5	20
2932293000	Butyrolactone	5	20
2932294000	Santonin	5	20
2932295000	Phenolphthalein	5	20
2932296000	Glucuronolactone	5	20
2932297000	Dehydracetic acid and its salts	5	20
2932298000	Acetyl ketene (diketene)	5	20
2932299010	Material for manufacturing agricultural chemicals (registered material under the Agricultural Chemicals Management Act)	2	20
2932299090	Other	5	20

2932910000	Isosafrole	6.5	20
2932920000	1-(1,3-Benzodioxol-5-yl)propane-2-one	6.5	20
2932930000	Piperonal	6.5	20
2932940000	Safrole	6.5	20
2932950000	Tetrahydrocannabinols (all isomers)	6.5	20
2932991000	Dioxanes	6.5	20
2932992000	Benzofuran (coumarone)	6.5	20
2933111000	Methylene bis(1-phenyl-2,3-dimethyl-4-methylamino pyrazolone-5)	6.5	20
2933119010	Phenazone (antipyrin)	6.5	20
2933119030	Sulpyrine	6.5	20
2933119040	Isopropyl antipyrin	6.5	20
2933119091	Material for manufacturing agricultural chemicals (registered material under the Agricultural Chemicals Management Act)	2	20
2933119099	Other	6.5	20
2933191000	Pyrazolone and its derivatives	6.5	20
2933199010	Phenyl butazone	6.5	20
2933199020	Pyrazolate	6.5	20
2933199099	Other	6.5	20
2933211000	Hydantoin	6.5	20
2933212000	Derivatives of hydantoin	6.5	20
2933291000	Lysidine	6.5	20
2933299010	Material for manufacturing agricultural chemicals (registered material under the Agricultural Chemicals Management Act)	2	20
2933329000	Salts of piperidine	6.5	20
2933330000	Alfentanil (INN), anileridine (INN), bezitramide (INN), bromazepam (INN), difenoxin (INN), diphenoxylate (INN) dipipanone (INN), fentanyl (INN), ketobemidone (INN), methylphenidate (INN), pentazocine (INN), pethidine (INN), pethidine (INN) intermediate A, phencyclidine (INN) (PCP), phenoperidine (INN), pipradrol (INN), piritramide (INN), propiram (INN) and trimeperidine (INN); salts thereof	6.5	20
2933391000	Isonicotinic acid hydrazide	6.5	20
2933393000	3-Hydroxy-1-methylpiperidine	6.5	20
2933394000	3-Quinuclidinyl benzilate	6.5	20
2933395000	Quinuclidin-3-ol	6.5	20
2933491000	Pyrvinium pamoate	6.5	20
2933499010	Material for manufacturing agricultural chemicals (registered material under the Agricultural Chemicals Management Act)	2	20
2933520000	Malonylurea (barbituric acid) and its salts	6.5	20
2933530000	Allobarbital (INN), amobarbital (INN), barbital (INN),	6.5	20

	butalbital (INN), butobarbital, cyclobarbital (INN), methylphenobarbital (INN), pentobarbital (INN), phenobarbital (INN), secbutabarbital (INN), secobarbital (INN) and vinylbital (INN); salts thereof		
2933540000	Other derivatives of malonylurea (barbituric acid); salts thereof	6.5	20
2933550000	Loprazolam (INN), mecloqualone (INN), methaqualone (INN) and zipeprol (INN); salts thereof	6.5	20
2933591100	5-fluorouracil	6.5	20
2933591910	Pyrimidine	6.5	20
2933591991	Material for manufacturing agricultural chemicals (registered material under the Agricultural Chemicals Management Act)	2	20
2933591999	Other	6.5	20
2933592020	Piperazine citrate	6.5	20
2933592030	Piperazine adipate	6.5	20
2933592040	1-amino-4-methylpiperazine	6.5	20
2933610000	Melamine	6.5	20
2933691000	Cyanuric chloride	3	20
2933692000	Hexamethylene tetramine	6.5	20
2933699010	Trimethylene trinitramine	6.5	20
2933699091	Material for manufacturing agricultural chemicals (registered material under the Agricultural Chemicals Management Act)	2	20
2933699099	Other	6.5	20
2933710000	6-Hexanelactam (epsilon-caprolactam)	3	20
2933720000	Clobazam (INN) and methyprylon (INN)	6.5	20
2933791000	Isatin	6.5	20
2933792000	2-hydroxyquinoline	6.5	20
2933793000	1-vinyl-2-pyrrolidone	6.5	20
2933910000	Alprazolam (INN), camazepam (INN), chlordiazepoxide (INN), clonazepam (INN), clorazepate, delorazepam (INN), diazepam (lNN), estazolam (INN), ethyl loflazepate (INN), fludiazepam (INN), flunitrazepam (INN), flurazepam (INN), halazepam (INN), lorazepam (INN), lormetazepam (INN), mazindol (INN), medazepam (INN), midazolam(INN), nimetazepam (INN), nitrazepam (INN), nordazepam (INN), oxazepam (INN), pinazepam (INN), prazepam (INN), pyrovalerone (INN), temazepam (INN) tetrazepam (INN) and triazolam (INN); salts thereof	6.5	20
2933991000	Indole and its derivatives	6.5	20
2934101000	Aminothiazole and its derivative	6.5	20
2934109010	Material for manufacturing agricultural chemicals (registered material under the Agricultural Chemicals Management Act)	2	20

2934109090	Other	6.5	20
2934201000	Benzothiazole	6.5	20
2934202000	Mercaptobenzothiazole	6.5	20
2934203000	Dibenzothiazolyl disulphide	6.5	20
2934209010	Material for manufacturing agricultural chemicals (registered material under the Agricultural Chemicals Management Act)	2	20
2934209090	Other	6.5	20
2934301000	Phenothiazine (thiodiphenyl amine)	6.5	20
2934309000	Other	6.5	20
2934910000	Aminorex (INN), brotizolam (INN), clotiazepam (INN), cloxazolam (INN), dextromoramide (INN), haloxazolam (INN), ketazolam (INN), mesocarb (INN), oxazolam (INN), pemoline (INN), phendimetrazine (INN), phenmetrazine (INN) and sufentanil (INN); salts thereof	6.5	20
2934991000	Morpholine	6.5	20
2935002000	5-amino-2-methyl-n-phenyl benzene sulfonamide	6.5	20
2935003000	Para-toluidine-3-sulfon anilide	6.5	20
2935007000	Sulfamethoxine	6.5	20
2935008010	Sulphamine	6.5	20
2935008020	Sulphapyridine	6.5	20
2935008030	Sulphadiazine	6.5	20
2935008040	Sulphamerazine	6.5	20
2935008050	Sulphathiazole	6.5	20
2935009020	Material for manufacturing agricultural chemicals (registered material under the Agricultural Chemicals Management Act)	2	20
2936230000	Vitamin B2 and its derivatives	6.5	20
2936240000	D- or DL-Pantothenic acid (Vitamin B3 or Vitamin B5) and its derivatives	6.5	20
2936250000	Vitamin B6 and its derivatives	6.5	20
2936260000	Vitamin B12 and its derivatives	6.5	20
2936271000	Ascorbic acid	6.5	20
2936272000	Sodium ascorbate	6.5	20
2936273000	Calcium ascorbate	6.5	20
2936279000	Other	6.5	20
2936281000	Alpha-tocoperol acetate	6.5	20
2936289000	Other	6.5	20
2936291010	Vitamin B9	6.5	20
2936291090	Other	6.5	20
2936292000	Vitamins D and their derivatives	6.5	20
2936293000	Vatamin H and its derivatives	6.5	20
2936901000	Provitamins, unmixed	6.5	20
2936909000	Other	6.5	20
2937111000	Of subheading 2933.9 or 2934.9	6.5	20

2937191000	Of subheading 2933.9 or 2934.9	6.5	20
2937292000	Of subheading 2914.50.	5.5	20
2937391000	Of subheading 2922.50.	6.5	20
2937501000	Of subheading 2918.19 or 2918.9	6.5	20
2937502000	Of subheading 2934.9	6.5	20
2938101000	Rutoside (rutin)	6.5	20
2938102000	Derivatives of rutoside	6.5	20
2938901000	Digitalis glycosides	6.5	20
2938903000	Saponins	6.5	20
2939114000	Concentrates of poppy straw containing not less than 50 % by weight of alkaloids	8	20
2940001010	Galactose	6.5	20
2940001020	Sorbose	6.5	20
2940001030	Xylose	6.5	20
2940001090	Other	6.5	20
2940002010	Hydroxypropyl sucrose	6.5	20
2940002090	Other	6.5	20
2941101000	Penicilline G potassium	6.5	20
2941109010	Penicilline G sodium	6.5	20
2941109020	Penicilline V	6.5	20
2941201000	Material for manufacturing agricultural chemicals (registered material under the Agricultural Chemicals Management Act)	2	20
2941209000	Other	6.5	20
2941301000	Chlorotetracycline	6.5	20
2941302000	Oxy-tetracycline hydrochloride	6.5	20
2941303000	Chlorotetracycline hydrochloride	6.5	20
2941400000	Chloramphenicol and its derivatives; salts thereof	6.5	20
2941902000	11-alpha-chloro-6-deoxy-6-demethyl-6-methylene-5-oxytetra cycline-paratoluene sulfonate	6.5	20
2941909020	Ledermycine	6.5	20
2941909030	Gentamycine sulfate	6.5	20
2941909091	Material for manufacturing agricultural chemicals (registered material under the Agricultural Chemicals Management Act)	2	20
2942001000	Ketens	6.5	20
2942009010	Copper acetoarsenite	6.5	20
2942009090	Other	6.5	20
3002903010	Saxitoxin	6.5	20
3002903020	Ricin	8	20
3003102000	Containing streptomycins or their derivatives	8	20
3003209010	Preparations containing chloramphenicol	8	20
3003310000	Containing insulin	8	20
3003391010	Preparations containing pituitary (anterior) hormones	8	20
3003392000	Preparations containing salivary gland hormones	8	20

3003393000	Preparations containing thyroid and parathyroid hormones	8	20
3003394000	Preparations containing anabolic steroids	8	20
3003396000	Preparations containing adrenal medulla hormones	8	20
3003397000	Preparations containing male sex hormones	8	20
3003398000	Preparations containing estrogens and gestagens, progestins	8	20
3003409110	Preparations containing morphine	8	20
3003409120	Preparations containing quinine	8	20
3003409130	Preparations containing theobromine	8	20
3003409210	Preparations containing caffeine	8	20
3003409220	Preparations containing strychnine	8	20
3003409230	Preparations containing ephedrine	8	20
3003409310	Preparations containing cocaine	8	20
3003409320	Preparations containing alkaloids of rye ergot	8	20
3003409330	Preparations containing nicotine	8	20
3003409400	Preparations containing atropine and homatropine	8	20
3003409500	Preparations containing arecoline	8	20
3003409600	Preparations containing piperine	8	20
3003409900	Other	8	20
3003909100	Preparations containing aspirin	8	20
3003909200	Preparations containing anti-allergic agents	8	20
3003909300	Preparations containing vitamins	8	20
3003909400	Preparations containing antler	8	20
3003909500	Preparations containing ginseng	8	20
3003909600	Preparations containing royal jelly	8	20
3004101000	Containing penicillins or derivatives thereof, with a penicillanic acid structure	8	20
3004102000	Containing streptomycins or their derivatives	8	20
3004209200	Preparations containing erythromycin	8	20
3004209400	Preparations containing kanamycin	8	20
3004209900	Other	8	20
3004310000	Containing insulin	8	20
3004391010	Preparations containing pituitary (anterior) hormones	8	20
3004391020	Preparations containing pituitary (posterior) hormones	8	20
3004392000	Preparations containing salivary gland hormones	8	20
3004393000	Preparations containing thyroid and parathyroid hormones	8	20
3004394000	Preparations contatining anabolic steroids	8	20
3004395000	Preparations containing adrenal medulla hormones	8	20
3004396000	Preparations cantaining male sex hormones	8	20
3004397000	Preparations containing estrogens and gestagens, progestins	8	20
3004401000	Anti-cancer preparations	8	20
3004409110	Preparations containing morphine	8	20
3004409120	Preparations containing quinine	8	20
3004409130	Preparations containing theobromine	8	20
3004409210	Preparations containing caffeine	8	20

3004409220	Preparations containing strychinine	8	20
3004409230	Preparations containing ephedrine	8	20
3004409310	Preparations containing cocaine	8	20
3004409320	Preparations containing alkaloids of rye ergot	8	20
3004409330	Preparations containing nicotine	8	20
3004409400	Preparations containing atropine and homatropine	8	20
3004409500	Preparations containing arecoline	8	20
3004409600	Preparations containing piperine	8	20
3004409900	Other	8	20
3004502010	Preparations containing vitamin B1	8	20
3004504000	Preparations containing vitamin D	8	20
3004505000	Preparations containing vitamin E	8	20
3004506000	Preparations containg vitamin H	8	20
3004507000	Preparations containg vitamin K	8	20
3004909100	Preparations containing aspirin	8	20
3004909300	Preparations containing antler	8	20
3004909400	Preparations containg ginseng	8	20
3004909500	Preparations containing royal jelly	8	20
3006105010	Of plastics	6.5	20
3006105020	Of knitted or crocheted fabrics	8	20
3006910000	Appliances identifiable for ostomy use	6.5	20
3006922031	Saxitoxin	6.5	20
3006922032	Ricin	8	20
3006923000	Of heading 30.03 or 30.04.	8	20
3006925000	Of subheading 3824.90	6.5	20
3101001010	Guano	6.5	20
3101001090	Other	6.5	20
3101002000	Vegetable fertilisers	6.5	20
3101003000	Fertilisers produced by the mixing or chemical treatment of animal or vegetable products	6.5	20
3102210000	Ammonium sulphate	6.5	20
3102291000	Double salts of ammonium sulphate and ammonium nitrate	6.5	20
3102292000	Mixtures of ammonium sulphate and ammonium nitrate	6.5	20
3102300000	Ammonium nitrate, whether or not in aqueous solution	6.5	20
3102400000	Mixtures of ammonium nitrate with calcium carbonate or other inorganic non-fertilising substances	6.5	20
3102501000	Natural	6.5	20
3102509000	Other	6.5	20
3102600000	Double salts and mixtures of calcium nitrate and ammonium nitrate	6.5	20
3102800000	Mixtures of urea and ammonium nitrate in aqueous or ammoniacal solution	6.5	20
3102901000	Double salts of calcium nitrate and magnesium nitrate	6.5	20
3103100000	Superphosphates	6.5	20

3103901000	Disintegrated (calcined) calcium phosphates	6.5	20
3103902000	Calcium hydrogenorthophosphate containing not less than 20 % by weight of fluorine	6.5	20
3103903000	Other calcium phosphate	6.5	20
3103904000	Mixtures of phosphatic fertilisers	6.5	20
3103909000	Other	6.5	20
3104301000	Not more than 52 % by weight of K2O	1	20
3104309000	Other	6.5	20
3104901010	Not more than 30 % by weight of K2O	1	20
3104901090	Other	6.5	20
3104909000	Other	1	20
3105100000	Goods of the this Chapter in tablets or similar forms or in packages of a gross weight not exceeding 10 kg	6.5	20
3105400000	Ammonium dihydrogenorthophosphate (monoammonium phosphate) and mixtures thereof with diammonium hydrogenorthophosphate (diammonium phosphate)	6.5	20
3105510000	Containing nitrates and phosphates	6.5	20
3105590000	Other	6.5	20
3105600000	Mineral or chemical fertilisers containing the two fertilising elements phosphorus and potassium	6.5	20
3105901000	Fertilisers containing nitrogen and potassium	6.5	20
3201100000	Quebracho extract	6.5	20
3201200000	Wattle extract	6.5	20
3201901010	Extracts from mangrove	6.5	20
3201901020	Extracts from myrobolans	6.5	20
3201901030	Extracts from sumach	6.5	20
3201901040	Extracts from gambier	6.5	20
3201901090	Other	6.5	20
3201902000	Tannins (tannic acids) and their salts	6.5	20
3201903000	Ethers or esters of tannins	6.5	20
3201904000	Other derivatives of tannins	6.5	20
3202101000	Aromatic syntans	6.5	20
3202102000	Alkylsulphonylchlorides	6.5	20
3202103000	Resinic tanning products	6.5	20
3202109000	Other	6.5	20
3202901000	Inorganic tanning products	6.5	20
3202902000	Artificial bates	6.5	20
3202909000	Other	6.5	20
3203001100	Natural indigo	6.5	20
3203001910	Logwood	6.5	20
3203001920	Sandal wood	6.5	20
3203001930	Chlorophyll	6.5	20
3203001990	Other	6.5	20
3203002010	Cochineal	6.5	20
3203002020	Kermes	6.5	20

3203002030	Sepia	6.5	20
3203002090	Other	6.5	20
3203003000	Preparations based on colouring matter of vegetable or animal origin	6.5	20
3204111000	Preparations based on disperse dyes (press cake)	4	20
3204121000	Acid dyes and preparations based thereon	8	20
3204122000	Mordant dyes and preparations based thereon	8	20
3204130000	Basic dyes and preparations based thereon	8	20
3204140000	Direct dyes and preparations based thereon	8	20
3204150000	Vat dyes (including those usable in that state as pigments) and preparations based thereon	8	20
3204160000	Reactive dyes and preparations based thereon	8	20
3204170000	Pigments and preparations based thereon	8	20
3204192000	Rapid dyes and preparations based thereon	8	20
3204193000	Sulphide dyes and sulphide vat dyes and preparations based thereon	8	20
3204199000	Other	8	20
3204901000	Synthetic organic products of the kind used as luminophores	6.5	20
3204909000	Other	6.5	20
3205001000	Pigment plastic colour bases	6.5	20
3205009000	Other	6.5	20
3206110000	Containing 80 % or more by weight of titanium dioxide calculated on the dry matter	6.5	20
3206190000	Other	6.5	20
3206200000	Pigments and preparations based on chromium compounds	6.5	20
3206411000	Ultramarine	6.5	20
3206419000	Other	6.5	20
3206421000	Lithopones	6.5	20
3206429000	Other	6.5	20
3206491000	Zinc grey	6.5	20
3206492000	Mineral black	6.5	20
3206493000	Coloured earths	6.5	20
3206494000	Soluble vandyke brown	6.5	20
3206495000	Pigments based on cobalt compounds	6.5	20
3206496000	Pigments and preparations based on cadmium compounds	6.5	20
3206499000	Other	6.5	20
3206500000	Inorganic products of a kind used as luminophores	6.5	20
3207100000	Prepared pigments, prepared opacifiers, prepared colours and similar preparations	6.5	20
3207201000	Vitrifiable enamels and glazes	6.5	20
3207202000	Engobes (slips)	6.5	20
3207209000	Other	6.5	20
3207301000	Of gold	6.5	20

3207302000	Of platinum	6.5	20
3207303000	Of palladium	6.5	20
3207304000	Of silver	6.5	20
3207309000	Other	6.5	20
3207400000	Glass frit and other glass, in the form of powder, granules or flakes	6.5	20
3208101010	Enamels	6.5	20
3208101090	Other	6.5	20
3208102000	Varnishes (including lacquers)	6.5	20
3208103000	Solutions as defined in Note 4 to this Chapter	6.5	20
3208201011	Enamels	6.5	20
3208201019	Other	6.5	20
3208201020	Varnishes (including lacquers)	6.5	20
3208201030	Solutions as defined in Note 4 to this Chapter	6.5	20
3208202011	Enamels	6.5	20
3208202019	Other	6.5	20
3208202020	Varnishes (including lacquers)	6.5	20
3208202030	Solutions as defined in Note 4 to this Chapter	6.5	20
3208901011	Enamels	6.5	20
3208901019	Other	6.5	20
3208901020	Varnishes (including lacquers)	6.5	20
3208901030	Solutions as defined in Note 4 to this Chapter	6.5	20
3208909011	Enamels	6.5	20
3208909019	Other	6.5	20
3208909020	Varnishes (including lacquers)	6.5	20
3208909030	Solutions as defined in Note 4 to this Chapter	6.5	20
3209101011	Enamels	6.5	20
3209101019	Other	6.5	20
3209101020	Varnishes (including lacquers)	6.5	20
3209102010	Paints (including enamels)	6.5	20
3209102020	Varnishes (including lacquers)	6.5	20
3209901011	Enamels	6.5	20
3209901019	Other	6.5	20
3209901020	Varnishes (including lacquers)	6.5	20
3209909011	Enamels	6.5	20
3209909019	Other	6.5	20
3209909020	Varnishes (including lacquers)	6.5	20
3210001011	Enamels	6.5	20
3210001019	Other	6.5	20
3210001091	Enamels	6.5	20
3210001099	Other	6.5	20
3210002010	Oil varnishes	6.5	20
3210002020	Varnishes and lacquers based on lac, natural gum or resins	6.5	20
3210002030	Varnishes based on bitumen,pitch or similar products	6.5	20

3210002040	Liquid varnishes containing no solvent	6.5	20
3210003010	Distempers	6.5	20
3211000000	Prepared driers.	6.5	20
3212100000	Stamping foils	6.5	20
3212901000	Dyes and other colouring matter put up in forms or packings for retail sale	6.5	20
3212909000	Other	6.5	20
3213101000	Oil colours	6.5	20
3213109000	Other	6.5	20
3213901000	Oil colours	6.5	20
3213902000	Water colours	6.5	20
3213909000	Other	6.5	20
3214101060	Based on rubber	6.5	20
3214101080	Resin mastics and cements	6.5	20
3214101090	Other	6.5	20
3214102000	Painters' fillings	6.5	20
3215110000	Black	6.5	20
3215190000	Other	6.5	20
3215901000	Writing ink	6.5	20
3215902000	Drawing ink	6.5	20
3215903000	Copying ink	6.5	20
3215904010	Of oil	6.5	20
3215904020	Of water	6.5	20
3215904030	Of oil and water	6.5	20
3215905000	Metalic ink	6.5	20
3215906010	Of oil	6.5	20
3215906020	Of water	6.5	20
3215906030	Of oil and water	6.5	20
3215909000	Other	6.5	20
3302102011	Compound alcoholic preparations	30	20
3302102019	Other	8	20
3302102090	Other	6.5	20
3304209000	Other	6.5	20
3304301000	Nail enamels	6.5	20
3304309000	Other	6.5	20
3304911000	Face powders	6.5	20
3304912000	Baby powders (including talcum powder)	6.5	20
3304919000	Other	6.5	20
3304991000	Skin care cosmetics	6.5	20
3304992000	Make-up cosmetics	6.5	20
3304993000	Baby cosmetics	6.5	20
3305200000	Preparations for permanent waving or straightening	6.5	20
3306201019	Other	8	20
3306201020	Of measuring per single yarn more than 50 tex	8	20
3307109000	Other	6.5	20

3307301000	Perfumed bath salts	6.5	20
3307410000	"Agarbatti" and other odoriferous preparations which operate by burning	6.5	20
3307909000	Other	6.5	20
3401111000	Medicated soaps	6.5	20
3401119000	Other	6.5	20
3401191010	Laundry soaps	6.5	20
3401191090	Other	6.5	20
3401192000	Paper, wadding, felt and nonwovens, impregnated, coated or covered with soap or detergent	6.5	20
3401300000	Organic surface-active products and preparations for washing the skin, in the form of liquid or cream and put up for retail sale, whether or not containing soap	6.5	20
3402110000	Anionic	8	20
3402120000	Cationic	8	20
3402131000	Material for manufacturing agricultural chemicals (registered material under the Agricultural Chemicals Management Act)	2	20
3402190000	Other	8	20
3402202000	Cleaning preparations	6.5	20
3402209000	Other	6.5	20
3402901000	Surface-active preparations	6.5	20
3402902000	Washing preparations	6.5	20
3402903000	Cleaning preparations	6.5	20
3403111000	Preparations for the treatment of textile materials	6.5	20
3403112000	Preparations for the treatment of leather or furskins	6.5	20
3403119000	Other	6.5	20
3403191000	Cutting oil preparations	6.5	20
3403192000	Bolt or nut release preparations	6.5	20
3403193000	Anti-rust or anti-corrosion preparations	6.5	20
3403194000	Mold release preparations	6.5	20
3403195000	Lubricating preparations used in wire-drawing	6.5	20
3403199000	Other	6.5	20
3403911000	Preparations for the treatment or textile materials	6.5	20
3403912000	Preparations for the treatment of leather or furskins	6.5	20
3403919000	Other	6.5	20
3403991000	Cutting oil preparations	6.5	20
3403992000	Lubricating preparations used in wire-drawing	6.5	20
3403999000	Other	6.5	20
3404901010	Of chloroparaffines	6.5	20
3404901020	Of opals	6.5	20
3404901030	Of polyalkylenes	6.5	20
3404901040	Of chemically modified lignite	6.5	20
3404902000	Prepared waxes	6.5	20
3405100000	Polishes, creams and similar preparations for footwear or	6.5	20

	leather		
3405200000	Polishes, creams and similar preparations for the maintenance of wooden furniture, floors or other woodwork	6.5	20
3405300000	Polishes and similar preparations for coachwork, other than metal polishes	6.5	20
3405400000	Scouring pastes and powders and other scouring preparations	6.5	20
3405901010	Based on chalk	6.5	20
3405901020	Based on kieselguhr	6.5	20
3405901030	Based on diamond powder or dust	6.5	20
3405901090	Other	6.5	20
3405909000	Other	6.5	20
3406000000	Candles, tapers and the like.	6.5	20
3407001000	Modelling pastes	6.5	20
3407003000	Other preparations for use in dentistry, with a basis of plaster	6.5	20
3506101000	Based on rubber	6.5	20
3506102000	Based on plastic (including artificial resins)	6.5	20
3506109000	Other	6.5	20
3506910000	Adhesives based on polymers of headings 39.01 to 39.13 or on rubber	6.5	20
3506991000	Vienna glues	6.5	20
3506992000	Glues obtained by chemically treating natural gums	6.5	20
3506993000	Glues based on silicates	6.5	20
3506999000	Other	6.5	20
3507901010	Trypsin	6.5	20
3507901020	Chymotrypsin	6.5	20
3507901030	Alpha-amylase	6.5	20
3507901040	Lipase	6.5	20
3507901090	Other	6.5	20
3507902000	Pepsin	6.5	20
3507903000	Malt enzymes	6.5	20
3507904010	Papain	6.5	20
3507904020	Bromelain	6.5	20
3507904030	Ficin	6.5	20
3507906020	Protease	6.5	20
3507908000	Cytochrome C	6.5	20
3601001000	Black powders	6.5	20
3601002000	Smokeless powders	6.5	20
3602000000	Prepared explosives, other than propellent powders.	6.5	20
3603001000	Safety fuses	6.5	20
3603002000	Detonating fuses	6.5	20
3603003000	Percussion or detonating caps	6.5	20
3603004000	Igniters	6.5	20

3603005000	Electric detonators	6.5	20
3604100000	Fireworks	6.5	20
3604901000	Signalling flares	6.5	20
3604909000	Other	6.5	20
3605001000	Yellow phosphorus match	6.5	20
3605009000	Other	6.5	20
3606100000	Liquid or liquefied-gas fuels in containers of a kind used for filling or refilling cigarette or similar lighters and of a capacity not exceeding 300cm³	6.5	20
3606901010	Meta fuel	6.5	20
3606901020	Hexamine	6.5	20
3606901030	Solidified alcohols	6.5	20
3606901090	Other	6.5	20
3606902010	Lighter flints	6.5	20
3606902090	Other	6.5	20
3606909010	Lighter flints	6.5	20
3606909090	Other	6.5	20
3701100000	For X-ray	6.5	20
3701200000	Instant print film	6.5	20
3701301000	For marking semiconductor	6.5	20
3701309100	For graphic art	6.5	20
3701309200	For printed circuit board	6.5	20
3701309910	For astonomy	6.5	20
3701309920	For aerial photography	6.5	20
3701309991	For Flat Panel Display (blank mask)	3	20
3701309999	Other	6.5	20
3701911000	For making semiconductor	6.5	20
3701919100	For graphic art	6.5	20
3701919200	For printed circuit board	6.5	20
3701919910	For astonomy	6.5	20
3701919920	For aerial photography	6.5	20
3701919990	Other	6.5	20
3701991000	For making semiconductor	3	20
3701999100	For graphic art	6.5	20
3701999200	For printed circtit board	6.5	20
3701999910	For astonomy	6.5	20
3701999920	For aerial photography	6.5	20
3701999990	Other	6.5	20
3702100000	For X-ray	6.5	20
3702311110	Negatives	6.5	20
3702311120	Positives	6.5	20
3702311210	Negatives	6.5	20
3702311220	Positives	6.5	20
3702311910	Negatives	6.5	20
3702311920	Positives	6.5	20

3702312000	For graphic art	6.5	20
3702313000	For printed circuit board	6.5	20
3702319010	For photo-electric sound recording	6.5	20
3702319020	For aerial photography	6.5	20
3702319090	Other	6.5	20
3702321110	Negatives	6.5	20
3702321120	Positives	6.5	20
3702321210	Negatives	6.5	20
3702321220	Positives	6.5	20
3702321910	Negatives	6.5	20
3702321920	Positives	6.5	20
3702322000	For graphic art	6.5	20
3702323000	For printed circuit board	6.5	20
3702329010	For photo-electric sound recording	6.5	20
3702329020	For aerial photography	6.5	20
3702329030	Instant print film	6.5	20
3702329090	Other	6.5	20
3702391110	Negatives	6.5	20
3702391120	Positives	6.5	20
3702391210	Negatives	6.5	20
3702391220	Positives	6.5	20
3702391910	Negatives	6.5	20
3702391920	Positives	6.5	20
3702392000	For graphic art	6.5	20
3702393000	For printed circuit board	6.5	20
3702399010	For photo-electric sound recording	6.5	20
3702399020	For aerial photography	6.5	20
3702399090	Other	6.5	20
3702411010	Negatives	6.5	20
3702411020	Positives	6.5	20
3702412000	For graphic art	6.5	20
3702413000	For printed circuit board	6.5	20
3702419010	For photo-electric sound recording	6.5	20
3702419020	For aerial photography	6.5	20
3702419090	Other	6.5	20
3702421010	Negatives	6.5	20
3702421020	Positives	6.5	20
3702422000	For graphic art	6.5	20
3702423000	For printed circuit board	6.5	20
3702429010	For photo-electric sound recording	6.5	20
3702429020	For aerial photography	6.5	20
3702429090	Other	6.5	20
3702431010	Negatives	6.5	20
3702431020	Positives	6.5	20
3702432000	For graphic art	6.5	20

3702433000	For printed circuit board	6.5	20
3702439010	For photo-electric sound recording	6.5	20
3702439020	For aerial photography	6.5	20
3702439090	Other	6.5	20
3702441010	Negatives	6.5	20
3702441020	Positives	6.5	20
3702442000	For graphic art	6.5	20
3702443000	For printed circuit board	6.5	20
3702449010	For photo-electric sound recording	6.5	20
3702449020	For aerial photography	6.5	20
3702449090	Other	6.5	20
3702511010	Negatives	6.5	20
3702511020	Positives	6.5	20
3702512000	For graphic art	6.5	20
3702513000	For printed circuit board	6.5	20
3702519010	For photo-electric sound recording	6.5	20
3702519020	For aerial photography	6.5	20
3702519090	Other	6.5	20
3702521010	Negatives	6.5	20
3702521020	Positives	6.5	20
3702522000	For graphic art	6.5	20
3702523000	For printed circuit board	6.5	20
3702529010	For photo-electric sound recording	6.5	20
3702529020	For aerial photography	6.5	20
3702529090	Other	6.5	20
3702530000	Of a width exceeding 16 mm but not exceeding 35 mm and of a length not exceeding 30 m, for slides	6.5	20
3702541010	Negatives	6.5	20
3702541020	Positives	6.5	20
3702542000	For graphic art	6.5	20
3702543000	For printed circuit board	6.5	20
3702549010	For photo-electric sound recording	6.5	20
3702549020	For aerial photography	6.5	20
3702549090	Other	6.5	20
3702551010	Negatives	6.5	20
3702551020	Positives	6.5	20
3702552000	For graphic art	6.5	20
3702553000	For printed circuit board	6.5	20
3702559010	For photo-electric sound recording	6.5	20
3702559020	For aerial photography	6.5	20
3702559090	Other	6.5	20
3702561010	Negatives	6.5	20
3702561020	Positives	6.5	20
3702562000	For graphic art	6.5	20
3702563000	For printed circuit board	6.5	20

3702569010	For photo-electric sound recording	6.5	20
3702569020	For aerial photography	6.5	20
3702569090	Other	6.5	20
3702911010	Negatives	6.5	20
3702911020	Positives	6.5	20
3702912000	For graphic art	6.5	20
3702913000	For printed circuit board	6.5	20
3702919010	For photo-electric sound recording	6.5	20
3702919020	For aerial photography	6.5	20
3702919090	Other	6.5	20
3702931010	Negatives	6.5	20
3702931020	Positives	6.5	20
3702932000	For graphic art	6.5	20
3702933000	For printed circuit board	6.5	20
3702939010	For photo-electric sound recording	6.5	20
3702939020	For aerial photography	6.5	20
3702939090	Other	6.5	20
3702941010	Negatives	6.5	20
3702941020	Positives	6.5	20
3702942000	For graphic art	6.5	20
3702943000	For printed circuit board	6.5	20
3702949010	For photo-electric sound recording	6.5	20
3702949020	For aerial photography	6.5	20
3702949090	Other	6.5	20
3702951010	Negatives	6.5	20
3702951020	Positives	6.5	20
3702952000	For graphic art	6.5	20
3702953000	For printed circuit board	6.5	20
3702959010	For photo-electric sound recording	6.5	20
3702959020	For aerial photography	6.5	20
3702959090	Other	6.5	20
3703101010	For x-ray	6.5	20
3703101020	For electro-cardiograph	6.5	20
3703101030	For photo-copying	6.5	20
3703101040	For recording	6.5	20
3703101090	Other	6.5	20
3703109010	For x-ray	6.5	20
3703109020	For electro-cardiograph	6.5	20
3703109030	For photo-copying	6.5	20
3703109040	For recording	6.5	20
3703109090	Other	6.5	20
3703201000	For x-ray	6.5	20
3703202000	For electro-cardiograph	6.5	20
3703203000	For photo-copying	6.5	20
3703204000	For recording	6.5	20

3703209000	Other	6.5	20
3703901000	For x-ray	6.5	20
3703902000	For electro-cardiograph	6.5	20
3703903000	For photo-copying	6.5	20
3703904000	For recording	6.5	20
3703909000	Other	6.5	20
3704002000	Photographic paper, paperboard and textiles	6.5	20
3705101000	For producing postcard, illastrated postcard, cards and calenders	6.5	20
3705901000	For making semiconductor	3	20
3706101000	Consisting only of sound track	195won/m or 6.5	20
3706102000	For news	4won/m or 6.5	20
3706103010	Rush	26won/m or 6.5	20
3706103020	Other negative joint-produced cinematography	468won/m or 6.5	20
3706103030	Other positive joint-produced cinematography	78won/m or 6.5	20
3706104000	Cinematograph film exposed overseas in the working of a motion picture by a republic of Korea producer (only pictured overseas scenery or only appeared actors of Republic of Korea in the film) and cinematograph film made by a Korean producer in Korea	26won/m or 6.5	20
3706105010	Negatives	1,092won/m or 6.5	20
3706105020	Positives	182won/m or 6.5	20
3706106010	Negatives	1,560won/m or 6.5	20
3706106020	Positives	260won/m or 6.5	20
3706901000	Consisting only of sound track	9won/m or 6.5	20
3706902000	For news	5won/m or 6.5	20
3706903010	Rush	26won/m or 6.5	20
3706903020	Other negative joint- produced cinematography	468won/m or 6.5	20
3706903030	Other positive joint-produced cinematography	78won/m or 6.5	20
3706904000	Cinematograph film exposed overseas in the working of a motion picture by a republic of Korea producer (only	26won/m or 6.5	20

	pictured overseas scenery or only appeared actors of Republic of Korea in the film) and cinmatograph film made by a Korean producer in Korea		
3706905010	Negatives	25won/m or 6.5	20
3706905020	Positives	8won/m or 6.5	20
3706906010	Negatives	1,092won/m or 6.5	20
3706906020	Positives	182won/m or 6.5	20
3707100000	Sensitising emulsions	6.5	20
3707901010	For making semiconductor	6.5	20
3707901090	Other	6.5	20
3707902100	For colour photography	6.5	20
3707902910	For X-ray	6.5	20
3707902920	For graphic art	6.5	20
3707902990	Other	6.5	20
3707903100	For colour photography	6.5	20
3707903910	For X-ray	6.5	20
3707903920	For graphic art	6.5	20
3707903990	Other	6.5	20
3707909100	Intensifiers and reducers	6.5	20
3707909200	Toners	6.5	20
3707909300	Clearing agents	6.5	20
3707909400	Flash light materials	6.5	20
3707909900	Other	6.5	20
3801101000	For manufacturing secondary battery	4	20
3801109000	Other	6.5	20
3801200000	Colloidal or semi-colloidal graphite	6.5	20
3801300000	Carbonaceous pastes for electrodes and similar pastes for furnace linings	6.5	20
3801900000	Other	6.5	20
3802100000	Activated carbon	6.5	20
3802901010	Activated diatomite	6.5	20
3802901020	Activated clays and activated earths	6.5	20
3802901090	Other	6.5	20
3802902000	Animal black (including spent animal black)	6.5	20
3803000000	Tall oil, whether or not refined.	5	20
3804001000	Liquid	6.5	20
3804009000	Other	6.5	20
3805101000	Gum spirits of turpentine	6.5	20
3805102000	Wood turpentine	6.5	20
3805103000	Sulphate turpentine	6.5	20
3805900000	Other	6.5	20

3806102000	Resin acids	6.5	20
3806201000	Salts of rosin	6.5	20
3806202000	Salts of resin acids	6.5	20
3806209000	Other	6.5	20
3806300000	Ester gums	6.5	20
3806902000	Run gum	6.5	20
3806903000	Rosin spirt and rogin oil	6.5	20
3806909000	Other	6.5	20
3807001000	Wood tar, wood tar oils and wood creosote	6.5	20
3807002000	Wood naphtha	6.5	20
3807003000	Vegetable pitch	6.5	20
3807009090	Other	6.5	20
3808501000	Material for manufacturing agricultural chemicals (registered material under the Agricultural Chemicals Management Act)	2	20
3808911000	Material for manufacturing agricultural chemicals (registered material under the Agricultural Chemicals Management Act)	2	20
3808921000	Material for manufacturing agricultural chemicals (registered material under the Agricultural Chemicals Management Act)	2	20
3808929000	Other	6.5	20
3808932000	Anti-sprouting products	6.5	20
3808933000	Plant-growth regulators	6.5	20
3808991000	Rodenticides	6.5	20
3809910000	Of a kind used in the textile or like industries	6.5	20
3809920000	Of a kind used in the paper or like industries	6.5	20
3809930000	Of a kind used in the leather or like industries	6.5	20
3810101000	Pickling preparations for metal surfaces	6.5	20
3810109000	Other	6.5	20
3810901000	Fluxes and other auxiliary preparations for soldering, brazing or welding	6.5	20
3810909000	Other	6.5	20
3811110000	Based on lead compounds	6.5	20
3811190000	Other	6.5	20
3811210000	Containing petroleum oils or oils obtained from bituminous minerals	5	20
3811290000	Other	5	20
3812101000	Based on diphenylguanidine	6.5	20
3812102000	Based on dithiocarbamates	6.5	20
3812103000	Based on thiuram sulphides	6.5	20
3812104000	Based on hexamethylene tetramine	6.5	20
3812106000	Based on dibenzothiazyle disulphide	6.5	20
3812109000	Other	6.5	20
3812200000	Compound plasticisers for rubber or plastics	6.5	20

3812301000	Anti-oxidising preparations	6.5	20
3812302000	Other compounds stabilisers	6.5	20
3813002000	Charges for fire-extinguishers	6.5	20
3813003000	Charged fire-extinguishing grenades	6.5	20
3814001010	Mixtures of acetones, methyl acetate and methanol	6.5	20
3814001020	Mixtures of ethyl acetate, butyl alcohol and toluene	6.5	20
3814001090	Other	6.5	20
3814002110	For making semiconductor	6.5	20
3814002190	Other	6.5	20
3815110000	With nickel or nickel compounds as the active substance	6.5	20
3815121000	With platinium metal or platinium compounds	6.5	20
3815122000	Of palladium or palladium compounds	6.5	20
3815129000	Other	6.5	20
3815191000	With iron or iron compounds as the active substance	6.5	20
3815192000	Of titanium or titanium compounds	6.5	20
3815199000	Other	6.5	20
3815901000	Reaction initiators	6.5	20
3815909000	Other	6.5	20
3816001000	Refractory cements	6.5	20
3816002000	Refractory mortars	6.5	20
3816003000	Refractory concretes	6.5	20
3819001000	Hydraulic brake fluids	6.5	20
3819002000	Other prepared liquids for hydraulic transmission	6.5	20
3820001000	Anti-freezing preparations	6.5	20
3820002000	Prepared de-icing fluids	6.5	20
3822001091	Of other plates, sheets, film, foil and strip of plastics	6.5	20
3822001099	Other	8	20
3822002091	Of other plates, sheets, film, foil and strip of plastics	6.5	20
3822002092	Other articles of plastics	6.5	20
3822003042	Of 1 % rate in the Tariff Schedules	1	20
3822003043	Of 2 % rate in the Tariff Schedules	2	20
3822003044	Of 3 % rate in the Tariff Schedules	3	20
3822003045	Of 4 % rate in the Tariff Schedules	4	20
3822003046	Of 5 % rate in the Tariff Schedules	5	20
3822003047	Of 5.4 % rate in the Tariff Schedules	5.4	20
3822003048	Of 6.5 % rate in the Tariff Schedules	6.5	20
3822003049	Of 7 % rate in the Tariff Schedules	7	20
3822003050	Of 8 % rate in the Tariff Schedules	8	20
3822003051	Of 10 % rate in the Tariff Schedules	10	20
3822003052	Of 20 % rate in the Tariff Schedules	20	20
3822003053	Of 27 % rate in the Tariff Schedules	27	20
3822003054	Of 30 % rate in the Tariff Schedules	30	20
3822003055	Of 36 % rate in the Tariff Schedules	36	20
3822003056	Of 40 % rate in the Tariff Schedules	40	20
3822003057	Of 50 % rate in the Tariff Schedules	50	20

3822003058	Of subheadings 3706.10.1000, 3706.10.5020 and 3706.90.6020	182won/m or 6.5	20
3822003059	Of subheadings 3706.120000 and 3706.920000	4won/m or 6.5	20
3822003060	Of subheadings 3706.10.3010, 3706.10.4000, 3706.90.3010 and 3706.90.4000	26won/m or 6.5	20
3822003061	Of subheadings 3706.10.3020 and 3706.90.3020	468won/m or 6.5	20
3822003062	Of subheadings 3706.10.3030 and 3706.90.3030	78won/m or 6.5	20
3822003063	Of subheadings 3706.10.5010 and 3706.90.6010	1,092won/m or 6.5	20
3822003064	Of subheading 3706.10.6010	1,560won/m or 6.5	20
3822003065	Of subheading 3706.10.6020	260won/m or 6.5	20
3822003066	Of subheadings 3706.90.1000 and 3706.90.5020	8won/m or 6.5	20
3822003067	Of subheading 3706.90.5010	25won/m or 6.5	20
3823110000	Stearic acid	8	20
3823120000	Oleic acid	8	20
3823130000	Tall oil fatty acids	8	20
3823191000	Palmitic acids	8	20
3823192000	Acid oils from refining	8	20
3823199000	Other	8	20
3823701000	Cetyl alcohol	5	20
3823702000	Stearyl alcohol	5	20
3823703000	Oleyl alcohol	5	20
3823704000	Lauryl alcohol	5	20
3823709010	Material for manufacturing agricultural chemicals (registered material under the Agricultural Chemicals Management Act)	2	20
3823709090	Other	5	20
3824100000	Prepared binders for foundry moulds or cores	6.5	20
3824300000	Non-agglomerated metal carbides mixed together or with metallic binders	6.5	20
3824400000	Prepared additives for cements, mortars or concretes	6.5	20
3824500000	Non-refractory mortars and concretes	6.5	20
3824711000	Detergents based on trichlorotrifluoroethane	6.5	20
3824730000	Containing hydrobromofluorocarbons (HBFCs)	6.5	20
3824750000	Containing carbon tetrachloride	6.5	20
3824770000	Containing bromomethane (methyl bromide) or bromochloromethane	6.5	20
3824901000	Roasted chromite	5	20

3824902100	Getters for vaccum tubes	6.5	20
3824902200	Preparations of carbon resistors or ceramic solid resistors	6.5	20
3824902490	Other	6.5	20
3824903100	Mistures consisting mainly of O-alkyl (≤C10, including cycloalkyl) alkyl (methyl, ethyl, n-propyl or isopropyl) phosphonofluoridates	6.5	20
3824903200	Mixtures consisting mainly of O-alkyl (≤C10, including cycloalkyl) N,N-dialkyl (methyl, ehtyl, n-propyl or isopropyl) phosphoramidocyanidates	6.5	20
3824903300	Mixtures consisting mainly of [S-2-(dialkyl (methyl, ethyl, n-propyl or isopropyl) amino)ethyl]hydrogen alkyl (methyl, ethyl, n-propyl or isopropyl) phosphonothioates and their O-alkyl (≤C10, including cycloalkyl) esters; mixtures consisting mainly of alkylated or protonated salts thereof	6.5	20
3824903400	Mixtures consisting mainly of alkyl (methyl, ethyl, n-propyl or isopropyl) phosphonyldifluorides	6.5	20
3824903500	Mixtures consisting mainly of[O-2-dialkyl (methyl, ethyl, n-propyl or isopropyl) aminoethyl] hydrogen alkyl (methyl, ethyl, n-propyl or isopropyl) phosphonites and their O-alkyl (≤C10, including cycloalkyl) esters; mixtures consisting mainly of alkylated or protoanted salts thereof	6.5	20
3824903600	Mixtures consisting mainly of N,N-dialkyl (methyl, ethyl, n-propyl or isopropyl) phosphoramidic dihalides	6.5	20
3824903700	Mixtures consisting mainly of dialkyl (methyl, ethyl, n-propyl or isopropyl) N,N-dialkyl (methyl, ethyl, n-propyl or isopropyl) phosphoramidates	6.5	20
3824903800	Mixtures consisting mainly of N,N-dialkyl (methyl, ethyl, n-propyl or isopropyl) 2-chloroethylamines or their protonated salts	6.5	20
3824903911	Mixtures consisting mainly of N,N dimethyl-2-amino-ethanol or N,N-diethyl-2-amino ethanol or their protonated salts	6.5	20
3824903919	Other	6.5	20
3824903920	Mixtures consisting mainly of N,N-dialkyl (methyl, ethyl, n-propyl or isopropyl) aminoethane-2-thiols or their protonated salts	6.5	20
3824903930	Other mixtures consisting mainly of chemicals containing a phosphorus atom to which is bonded one methyl, ethyl, n-propyl or isopropyl group but not further carbon atoms	6.5	20
3824903990	Other	6.5	20
3824904100	Mixed polyethylene glycol	6.5	20
3824904200	Ion-exchangers	6.5	20
3824904300	Anti-scaling compounds	6.5	20
3824904400	Additives to harden varnish or glue	6.5	20
3824905100	Ink-removers	6.5	20

3824905200	Stencil correctors	6.5	20
3824905300	Correcting fluids	6.5	20
3824906100	Compounded extenders for paints	6.5	20
3824906300	Soda-lime	6.5	20
3824906400	Hydrated silica gel	6.5	20
3824906500	Anti-rust preparations	6.5	20
3824906600	Preparations for the manufacture of ceramic condenser and ferrite core	6.5	20
3824907100	Metal plating preparations	6.5	20
3824907200	Chlorinated paraffin	6.5	20
3824907300	Anti-foaming agent	6.5	20
3824907400	Foaming agent	6.5	20
3824907600	Liquid crystal preparations	6.5	20
3824907700	Ammoniacal gas liquors	6.5	20
3824908010	Based on methyl ethyl ketone peroxide	6.5	20
3824908090	Other	6.5	20
3824909010	Micro-element fertilisers (other than products of Chapter 31)	6.5	20
3824909030	Chewing gum base	6.5	20
3824909050	Naphthenic acids, their water-insoluble salts and their esters	6.5	20
3825100000	Municipal waste	6.5	20
3825200000	Sewage sludge	6.5	20
3825302000	Of subheading 3824.90	6.5	20
3825303000	Of subheading 4015.11	8	20
3825304000	Of subheading 9018.3	8	20
3825410000	Halogenated	6.5	20
3825490000	Other	6.5	20
3825500000	Wastes of metal pickling liquors, hydraulic fluids, brake fluids and anti-freeze fluids	6.5	20
3825610000	Mainly containing organic constituents	6.5	20
3825690000	Other	6.5	20
3825900000	Other	6.5	20
3901201000	Of pulp	6.5	20
3901300000	Ethylene-vinyl acetate copolymers	6.5	20
3904210000	Non-plasticised	6.5	20
3904220000	Plasticised	6.5	20
3904500000	Vinylidene chloride polymers	6.5	20
3904610000	Polytetrafluoroethylene	6.5	20
3904690000	Other	6.5	20
3904900000	Other	6.5	20
3905120000	In aqueous dispersion	6.5	20
3905190000	Other	6.5	20
3905290000	Other	6.5	20
3905300000	Poly(vinyl alcohol), whether or not containing	8	20

	unhydrolysed acetate groups		
3905910000	Copolymers	6.5	20
3905990000	Other	6.5	20
3907201000	Polyoxyethylene (polyethylene glycol)	6.5	20
3907203000	Poly phenylene oxide	6.5	20
3907500000	Alkyd resins	6.5	20
3907700000	Poly(lactic acid)	6.5	20
3908103000	Polyamide-11, -12, -6,9, -6,10, -6,12	6.5	20
3909102000	Thiourea resins	6.5	20
3910001000	For making semiconductor	6.5	20
3911101000	Petroleum resins	8	20
3911102000	Coumarone, indene or coumarone-indene resins	8	20
3911103000	Polyterpenes	8	20
3911901000	Polysulphides	6.5	20
3911902000	Polysulphones	6.5	20
3911903000	Furan resin	6.5	20
3912110000	Non-plasticised	5	20
3912120000	Plasticised	5	20
3912200000	Cellulose nitrates (including collodions)	6.5	20
3912311000	Sodium carboxymethyl cellulose	6.5	20
3912399000	Other	6.5	20
3912901000	Regenerated cellulose	6.5	20
3912909000	Other	6.5	20
3913101000	Sodium alginate	6.5	20
3913102000	Propylene glycol alginate	6.5	20
3913109000	Other	6.5	20
3913901000	Hardened proteins	6.5	20
3913902010	Chlorinated rubber	6.5	20
3913902020	Rubber hydrochloride	6.5	20
3913902030	Oxidised rubber	6.5	20
3913902040	Cyclised rubber	6.5	20
3913902090	Other	6.5	20
3913909010	Dextran	6.5	20
3914001000	Cationic	6.5	20
3914009000	Other	6.5	20
3915101000	Film, sheets, plates and foil before they became wastes	6.5	20
3915102000	Pipes and hoses before they became wastes	6.5	20
3915109000	Other	6.5	20
3915200000	Of polymers of styrene	6.5	20
3915300000	Of polymers of vinyl chloride	6.5	20
3915901000	Of polymers of propylene	6.5	20
3915902000	Of acrylic polymers	6.5	20
3915903000	Of polyacetals	6.5	20
3915904000	Of polycarbonates	6.5	20
3915905000	Of polyamides	6.5	20

3916100000	Of polymers of ethylene	6,5	20
3916200000	Of polymers of vinyl chloride	6,5	20
3916901000	Of polymers of styrene	6,5	20
3916902000	Of polymers of propylene	6,5	20
3916903000	Of acrylic polymers	6,5	20
3916904000	Of polyamides	6,5	20
3916909000	Other	6,5	20
3917101000	Of hardened protein	6,5	20
3917102000	Of cellulosic materials	6,5	20
3917210000	Of polymers of ethylene	6,5	20
3917220000	Of polymers of propylene	6,5	20
3917230000	Of polymers of vinyl chloride	6,5	20
3917291000	Of polymers of styrene	6,5	20
3917292000	Of polyamides	6,5	20
3917299000	Other	6,5	20
3917311000	Of polymers of ethylene	6,5	20
3917312000	Of polymers of vinyl chloride	6,5	20
3917319000	Other	6,5	20
3917321000	Of polymers of ethylene	6,5	20
3917322000	Of polymers of vinyl chloride	6,5	20
3917329000	Other	6,5	20
3917331000	Of polymers of ethylene	6,5	20
3917332000	Of polymers of vinyl chloride	6,5	20
3917339000	Other	6,5	20
3917391000	Of polymers of ethylene	6,5	20
3917392000	Of polymers of vinyl chloride	6,5	20
3917399000	Other	6,5	20
3917400000	Fittings	6,5	20
3918101000	Of polyvinyl chloride	6,5	20
3918102000	Of copolymers of vinyl chloride and vinyl acetate	6,5	20
3918109000	Other	6,5	20
3918900000	Of other plastics	6,5	20
3919100000	In rolls of a width not exceeding 20 cm	6,5	20
3919900000	Other	6,5	20
3920100000	Of polymers of ethylene	6,5	20
3920200000	Of polymers of propylene	6,5	20
3920300000	Of polymers of styrene	6,5	20
3920430000	Containing by weight not less than 6 % of plasticisers	6,5	20
3920490000	Other	6,5	20
3920620000	Of poly(ethylene terephthalate)	6,5	20
3920630000	Of unsaturated polyesters	6,5	20
3920690000	Of other polyesters	6,5	20
3920710000	Of regenerated cellulose	6,5	20
3920730000	Of cellulose acetate	6,5	20
3920791000	Of vulcanised fibre	6,5	20

3920799000	Other	6.5	20
3920920000	Of polyamides	6.5	20
3920930000	Of amino-resins	6.5	20
3920940000	Of phenolic resins	6.5	20
3920991000	For aircrafts	6.5	20
3920999010	Polyimides film, for manufacturing Printed Circuit Board with the function of lead frame	4	20
3920999090	Other	6.5	20
3921110000	Of polymers of styrene	6.5	20
3921120000	Of polymers of vinyl chloride	6.5	20
3921130000	Of polyurethanes	6.5	20
3921140000	Of regenerated cellulose	6.5	20
3921191010	Separator, for manufacturing secondary battery	4	20
3921191090	Other	6.5	20
3921192010	Separator, for manufacturing secondary battery	4	20
3921192090	Other	6.5	20
3921193010	Of polymethyl methacrylate	6.5	20
3921193090	Other	6.5	20
3921194010	Of polycarbonates	6.5	20
3921194020	Of polyethylene terephthalate	6.5	20
3921194030	Of unsaturated polyesters	6.5	20
3921194090	Other	6.5	20
3921195010	Of vulcanised fibre	6.5	20
3921195020	Of cellulose acetate	6.5	20
3921195090	Other	6.5	20
3921199010	Of polyvinyl butyral	6.5	20
3921199020	Of polyamides	6.5	20
3921199030	Of amino-resins	6.5	20
3921199040	Of phenolic resins	6.5	20
3921199090	Other	6.5	20
3921901000	Of polymers of ethylene	6.5	20
3921902000	Of polymers of propylene	6.5	20
3921903000	Of polymers of styrene	6.5	20
3921904010	Rigid	6.5	20
3921904020	Flexible	6.5	20
3921905010	Of polymethyl methacrylate	6.5	20
3921905090	Other	6.5	20
3921906010	Of polycarbonates	6.5	20
3921906020	Of polyethylene terephthalate	6.5	20
3921906030	Of unsaturated polyesters	6.5	20
3921907010	Of regenerated cellulose	6.5	20
3921907020	Of vulcanised fibre	6.5	20
3921907030	Of cellulose acetate	6.5	20
3921907090	Other	6.5	20
3921909010	Of polyvinyl butyral	6.5	20

3921909020	Of polyamides	6.5	20
3921909030	Of amino-resins	6.5	20
3921909050	Of polyurethanes	6.5	20
3921909090	Other	6.5	20
3922101000	Baths and shower baths	6.5	20
3922102000	Wash-basins	6.5	20
3922103000	Sinks	6.5	20
3922200000	Lavatory seats and covers	6.5	20
3922901000	Bidets	6.5	20
3923210000	Of polymers of ethylene	6.5	20
3923290000	Of other plastics	6.5	20
3923300000	Carboys, bottles, flasks and similar articles	6.5	20
3923400000	Spools, cops, bobbins and similar supports	6.5	20
3924100000	Tableware and kitchenware	6.5	20
3924901000	Soap dishes and boxes	6.5	20
3924902000	Table cloths and other similar articles	6.5	20
3925100000	Reservoirs, tanks, vats and similar containers, of a capacity exceeding 300ℓ	6.5	20
3925200000	Doors, windows and their frames and thresholds for doors	6.5	20
3925300000	Shutters, blinds (including Venetian blinds) and similar articles and parts thereof	6.5	20
3925900000	Other	6.5	20
3926101000	Pencil cases and erasers	6.5	20
3926102000	Binders and albums	6.5	20
3926109000	Other	6.5	20
3926200000	Articles of apparel and clothing accessories (including gloves, mittens and mitts)	6.5	20
3926300000	Fittings for furniture, coachwork or the like	6.5	20
3926400000	Statuettes and other ornamental articles	6.5	20
3926901000	Parts for use in machinery and mechanical appliances	6.5	20
3926902000	Fans and hand screens non-mechanical; frams and handles therefor and parts of such frames and handles	6.5	20
3926903000	Lables and tags	6.5	20
3926904000	Adhesive tapes with case	6.5	20
3926905000	Frames for painting, photographs, mirrors and the like	6.5	20
3926909000	Other	6.5	20
4001301000	Chicle gum	2	20
4001309000	Other	2	20
4002201000	Latex	8	20
4002209000	Other	8	20
4002311000	Latex	5	20
4002319000	Other	5	20
4002391000	Latex	5	20
4002399010	Of chlorinated-isobutene-isoprene rubber (CIIR)	5	20
4002399020	Of brominated-isobutene-isoprene rubber (BIIR)	5	20

4002410000	Latex	8	20
4002490000	Other	8	20
4002510000	Latex	8	20
4002601000	Latex	8	20
4002609000	Other	8	20
4002701000	Latex	8	20
4002801000	Latex	8	20
4002809000	Other	8	20
4002991000	Of carboxylated acrylonitile-butadiene rubbers (XNBR)	8	20
4002992000	Of acrylonitile-isoprene rubbers (NIR)	8	20
4002993000	Thioplasts (TM)	8	20
4003000000	Reclaimed rubber in primary forms or in plates, sheets or strip.	8	20
4004000000	Waste, parings and scrap of rubber (other than hard rubber) and powders and granules obtained therefrom.	3	20
4005101000	Plates, sheets and strip	8	20
4005109000	Other	8	20
4005200000	Solutions; dispersions other than those of subheading 4005.10	8	20
4005910000	Plates, sheets and strip	8	20
4005991000	Compounded rubber latex	8	20
4005999000	Other	8	20
4006100000	"Camel-back" strips for retreading rubber tyres	8	20
4006901000	Rubber rods	8	20
4006902000	Rubber tubes	8	20
4006903000	Rubber profile shapes	8	20
4006904000	Rubber discs, rings and washers	8	20
4006905000	Rubber thread	8	20
4006909000	Other	8	20
4007001000	Rubber thread	8	20
4008111000	Combined with textile fabrics for reinforcing purposes	8	20
4008119000	Other	8	20
4008191000	Combined with textile fabrics for reinforcing purposes	8	20
4008199000	Other	8	20
4008211000	Combined with textile fabrics for reinforcing purposes	8	20
4008219000	Other	8	20
4008291000	Combined with textile fabrics for reinforcing purposes	8	20
4009120000	With fittings	8	20
4009220000	With fittings	8	20
4009310000	Without fittings	8	20
4009320000	With fittings	8	20
4009410000	Without fittings	8	20
4009420000	With fittings	8	20
4010110000	Reinforced only with metal	8	20
4010120000	Reinforced only with textile materials	8	20

4010191000	Reinforced only with plastics	8	20
4010199000	Other	8	20
4010310000	Endless transmission belts of trapezoidal cross-section (V-belts), V-ribbed, of an outside circumference exceeding 60 cm but not exceeding 180 cm	8	20
4010320000	Endless transmission belts of trapezoidal cross-section (V-belts), other than V-ribbed, of an outside circumference exceeding 60 cm but not exceeding 180 cm	8	20
4010330000	Endless transmission belts of trapezoidal cross-section (V-belts), V-ribbed, of an outside circumference exceeding 180 cm but not exceeding 240 cm	8	20
4010340000	Endless transmission belts of trapezoidal cross-section (V-belts), other than V-ribbed, of an outside circumference exceeding 180 cm but not exceeding 240 cm	8	20
4010350000	Endless synchronous belts, of an outside circumference exceeding 60 cm but not exceeding 150 cm	8	20
4010360000	Endless synchronous belts, of an outside circumference exceeding 150 cm but not exceeding 198 cm	8	20
4010390000	Other	8	20
4011101000	Of radial carcass	8	20
4011102000	Of biased carcass	8	20
4011109000	Other	8	20
4011201010	For use on a rim measuring less than 49.53 cm in diameter	8	20
4011201090	Other	8	20
4011202010	For use on a rim measuring less than 49.53 cm in diameter	8	20
4011202090	Other	8	20
4011209000	Other	8	20
4011300000	Of a kind used on aircraft	5	20
4011400000	Of a kind used on motorcycles	8	20
4011500000	Of a kind used on bicycles	8	20
4011610000	Of a kind used on agricultural or forestry vehicles and machines	8	20
4011620000	Of a kind used on construction or industrial handling vehicles and machines and having a rim size not exceeding 61 cm	8	20
4011630000	Of a kind used on construction or industrial handling vehicles and machines and having a rim size exceeding 61 cm	8	20
4011690000	Other	8	20
4011920000	Of a kind used on agricultural or forestry vehicles and machines	8	20
4011930000	Of a kind used on construction or industrial handling vehicles and machines and having a rim size not exceeding 61 cm	8	20
4011940000	Of a kind used on construction or industrial handling	8	20

	vehicles and machines and having a rim size exceeding 61 cm		
4012110000	Of a kind used on motor cars (including station wagons and racing cars)	8	20
4012120000	Of a kind used on buses or lorries	8	20
4012130000	Of a kind used on aircraft	5	20
4012190000	Other	8	20
4012201000	Of a kind used on aircraft	5	20
4012209010	Of a kind used on motor cars (including station wagons and racing cars)	8	20
4012209020	Of a kind used on buses or lorries	8	20
4012209090	Other	8	20
4012901010	Solid tyres	5	20
4012901020	Cushion tyres	5	20
4012901030	Tyre treads	5	20
4012901040	Tyre flaps	5	20
4012909010	Solid tyres	8	20
4012909020	Cushion tyres	8	20
4012909030	Tyre treads	8	20
4012909040	Tyre flaps	8	20
4012909090	Other	8	20
4013101000	Of a kind used on motor cars (including station wagons and racing cars)	8	20
4013102000	Of a kind used on buses or lorries	8	20
4013200000	Of a kind used on bicycles	8	20
4013901000	Of a kind used on aircraft	5	20
4013909010	Of a kind used on motorcycles or motor scooters	8	20
4013909020	Of a kind used on industrial vehicles or agricultural machinery	8	20
4013909090	Other	8	20
4014100000	Sheath contraceptives	8	20
4014909000	Other	8	20
4015110000	Surgical	8	20
4015901000	Protective clothing for divers	8	20
4016100000	Of cellular rubber	8	20
4016910000	Floor coverings and mats	8	20
4016920000	Erasers	8	20
4016940000	Boat or dock fenders, whether or not inflatable	8	20
4016951000	Pneumatic mattresses	8	20
4016952000	Pillows	8	20
4016953000	Cushions	8	20
4016959000	Other	8	20
4016991090	Other	8	20
4016993000	Stoppers and rings for bottles	8	20
4016999000	Other	8	20

4017001000	Hard rubber	8	20
4017002000	Articles of hard rubber	8	20
4101202000	Hides and skins, which have undergone a tanning (including pre-tanning) process which is reversible	5	20
4101501011	Cow hide	1	20
4101501012	Steer hide	1	20
4101501013	Ox hide	1	20
4101501014	Bull hide	1	20
4101501019	Other	1	20
4101501021	Cow hide	1	20
4101501022	Steer hide	1	20
4101501023	Ox hide	1	20
4101501024	Bull hide	1	20
4101501029	Other	1	20
4101501090	Other	1	20
4101502000	Hides and skins, which have undergone a tanning (including pre-tanning) process which is reversible	5	20
4101901011	Of calf skin	1	20
4101901091	Of calf skin	1	20
4101901099	Other	1	20
4101902000	Hides and skins, which have undergone a tanning (including pre-tanning) process which is reversible	5	20
4102100000	With wool on	1	20
4102212000	Hides and skins, which have undergone a tanning (including pre-tanning) process which is reversible	5	20
4102292000	Hides and skins, which have undergone a tanning (including pre-tanning) process which is reversible	5	20
4103201020	Of lizard	1	20
4103201090	Other	1	20
4103202000	Hides and skins, which have undergone a tanning (including pretanning) process which is reversible	5	20
4103301000	Hides and skins, untanned	1	20
4103302000	Hides and skins, which have undergone a tanning (including pretanning) process which is reversible	5	20
4103901010	Of eels	1	20
4103901020	Of kangaroo	1	20
4103901030	Of camels (including dromedaries)	1	20
4103902010	Of camels (including dromedaries)	3	20
4103902090	Other	5	20
4104190000	Other	5	20
4104410000	Full grains, unsplit; grain splits	5	20
4104490000	Other	5	20
4105100000	In the wet state (including wet-blue)	5	20
4105300000	In the dry state (crust)	5	20
4106210000	In the wet state (including wet-blue)	5	20

4106220000	In the dry state (crust)	5	20
4106310000	In the wet state (including wet-blue)	5	20
4106320000	In the dry state (crust)	5	20
4106400000	Of reptiles	5	20
4106910000	In the wet state (including wet-blue)	5	20
4106920000	In the dry state (crust)	5	20
4107120000	Grain splits	5	20
4107910000	Full grains, unsplit	5	20
4107920000	Grain splits	5	20
4107990000	Other	5	20
4112000000	Leather further prepared after tanning or crusting, including parchment-dressed leather, of sheep or lamb, without wool on, whether or not split, other than leather of heading 41.14.	5	20
4113100000	Of goats or kids	5	20
4113200000	Of swine	5	20
4113300000	Of reptiles	5	20
4114100000	Chamois (including combination chamois) leather	5	20
4114201000	Patent leather	5	20
4114202000	Patent laminated leather	5	20
4114203000	Metallised leather	5	20
4115100000	Composition leather with a basis of leather or leather fibre, in slabs, sheets or strip, whether or not in rolls	8	20
4115200000	Parings and other waste of leather or of composition leather, not suitable for the manufacture of leather articles; leather dust, powder and flour	3	20
4201001000	Of reptile leather	8	20
4201009010	Saddles and saddle cloths	8	20
4201009020	Traces	8	20
4201009030	Leads	8	20
4201009040	Muzzles	8	20
4201009090	Other	8	20
4202111010	Of snake	8	20
4202111020	Of lizard	8	20
4202111030	Of crocodile	8	20
4202111040	Of eels	8	20
4202111050	Of kangaroo	8	20
4202111090	Other	8	20
4202112000	Of composition leather	8	20
4202113000	Of patent leather	8	20
4202121010	Of polyvinylchloride	8	20
4202121020	Of polyurethane	8	20
4202121090	Other	8	20
4202122000	Of textile materials	8	20
4202191000	Of paper board	8	20

4202199000	Other	8	20
4202211010	Of snake	8	20
4202211020	Of lizard	8	20
4202211030	Of crocodile	8	20
4202211040	Of eels	8	20
4202211050	Of kangaroo	8	20
4202211090	Other	8	20
4202212000	Of composition leather	8	20
4202213000	Of patent leather	8	20
4202221010	Of polyvinylchloride	8	20
4202221020	Of polyurethane	8	20
4202221090	Other	8	20
4202222000	Of textile materials	8	20
4202291000	Of paper-board	8	20
4202299000	Other	8	20
4202311010	Of snake	8	20
4202311020	Of lizard	8	20
4202311030	Of crocodile	8	20
4202311040	Of eels	8	20
4202311050	Of kangaroo	8	20
4202311090	Other	8	20
4202312000	Of composition leather	8	20
4202313000	Of patent leather	8	20
4202321010	Of polyvinylchloride	8	20
4202321020	Of polyurethane	8	20
4202321090	Other	8	20
4202322000	Of textile materials	8	20
4202391000	Of paper board	8	20
4202399000	Other	8	20
4202911010	Of snake	8	20
4202911020	Of lizard	8	20
4202911030	Of crocodile	8	20
4202911040	Of eels	8	20
4202911050	Of kangaroo	8	20
4202911090	Other	8	20
4202912000	Of composition leather	8	20
4202913000	Of patent leather	8	20
4202921010	Of polyvinylchloride	8	20
4202921020	Of polyurethane	8	20
4202921090	Other	8	20
4202922000	Of textile materials	8	20
4202991000	Of paper board	8	20
4203101010	Coats	13	20
4203101020	Jackets, blazers and jumpers	13	20
4203101050	Vests	13	20

4203101060	Pants and trousers	13	20
4203101070	Skirts	13	20
4203101080	Overalls	13	20
4203101090	Other	13	20
4203102010	Coats	13	20
4203102020	Jackets, blazers and jumpers	13	20
4203102050	Vests	13	20
4203102060	Pants and trousers	13	20
4203102070	Skirts	13	20
4203102080	Overalls	13	20
4203102090	Other	13	20
4203103010	Coats	13	20
4203103020	Jackets, blazers and jumpers	13	20
4203103050	Vests	13	20
4203103060	Pants and trousers	13	20
4203103070	Skirts	13	20
4203103080	Overalls	13	20
4203103090	Other	13	20
4203109010	Coats	13	20
4203109020	Jackets, blazers and jumpers	13	20
4203109050	Vests	13	20
4203109060	Pants and trousers	13	20
4203109070	Skirts	13	20
4203109080	Overalls	13	20
4203109090	Other	13	20
4203211000	Baseball glove	13	20
4203212000	Golf glove	13	20
4203213000	Ski glove	13	20
4203214000	Motor cycle glove	13	20
4203215000	Batting glove	13	20
4203216000	Tennis glove	13	20
4203217000	Ice hockey glove	13	20
4203219000	Other	13	20
4203291000	Working glove	13	20
4203292000	Dress glove	13	20
4203293000	Driver's glove	13	20
4203299000	Other	13	20
4203301010	Of snake	13	20
4203301020	Of lizard	13	20
4203301030	Of crocodile	13	20
4203301040	Of eels	13	20
4203309000	Other	13	20
4203400000	Other clothing accessories	13	20
4205001110	Belts	8	20
4205001190	Other	8	20

4205001900	Other articles of leather	8	20
4205002110	Belts	8	20
4205002190	Other	8	20
4205002900	Other articles of composition leather	8	20
4206001000	Catgut	8	20
4206009000	Other	8	20
4301100000	Of mink, whole, with or without head, tail or paws	3	20
4301300000	Of lamb, the following : Astrakhan, Broadtail, Caracul, Persian and similar lamb, Indian, Chinese, Mongolian or Tibetan lamb, whole, with or without head, tail or paws	3	20
4301600000	Of fox, whole, with or without head, tail or paws	3	20
4301801000	Of chinchila	3	20
4301802000	Of opossum	3	20
4301803000	Of raccoon	3	20
4301804000	Of coyote	3	20
4301805000	Of rabbit or hare	3	20
4301806000	Of musk-rat	3	20
4301809000	Other	3	20
4301900000	Heads, tails, paws and other pieces or cuttings, suitable for furriers' use	3	20
4302110000	Of mink	5	20
4302191000	Of beaver	5	20
4302192000	Of musk-rat	5	20
4302193000	Of fox	5	20
4302195000	Of chinchila	5	20
4302196000	Of opossum	5	20
4302197000	Of reccoon	5	20
4302198000	Of coyote	5	20
4302199010	Of sheep	5	20
4302199020	Of lamb, the following : Astrakhan, Broadtail, Caracul, Persian and similar lamb, Indian, Chinese, Mongolian or Tibetan lamb	5	20
4302199090	Other	5	20
4302201000	Of mink	5	20
4302202000	Of rabbit or hare	5	20
4302203000	Of beaver	5	20
4302204000	Of musk-rat	5	20
4302205000	Of fox	5	20
4302207000	Of chinchila	5	20
4302209010	Of opossum	5	20
4302209020	Of raccoon	5	20
4302209030	Of coyote	5	20
4302209090	Other	5	20
4302300000	Whole skins and pieces or cuttings thereof, assembled	5	20
4303101100	Of mink	16	20

4303101200	Of rabbit or hare	16	20
4303101300	Of lamb	16	20
4303101400	Of beaver	16	20
4303101500	Of musk-rat	16	20
4303101600	Of fox	16	20
4303101800	Of chinchila	16	20
4303101910	Of opossum	16	20
4303101920	Of raccoon	16	20
4303101930	Of coyote	16	20
4303101990	Other	16	20
4303102100	Of mink	16	20
4303102200	Of rabbit or hare	16	20
4303102300	Of lamb	16	20
4303102400	Of beaver	16	20
4303102500	Of musk-rat	16	20
4303102600	Of fox	16	20
4303102800	Of chinchila	16	20
4303102910	Of opossum	16	20
4303102920	Of raccoon	16	20
4303102930	Of coyote	16	20
4303102990	Other	16	20
4303900000	Other	16	20
4304001000	Artificial fur	8	20
4304002000	Articles of artificial fur	8	20
4408109100	For manufacturing plywood	3	20
4408319011	For manufacturing plywood	3	20
4408319021	For manufacturing plywood	3	20
4408399011	For manufacturing plywood	3	20
4408399021	For manufacturing plywood	3	20
4408399031	For manufacturing plywood	3	20
4408399041	For manufacturing plywood	3	20
4408399051	For manufacturing plywood	3	20
4408399091	For manufacturing plywood	3	20
4408909150	For manufacturing plywood	3	20
4408909210	For manufacturing plywood	3	20
4408909370	For manufacturing plywood	3	20
4408909410	For manufacturing plywood	3	20
4408909912	For manufacturing plywood	3	20
4408909991	For manufacturing plywood	3	20
4601211000	Mats and matting	8	20
4601212000	Screens	8	20
4601221000	Mats and matting	8	20
4601222000	Screens	8	20
4601291000	Mats and matting	8	20
4601292000	Screens	8	20

4601921000	Eunjukbaljang (of width less than 35 cm)	8	20
4601929000	Other	8	20
4601930000	Of rattan	8	20
4601941000	Eunjukbaljang (of width less than 35 cm)	8	20
4601949000	Other	8	20
4601991000	Articles in sheets plaitied with plastics	8	20
4601999000	Other	8	20
4602191000	Articles of rush	8	20
4602199000	Other	8	20
4602900000	Other	8	20
5004000000	Silk yarn (other than yarn spun from silk waste) not put up for retail sale.	8	20
5005001000	Hand made yarn	8	20
5005002000	Yarn spun from silk waste	8	20
5005003000	Yarn spun from noil silk	8	20
5006001000	Silk yarn	8	20
5006002000	Hand made yarn	8	20
5006003000	Yarn spun from silk waste	8	20
5006004000	Yarn spun from noil silk	8	20
5006005000	Silk worm gut	8	20
5007100000	Fabrics of noil silk	13	20
5007201000	Silk fabrics, grey	13	20
5007202010	Shibori	13	20
5007202020	Satin	13	20
5007202030	Crepe de chine	13	20
5007202090	Other	13	20
5007209000	Other	13	20
5007901000	Silk fabrics, grey	13	20
5007902000	Silk woven fabrics, mixed with acetate yarn	13	20
5007903000	Silk woven fabrics, mixed with other man-made fiber	13	20
5007904000	Silk woven fabrics, mixed with wool	13	20
5007909000	Other	13	20
5106109000	Other	8	20
5106201000	Mixed with polyester fiber	8	20
5106202000	Mixed with polyamide fiber	8	20
5106203000	Mixed with acrylic fiber	8	20
5106204000	Mixed with other synthetic fiber	8	20
5106209000	Other	8	20
5107102000	Mixed with synthetic fiber	8	20
5107109000	Mixed with other fiber	8	20
5107202000	Mixed with polyamide fiber	8	20
5107203000	Mixed with acrylic fiber	8	20
5107204000	Mixed with other synthetic fiber	8	20
5107209000	Mixed with other fiber	8	20
5108100000	Carded	8	20

5108200000	Combed	8	20
5109909000	Yarn of fine animal hair	8	20
5110000000	Yarn of coarse animal hair or of horsehair (including gimped horsehair yarn), whether or not put up for retail sale.	8	20
5111112000	Of fine animal hair	13	20
5111200000	Other, mixed mainly or solely with man-made filaments	13	20
5111300000	Other, mixed mainly or solely with man-made staple fibres	13	20
5112112000	Of fine animal hair	13	20
5113000000	Woven fabrics of coarse animal hair or of horsehair.	13	20
5204110000	Containing 85 % or more by weight of cotton	8	20
5204190000	Other	8	20
5204200000	Put up for retail sale	8	20
5205121010	Measuring not more than 370.37 decitex but not less than 232.56 decitex (not less than 27 metric number but not exceeding 43 metric number). excluding open end yarn	4	20
5205151000	Unbleached or not mercerized	8	20
5205159000	Other	8	20
5205211000	Unbleached or not mercerized	8	20
5205219000	Other	8	20
5205281000	Unbleached or not mercerized	8	20
5205289000	Other	8	20
5205311000	Unbleached or not mercerized	8	20
5205319000	Other	8	20
5205321010	Measuring not more than 370.37 decitex but not less than 232.56 decitex(not less than 27 metric number but not exceeding 43 metric number). excluding open end yarn	4	20
5205321090	Other	8	20
5205329000	Other	8	20
5205331000	Unbleached or not mercerized	8	20
5205339000	Other	8	20
5205341000	Unbleached or not mercerized	8	20
5205349000	Other	8	20
5205351000	Unbleached or not mercerized	8	20
5205359000	Other	8	20
5205411000	Unbleached or not mercerized	8	20
5205419000	Other	8	20
5205421000	Unbleached or not mercerized	8	20
5205429000	Other	8	20
5205431000	Unbleached or not mercerized	8	20
5205439000	Other	8	20
5205441000	Unbleached or not mercerized	8	20
5205449000	Other	8	20
5205461000	Unbleached or not mercerized	8	20
5205469000	Other	8	20

5205471000	Unbleached or not mercerized	8	20
5205479000	Other	8	20
5205481000	Unbleached or not mercerized	8	20
5205489000	Other	8	20
5206141000	Unbleached or not mercerized	8	20
5206149000	Other	8	20
5206151000	Unbleached or not mercerized	8	20
5206159000	Other	8	20
5206211000	Unbleached or not mercerized	8	20
5206219000	Other	8	20
5206311000	Unbleached or not mercerized	8	20
5206319000	Other	8	20
5206321000	Unbleached or not mercerized	8	20
5206329000	Other	8	20
5206331000	Unbleached or not mercerized	8	20
5206339000	Other	8	20
5206341000	Unbleached or not mercerized	8	20
5206349000	Other	8	20
5206351000	Unbleached or not mercerized	8	20
5206359000	Other	8	20
5206411000	Unbleached or not mercerized	8	20
5206419000	Other	8	20
5206421000	Unbleached or not mercerized	8	20
5206429000	Other	8	20
5206431000	Unbleached or not mercerized	8	20
5206439000	Other	8	20
5206441000	Unbleached or not mercerized	8	20
5206449000	Other	8	20
5206451000	Unbleached or not mercerized	8	20
5206459000	Other	8	20
5207101000	Unbleached or not mercerized	8	20
5207109000	Other	8	20
5207901000	Unbleached or not mercerized	8	20
5207909000	Other	8	20
5208110000	Plain weave, weighing not more than 100 g/m^2	10	20
5208120000	Plain weave, weighing more than 100 g/m^2	10	20
5208130000	3-thread or 4-thread twill, including cross twill	10	20
5208210000	Plain weave, weighing not more than 100 g/m^2	10	20
5208220000	Plain weave, weighing more than 100 g/m^2	10	20
5208230000	3-thread or 4-thread twill, including cross twill	10	20
5208290000	Other fabrics	10	20
5208310000	Plain weave, weighing not more than 100 g/m^2	10	20
5208320000	Plain weave, weighing more than 100 g/m^2	10	20
5208330000	3-thread or 4-thread twill, including cross twill	10	20
5208390000	Other fabrics	10	20

5208410000	Plain weave, weighing not more than 100 g/m²	10	20
5208420000	Plain weave, weighing more than 100 g/m²	10	20
5208430000	3-thread or 4-thread twill, including cross twill	10	20
5208490000	Other fabrics	10	20
5208510000	Plain weave, weighing not more than 100 g/m²	10	20
5208520000	Plain weave, weighing more than 100 g/m²	10	20
5208591000	3-thread or 4-thread twill, including cross twill	10	20
5208599000	Other	10	20
5209120000	3-thread or 4-thread twill, including cross twill	10	20
5209190000	Other fabrics	10	20
5209210000	Plain weave	10	20
5209220000	3-thread or 4-thread twill, including cross twill	10	20
5209290000	Other fabrics	10	20
5209310000	Plain weave	10	20
5209320000	3-thread or 4-thread twill, including cross twill	10	20
5209390000	Other fabrics	10	20
5209410000	Plain weave	10	20
5209420000	Denim	10	20
5209430000	Other fabrics of 3-thread or 4-thread twill, including cross twill	10	20
5209490000	Other fabrics	10	20
5209510000	Plain weave	10	20
5209520000	3-thread or 4-thread twill, including cross twill	10	20
5209590000	Other fabrics	10	20
5210110000	Plain weave	10	20
5210191000	3-thread or 4-thread twill, including cross twill	10	20
5210199000	Other	10	20
5210210000	Plain weave	10	20
5210291000	3-thread or 4-thread twill, including cross twill	10	20
5210299000	Other	10	20
5210310000	Plain weave	10	20
5210320000	3-thread or 4-thread twill, including cross twill	10	20
5210390000	Other fabrics	10	20
5210410000	Plain weave	10	20
5210491000	3-thread or 4-thread twill, including cross twill	10	20
5210499000	Other	10	20
5210510000	Plain weave	10	20
5210590000	Other fabrics	10	20
5211110000	Plain weave	10	20
5211120000	3-thread or 4-thread twill, including cross twill	10	20
5211190000	Other fabrics	10	20
5211200000	Bleached	10	20
5211310000	Plain weave	10	20
5211320000	3-thread or 4-thread twill, including cross twill	10	20
5211390000	Other fabrics	10	20

5211410000	Plain weave	10	20
5211420000	Denim	10	20
5211430000	Other fabrics of 3-thread or 4-thread twill, including cross twill	10	20
5211490000	Other fabrics	10	20
5211510000	Plain weave	10	20
5211520000	3-thread or 4-thread twill, including cross twill	10	20
5211590000	Other fabrics	10	20
5212110000	Unbleached	10	20
5212120000	Bleached	10	20
5212130000	Dyed	10	20
5212140000	Of yarns of different colours	10	20
5212150000	Printed	10	20
5212210000	Unbleached	10	20
5212220000	Bleached	10	20
5212230000	Dyed	10	20
5212240000	Of yarns of different colours	10	20
5212250000	Printed	10	20
5301100000	Flax, raw or retted	2	20
5301210000	Broken or scutched	2	20
5301290000	Other	2	20
5301301000	Flax tow	2	20
5301302000	Flax waste	2	20
5302100000	True hemp, raw or retted	2	20
5302901000	True hemp, broken, scutched, hackled or otherwise processed, but not spun.	2	20
5302902010	Tow of true hemp	2	20
5302902020	Waste of true hemp	2	20
5303101000	Jute	2	20
5303102000	Other textile bast fibres	2	20
5303901010	Jute	2	20
5303901090	Other textile bast fibres	2	20
5303909010	Tow and waste of jute	2	20
5303909090	Tow and waste of other taxtile bast fibres	2	20
5305001010	Raw	2	20
5305001090	Other	2	20
5305002010	Raw	2	20
5305002090	Other	2	20
5305003010	Raw	2	20
5305003090	Other	2	20
5305009010	Raw	2	20
5305009090	Other	2	20
5306101000	Of all flax	8	20
5306102000	Of mixed	8	20
5306201000	Of all flax	8	20

5306202000	Of mixed	8	20
5307101000	Of jute	8	20
5307109000	Other	8	20
5307201000	Of jute	8	20
5307209000	Other	8	20
5308100000	Coir yarn	8	20
5308200000	True hemp yarn	8	20
5308901000	Ramie yarn	8	20
5308909000	Other	8	20
5309110000	Unbleached or bleached	2	20
5309190000	Other	2	20
5309210000	Unbleached or bleached	2	20
5309290000	Other	2	20
5310101000	Jute fabrics	8	20
5310109000	Other	8	20
5310901000	Jute fabrics	8	20
5310909000	Other	8	20
5311001000	Of ramie	8	20
5311002000	Of true hemp	8	20
5311003000	Of paper yarn	8	20
5311009000	Other	8	20
5401101000	Of nylon or other polyamides	8	20
5401102000	Of polyesters	8	20
5401103000	Of acrylic polymers	8	20
5401109000	Other	8	20
5401201000	Of viscose rayon	8	20
5401202000	Of cellulose acetate	8	20
5401209000	Other	8	20
5402110000	Of aramids	8	20
5402191011	For tire cord	8	20
5402191012	For fishing net	8	20
5402191019	For other	8	20
5402191021	For tire cord	8	20
5402191022	For fishing net	8	20
5402191029	For other	8	20
5402191090	Other	8	20
5402199000	Other	8	20
5402200000	High tenacity yarn of polyesters	8	20
5402311010	Of nylon 6	8	20
5402311020	Of nylon 66	8	20
5402311090	Other	8	20
5402319000	Other	8	20
5402321010	Of nylon 6	8	20
5402321020	Of nylon 66	8	20
5402321090	Other	8	20

5402329000	Other	8	20
5402339000	Other	8	20
5402340000	Of polypropylene	8	20
5402390000	Other	8	20
5402440000	Elastomeric	8	20
5402451010	Of nylon 6	8	20
5402451020	Of nylon 66	8	20
5402451090	Other	8	20
5402459000	Other	8	20
5402461000	Of poly trimethylene terephthalate	8	20
5402469000	Other	8	20
5402471000	Of poly trimethylene terephthalate	8	20
5402479000	Other	8	20
5402480000	Other, of polypropylene	8	20
5402491000	Of acrylic polymers	8	20
5402499000	Other	8	20
5402510000	Of nylon or other polyamides	8	20
5402520000	Of polyesters	8	20
5402591000	Of acrylic polymers	8	20
5402599000	Other	8	20
5402692000	Of polyvinyl alcohol	8	20
5402699000	Other	8	20
5403100000	High tenacity yarn of viscose rayon	2	20
5403311000	Textured yarn	2	20
5403319000	Other	2	20
5403321000	Textured yarn	2	20
5403329000	Other	2	20
5403331000	Textured yarn	8	20
5403339000	Other	8	20
5403391000	Textured yarn	8	20
5403399000	Other	8	20
5403411000	Textured yarn	2	20
5403419000	Other	2	20
5403421000	Textured yarn	8	20
5403429000	Other	8	20
5403491000	Textured yarn	8	20
5403499000	Other	8	20
5404110000	Elastomeric	8	20
5404120000	Other, of polypropylene	8	20
5404192000	Of polyurethane	8	20
5404193000	Of polyvinyl alcohol	8	20
5404199000	Other	8	20
5404901000	Of strip	8	20
5404909000	Other	8	20
5405001000	Monofilament	8	20

5405009000	Other	8	20
5406001000	Synthetic filament yarn	8	20
5406002000	Artificial filament yarn	8	20
5407101000	Of nylon or other polyamides	8	20
5407102000	Of polyesters	8	20
5407200000	Woven fabrics obtained from strip or the like	8	20
5407300000	Fabrics specified in note 9 to section XI	8	20
5407410000	Unbleached or bleached	8	20
5407420000	Dyed	8	20
5407430000	Of yarns of different colours	8	20
5407440000	Printed	8	20
5407510000	Unbleached or bleached	8	20
5407520000	Dyed	8	20
5407530000	Of yarns of different colours	8	20
5407540000	Printed	8	20
5407611000	Unbleached or bleached	8	20
5407612000	Dyed	8	20
5407613000	Of yarns of different colours	8	20
5407614000	Printed	8	20
5407691000	Unbleached or bleached	8	20
5407692000	Dyed	8	20
5407693000	Of yarns of different colours	8	20
5407694000	Printed	8	20
5407711000	Of acrylic polymers	8	20
5407719000	Other	8	20
5407721000	Of acrylic polymers	8	20
5407729000	Other	8	20
5407731000	Of acrylic polymers	8	20
5407739000	Other	8	20
5407741000	Of acrylic polymers	8	20
5407749000	Other	8	20
5407811000	Of nylon or other polyamides	8	20
5407812000	Of polyesters	8	20
5407813000	Of acrylic polymers	8	20
5407819000	Other	8	20
5407821000	Of nylon or other polyamides	8	20
5407822000	Of polyesters	8	20
5407823000	Of acrylic polymers	8	20
5407829000	Other	8	20
5407831000	Of nylon or other polyamides	8	20
5407832000	Of polyesters	8	20
5407833000	Of acrylic polymers	8	20
5407839000	Other	8	20
5407841000	Of nylon or other polyamides	8	20
5407842000	Of polyesters	8	20

5407843000	Of acrylic polymers	8	20
5407849000	Other	8	20
5407911000	Of nylon or other polyamides	8	20
5407912000	Of polyesters	8	20
5407913000	Of acrylic polymers	8	20
5407919000	Other	8	20
5407921000	Of nylon or other polyamides	8	20
5407922000	Of polyesters	8	20
5407923000	Of acrylic polymers	8	20
5407929000	Other	8	20
5407931000	Of nylon or other polyamides	8	20
5407932000	Of polyesters	8	20
5407933000	Of acrylic polymers	8	20
5407939000	Other	8	20
5407941000	Of nylon or other polyamides	8	20
5407942000	Of polyesters	8	20
5407943000	Of acrylic polymers	8	20
5407949000	Other	8	20
5408100000	Woven fabrics obtained from high tenacity yarn of viscose rayon	8	20
5408210000	Unbleached or bleached	8	20
5408220000	Dyed	8	20
5408230000	Of yarns of different colours	8	20
5408240000	Printed	8	20
5408310000	Unbleached or bleached	8	20
5408320000	Dyed	8	20
5408330000	Of yarns of different colours	8	20
5408340000	Printed	8	20
5501100000	Of nylon or other polyamides	8	20
5501200000	Of polyesters	8	20
5501301000	Acrylic	8	20
5501302000	Modacrylic	8	20
5501400000	Of polypropylene	8	20
5501900000	Other	8	20
5502001000	Of viscose rayon	7.5	20
5502002010	Less than 44,000 decitex	7.5	20
5502002020	Not less than 44,000 decitex	7.5	20
5502009000	Other	7.5	20
5503111000	Of special section face	8	20
5503119000	Other	8	20
5503191000	Of special section face	8	20
5503199000	Other	8	20
5503201000	Of special scetion face	8	20
5503209010	Of poly trimethylene terephthalate	8	20
5503209090	Other	8	20

5503301010	Of special scetion face	8	20
5503301020	Of conjugated section face	8	20
5503301090	Other	8	20
5503302010	Of special section face	8	20
5503302020	Of conjugated section face	8	20
5503302090	Other	8	20
5503400000	Of polypropylene	8	20
5503900000	Other	8	20
5504901000	Of cellulose acetate	8	20
5504902000	Of lyocell	4	20
5504909000	Other	8	20
5505200000	Of artificial fibres	2	20
5506101000	Of special section face	8	20
5506109000	Other	8	20
5506201000	Of special section face	8	20
5506209000	Other	8	20
5506301010	Of special section face	8	20
5506301020	Of conjugated section face	8	20
5506301090	Other	8	20
5506302010	Of special section face	8	20
5506302020	Of conjugated section face	8	20
5506302090	Other	8	20
5506900000	Other	8	20
5507001010	Of special section face	8	20
5507001020	Of polynosic section face	8	20
5507002000	Of cellulose acetate	8	20
5507009000	Other	8	20
5508101000	Of nylon or other polyamides	8	20
5508102000	Of polyesters	8	20
5508103000	Acrylic or modacrylic	8	20
5508109000	Other	8	20
5508201000	Of viscose rayon	8	20
5508202000	Of cellulose acetate	8	20
5508209000	Other	8	20
5509111000	High tenacity yarn	8	20
5509119000	Other	8	20
5509121000	High tanacity yarn	8	20
5509129000	Other	8	20
5509312000	Modacrylic	8	20
5509410000	Single yarn	8	20
5509420000	Multiple (folded) or cabled yarn	8	20
5509520000	Mixed mainly or solely with wool or fine animal hair	8	20
5509612000	Modacrylic	8	20
5509621000	Acrylic	8	20
5509622000	Modacrylic	8	20

5509691020	Modacrylic	8	20
5509692020	Modacrylic	8	20
5509911000	Of nylon or other polyamides	8	20
5509919000	Other	8	20
5509921000	Of nylon or other polyamides	8	20
5509929000	Other	8	20
5509990000	Other	8	20
5510112000	Of cellulose acetate	8	20
5510122000	Of cellulose acetate	8	20
5510129000	Other	8	20
5510201000	Of viscose rayon	8	20
5510202000	Of cellulose acetate	8	20
5510209000	Other	8	20
5510302000	Of cellulose acetate	8	20
5510902000	Of cellulose acetate	8	20
5511101000	Of nylon or other polyamides	8	20
5511102000	Of polyesters	8	20
5511103000	Acrylic or modacrylic	8	20
5511109000	Other	8	20
5511201000	Of nylon or other polyamides	8	20
5511202000	Of polyesters	8	20
5511203000	Acrylic or modacrylic	8	20
5511209000	Other	8	20
5511301000	Of viscose rayon	8	20
5511302000	Of cellulose acetate	8	20
5511309000	Other	8	20
5512191000	Dyed	10	20
5512192000	Of yarns of different colours	10	20
5512193000	Printed	10	20
5512211000	Acrylic	10	20
5512212000	Modacrylic	10	20
5512290000	Other	10	20
5512911000	Of nylon or other polyamides	10	20
5512919000	Other	10	20
5512991000	Of nylon or other polyamides	10	20
5512999000	Other	10	20
5513130000	Other woven fabrics of polyester staple fibres	10	20
5513191000	Of nylon or other polyamides	10	20
5513192010	Acrylic	10	20
5513192020	Modacrylic	10	20
5513199000	Other	10	20
5513210000	Of polyester staple fibres, plain weave	10	20
5513231000	3-thread or 4-thread twill, including cross twill, of polyester staple fibres	10	20
5513239000	Other	10	20

5513291000	Of nylon or other polyamides	10	20
5513292010	Acrylic	10	20
5513292020	Modacrylic	10	20
5513299000	Other	10	20
5513310000	Of polyester staple fibres, plain weave.	10	20
5513391000	Of nylon or other polyamides	10	20
5513392010	Acrylic	10	20
5513392020	Modacrylic	10	20
5513399000	Other	10	20
5513410000	Of polyester staple fibres, plain weave	10	20
5513491000	Of nylon or other polyamides	10	20
5513492010	Acrylic	10	20
5513492020	Modacrylic	10	20
5513499000	Other	10	20
5514110000	Of polyester staple fibres, plain weave	10	20
5514191000	Of nylon or other polyamides	10	20
5514192010	Acrylic	10	20
5514192020	Modacrylic	10	20
5514193000	Other woven fabrics of polyester staple fibres	10	20
5514199000	Other	10	20
5514210000	Of polyester staple fibres, plain weave	10	20
5514220000	3-thread or 4-thread twill, including cross twill, of polyester staple fibres	10	20
5514230000	Other woven fabrics of polyester staple fibres	10	20
5514291000	Of nylon or other polyamides	10	20
5514292010	Acrylic	10	20
5514292020	Modacrylic	10	20
5514299000	Other	10	20
5514300000	Of yarns of different colours	10	20
5514410000	Of polyester staple fibres, plain weave	10	20
5514420000	3-thread or 4-thread twill, including cross twill, of polyester staple fibres	10	20
5514430000	Other woven fabrics of polyester staple fibres	10	20
5514491000	Of nylon or other polyamides	10	20
5514492010	Acrylic	10	20
5514492020	Modacrylic	10	20
5514499000	Other	10	20
5515111000	Unbleached or bleached	10	20
5515121000	Unbleached or bleached	10	20
5515129000	Other	10	20
5515131000	Unbleached or bleached	10	20
5515139000	Other	10	20
5515191000	Unbleached or bleached	10	20
5515199000	Other	10	20
5515211000	Unbleached or bleached	10	20

5515219000	Other	10	20
5515221000	Unbleached or bleached	10	20
5515229000	Other	10	20
5515291000	Unbleached or bleached	10	20
5515299000	Other	10	20
5515911000	Unbleached or bleached	10	20
5515919000	Other	10	20
5515991000	Unbleached or bleached	10	20
5515999000	Other	10	20
5516111000	Of viscose rayon	10	20
5516112000	Of cellulose acetate	10	20
5516119000	Other	10	20
5516121000	Of viscose rayon	10	20
5516122000	Of cellulose acetate	10	20
5516129000	Other	10	20
5516131000	Of viscose rayon	10	20
5516132000	Of cellulose acetate	10	20
5516139000	Other	10	20
5516141000	Of viscose rayon	10	20
5516142000	Of cellulose acetate	10	20
5516149000	Other	10	20
5516211000	Of viscose rayon	10	20
5516212000	Of cellulose acetate	10	20
5516219000	Other	10	20
5516221000	Of viscose rayon	10	20
5516222000	Of cellulose acetate	10	20
5516229000	Other	10	20
5516231000	Of viscose rayon	10	20
5516232000	Of cellulose acetate	10	20
5516239000	Other	10	20
5516241000	Of viscose rayon	10	20
5516242000	Of cellulose acetate	10	20
5516249000	Other	10	20
5516311000	Of viscose rayon	10	20
5516312000	Of cellulose acetate	10	20
5516319000	Other	10	20
5516321000	Of viscose rayon	10	20
5516322000	Of cellulose acetate	10	20
5516329000	Other	10	20
5516331000	Of viscose rayon	10	20
5516332000	Of cellulose acetate	10	20
5516339000	Other	10	20
5516341000	Of viscose rayon	10	20
5516342000	Of cellulose acetate	10	20
5516349000	Other	10	20

5516411000	Of viscose rayon	10	20
5516412000	Of cellulose acetate	10	20
5516419000	Other	10	20
5516421000	Of viscose rayon	10	20
5516422000	Of cellulose acetate	10	20
5516429000	Other	10	20
5516431000	Of viscose rayon	10	20
5516432000	Of cellulose acetate	10	20
5516439000	Other	10	20
5516441000	Of viscose rayon	10	20
5516442000	Of cellulose acetate	10	20
5516449000	Other	10	20
5516911000	Of viscose rayon	10	20
5516912000	Of cellulose acetate	10	20
5516919000	Other	10	20
5516921000	Of viscose rayon	10	20
5516922000	Of cellulose acetate	10	20
5516929000	Other	10	20
5516931000	Of viscose rayon	10	20
5516932000	Of cellulose acetate	10	20
5516939000	Other	10	20
5516941000	Of viscose rayon	10	20
5516942000	Of cellulose acetate	10	20
5516949000	Other	10	20
5601100000	Sanitary towels and tampons, napkins and napkin liners for babies and similar sanitary articles, of wadding	8	20
5601210000	Of cotton	8	20
5601220000	Of man-made fibres	8	20
5601290000	Other	8	20
5601301000	Textile flock	8	20
5601309000	Other	8	20
5602101000	Needleloom felt	8	20
5602102000	Stitch-bonded fiber fabrics	8	20
5602211000	Piano felt	8	20
5602219000	Other	8	20
5602290000	Of other textile materials	8	20
5602900000	Other	8	20
5603111000	Impregnated, coated, covered or laminated	8	20
5603121000	Impregnated, coated, covered or laminated	8	20
5603129000	Other	8	20
5603131000	Impregnated, coated, covered or laminated	8	20
5603141000	Impregnated, coated, covered or laminated	8	20
5603910000	Weighing not more than 25 g/m²	8	20
5603920000	Weighing more than 25 g/m² but not more than 70 g/m²	8	20
5603940000	Weighing more than 150 g/m²	8	20

5604100000	Rubber thread and cord, textile covered	8	20
5604901000	Imitation catguts consisting of textile yarn	8	20
5604902000	High tenacity yarn of polyesters, of nylon or other polyamides or of viscose rayon, impregnated or coated	8	20
5604909000	Other	8	20
5605000000	Metallised yarn, whether or not gimped,being textile yarn, or strip or the like of heading 54.04 or 54.05, combined with metal in the form of thread, strip or powder or covered with metal.	8	20
5606001000	Gimped yarn	8	20
5606002000	Chenill yarn	8	20
5606003000	Loop wale-yarn	8	20
5606009000	Other	8	20
5607210000	Binder or baler twine	10	20
5607290000	Other	10	20
5607410000	Binder or baler twine	10	20
5607490000	Other	10	20
5607500000	Of other synthetic fibres	10	20
5607901000	Of jute or other textile bast fibres of heading 53.03	10	20
5607909000	Other	10	20
5608111000	Of synthetic fibres	10	20
5608119000	Other	10	20
5608191000	Of synthetic fibres	10	20
5608199000	Other	10	20
5608901000	Of cotton	10	20
5608909000	Other	10	20
5609001000	Of cotton	8	20
5609002000	Of vegetable fibres, except cotton	8	20
5609003000	Of man-made fibres	8	20
5701100000	Of wool or fine animal hair	10	20
5701900000	Of other textile materials	10	20
5702100000	"Kelem", "Schumacks", "Karamanie" and similar hand-woven rugs	10	20
5702200000	Floor coverings of coconut fibres (coir)	10	20
5702310000	Of wool or fine animal hair	10	20
5702320000	Of man-made textile materials	10	20
5702390000	Of other textile materials	10	20
5702410000	Of wool or fine animal hair	10	20
5702420000	Of man-made textile materials	10	20
5702490000	Of other textile materials	10	20
5702500000	Other, not of pile construction, not made up	10	20
5702910000	Of wool or fine animal hair	10	20
5702920000	Of man-made textile materials	10	20
5702990000	Of other textile materials	10	20
5703100000	Of wool or fine animal hair	10	20

5703200000	Of nylon or other polyamides	10	20
5703300000	Of other man-made textile materials	10	20
5703900000	Of other texteile materials	10	20
5704100000	Tiles, having a maximum surface area or $0.3m^2$	10	20
5705000000	Other carpets and other textile floor coverings, whether or not made up.	10	20
5801101000	Pile fabrics	13	20
5801102000	Chenille fabrics	13	20
5801210000	Uncut weft pile fabrics	13	20
5801220000	Cut corduroy	13	20
5801230000	Other weft pile fabrics	13	20
5801240000	Warp pile fabrics, épinglé (uncut)	13	20
5801250000	Warp pile fabrics, cut	13	20
5801260000	Chenille fabrics	13	20
5801310000	Uncut weft pile fabrics	13	20
5801320000	Cut corduroy	13	20
5801330000	Other weft pile fabrics	13	20
5801340000	Warp pile fabrics, épinglé (uncut)	13	20
5801350000	Warp pile fabrics, cut	13	20
5801360000	Chenille fabrics	13	20
5801900000	Of other textile materials	13	20
5802110000	Unbleached	8	20
5802190000	Other	8	20
5802200000	Terry towelling and similar woven terry fabrics, of other textile materials	8	20
5802300000	Tufted textile fabrics	8	20
5803000000	Gauze, other than narrow fabrics of heading 58.06.	8	20
5804101000	Of silk	13	20
5804102000	Of cotton	13	20
5804103000	Of man-made fibres	13	20
5804109000	Other	13	20
5804210000	Of man-made fibres	13	20
5804291000	Of silk	13	20
5804292000	Of cotton	13	20
5804299000	Other	13	20
5804300000	Hand-made lace	13	20
5805001010	Of wool or fine animal hair	8	20
5805001090	Other	8	20
5805002000	Needle-worked tapestries	8	20
5806101000	Of wool or fine animal hair	8	20
5806102000	Of cotton	8	20
5806103000	Of man-made fibres	8	20
5806109000	Other	8	20
5806200000	Other woven fabrics, containing by weight 5 % or more of elastomeric yarn or rubber thread	8	20

5806310000	Of cotton	8	20
5806320000	Of man-made fibres	8	20
5806391000	Of wool or fine animal hair	8	20
5806392000	Of vegetable fibres, except cotton	8	20
5806400000	Fabrics consisting of warp without weft assembled by means of an adhesive (bolducs)	8	20
5807101000	Labels	8	20
5807109000	Other	8	20
5807901000	Labels	8	20
5807909000	Other	8	20
5808100000	Braids in the piece	8	20
5808901000	Ornamental trimmings	8	20
5808909000	Other	8	20
5809000000	Woven fabrics of metal thread and woven fabrics of metallised yarn of heading 56.05, of a kind used in apparel, as furnishing fabrics or for similar purposes, not elsewhere specified or included.	8	20
5810100000	Embroidery without visible ground	13	20
5810910000	Of cotton	13	20
5810920000	Of man-made fibres	13	20
5811001000	Of silk	8	20
5811002000	Of wool or fine animal hair	8	20
5811003000	Of cotton	8	20
5811004000	Of man-made fibres	8	20
5811009000	Other	8	20
5901100000	Textile fabrics coated with gum or amylaceous substances, of a kind used for the outer covers of books or the like	8	20
5901901000	Tracing cloth	8	20
5901902000	Prepaired painting canvas	8	20
5901903000	Buckram and similar stiffened textile fabrics	8	20
5902100000	Of nylon or other polyamides	8	20
5902200000	Of polyesters	8	20
5902900000	Other	8	20
5903100000	With poly (vinyl chloride)	10	20
5903200000	With polyurethane	10	20
5903900000	Other	10	20
5904100000	Linoleum	8	20
5904900000	Other	8	20
5905000000	Textile wall converings.	8	20
5906100000	Adhesive tape of a width not exceeding 20 cm	8	20
5906910000	Knitted or crocheted	8	20
5907001000	Textile fabrics coated or impregnated with oil or preparations with a basis of drying oil	8	20
5907002000	Painted canvas being theatrical scenery, studio back-cloth or the like	8	20

5907009000	Other	8	20
5908001000	Wicks	8	20
5908009000	Other	8	20
5909000000	Textile hosepiping and similar textile tubing, with or without lining, armour or accessories of other materials.	8	20
5910000000	Transmission or conveyor belts or belting,of textile material, whether or not impregnated, coated, covered or laminated with plastics, or reinforced with metal or other material.	8	20
5911101000	Of narrow fabrics	8	20
5911109000	Other	8	20
5911200000	Bolting cloth, whether or not made up	8	20
5911310000	Weighing less than 650 g/m²	8	20
5911320000	Weighing 650 g/m² or more	8	20
5911900000	Other	8	20
6001101000	Of cotton	10	20
6001102000	Of man-made fibres	10	20
6001109000	Other	10	20
6001210000	Of cotton	10	20
6001220000	Of man-made fibres	10	20
6001290000	Of other textile materials	10	20
6001910000	Of cotton	10	20
6001920000	Of man-made fibres	10	20
6001990000	Of other textile materials	10	20
6002400000	Containing by weight 5 % or more of elastomeric yarn but not containing rubber thread	10	20
6002900000	Other	10	20
6003100000	Of wool or fine animal hair	10	20
6003200000	Of cotton	10	20
6003300000	Of synthetic fibres	10	20
6003400000	Of artificial fibres	10	20
6003900000	Other	10	20
6004100000	Containing by weight 5 % or more of elastomeric yarn but not containing rubber thread	10	20
6004900000	Other	10	20
6005210000	Unbleached or bleached	10	20
6005220000	Dyed	10	20
6005230000	Of yarns of different colours	10	20
6005240000	Printed	10	20
6005310000	Unbleached or bleached	10	20
6005320000	Dyed	10	20
6005330000	Of yarns of different colours	10	20
6005340000	Printed	10	20
6005410000	Unbleached or bleached	10	20
6005420000	Dyed	10	20

6005430000	Of yarns of different colours	10	20
6005440000	Printed	10	20
6005900000	Other	10	20
6006100000	Of wool or fine animal hair	10	20
6006210000	Unbleached or bleached	10	20
6006220000	Dyed	10	20
6006230000	Of yarns of different colours	10	20
6006240000	Printed	10	20
6006310000	Unbleached or bleached	10	20
6006320000	Dyed	10	20
6006330000	Of yarns of different colours	10	20
6006340000	Printed	10	20
6006410000	Unbleached or bleached	10	20
6006420000	Dyed	10	20
6006430000	Of yarns of different colours	10	20
6006440000	Printed	10	20
6006900000	Other	10	20
6101302000	Of artificial fibres	13	20
6101900000	Of other textile materials	13	20
6102100000	Of wool or fine animal hair	13	20
6102302000	Of artificial fibres	13	20
6102900000	Of other textile materials	13	20
6103101000	Of wool or fine animal hair	13	20
6103102000	Of synthetic fibres	13	20
6103109000	Of other textile materials	13	20
6103220000	Of cotton	13	20
6103230000	Of synthetic fibres	13	20
6103290000	Of other textile materials	13	20
6103310000	Of wool or fine animal hair	13	20
6103390000	Of other textile materials	13	20
6103410000	Of wool or fine animal hair	13	20
6103490000	Of other textile materials	13	20
6104191000	Of cotton	13	20
6104199000	Other	13	20
6104220000	Of cotton	13	20
6104230000	Of synthetic fibres	13	20
6104290000	Of other textile materials	13	20
6104310000	Of wool or fine animal hair	13	20
6104390000	Of other textile materials	13	20
6104410000	Of wool or fine animal hair	13	20
6104491000	Of silk	13	20
6104499000	Other	13	20
6104510000	Of wool or fine animal hair	13	20
6104610000	Of wool or fine animal hair	13	20
6104690000	Of other textile materials	13	20

6105202000	Of artificial fibres	13	20
6105901000	Of silk	13	20
6105902000	Of wool or fine animal hair	13	20
6105909000	Other	13	20
6106901000	Of silk	13	20
6106902000	Of wool or fine animal hair	13	20
6106909000	Other	13	20
6107122000	Of artificial fibres	13	20
6107190000	Of other textile materials	13	20
6107210000	Of cotton	13	20
6107221000	Of synthetic fibres	13	20
6107222000	Of artificial fibres	13	20
6107290000	Of other textile materials	13	20
6107991000	Of wool or fine animal hair	13	20
6108111000	Of synthetic fibres	13	20
6108112000	Of artificial fibres	13	20
6108191000	Of cotton	13	20
6108199000	Other	13	20
6108222000	Of artificial fibres	13	20
6108290000	Of other textile materials	13	20
6108321000	Of synthetic fibres	13	20
6108322000	Of artificial fibres	13	20
6108390000	Of other textile materials	13	20
6108922000	Of artificial fibres	13	20
6108991000	Of wool or fine animal hair	13	20
6108999000	Other	13	20
6109901010	T-shirts	13	20
6109901090	Other	13	20
6110120000	Of Kashmir (cashmere) goats	13	20
6110190000	Other	13	20
6110901000	Of silk	13	20
6111202000	Accessories	13	20
6111302000	Accessories	13	20
6111902000	Accessories	13	20
6112190000	Of other textile materials	13	20
6112201000	Of man-made fibres	13	20
6112209000	Other	13	20
6113001000	Of heading 59.03	13	20
6113002000	Of heading 59.06	13	20
6113003000	Of heading 59.07	13	20
6114302000	Of artificial fibres	13	20
6114901000	Of silk	13	20
6115100000	Graduated compression hosiery (for example, stockings for varicose veins)	13	20
6115210000	Of synthetic fibres, measuring per single yarn less than 67	13	20

	decitex		
6115220000	Of synthetic fibres, measuring per single yarn 67 decitex or more	13	20
6115290000	Of other textile materials	13	20
6115301000	Of man-made fibres	13	20
6115309000	Other	13	20
6115940000	Of wool or fine animal hair	13	20
6115960000	Of synthetic fibres	13	20
6115990000	Of other textile materials	13	20
6116910000	Of wool or fine animal hair	8	20
6116929000	Other	8	20
6116930000	Of synthetic fibres	8	20
6116990000	Of other textile materials	8	20
6117101000	Of silk	13	20
6117104000	Of man-made fibres	13	20
6117109000	Other	13	20
6117801000	Ties, bow ties and cravats	13	20
6117809000	Other	13	20
6117900000	Parts	13	20
6201132000	Of artificial fibres	13	20
6201910000	Of wool or fine animal hair	13	20
6201990000	Of other textile materials	13	20
6202132000	Of artificial fibres	13	20
6202190000	Of other textile materials	13	20
6202932000	Of artificial fibres	13	20
6203110000	Of wool or fine animal hair	13	20
6203220000	Of cotton	13	20
6203230000	Of synthetic fibres	13	20
6203291000	Of wool or fine animal hair	13	20
6203299000	Other	13	20
6204110000	Of wool or fine animal hair	13	20
6204130000	Of synthetic fibres	13	20
6204191000	Of silk	13	20
6204210000	Of wool or fine animal hair	13	20
6204220000	Of cotton	13	20
6204230000	Of synthetic fibres	13	20
6204291000	Of silk	13	20
6204299000	Other	13	20
6204391000	Of silk	13	20
6204591000	Of silk	13	20
6204691000	Of silk	13	20
6205302000	Of artificial fibres	13	20
6205901000	Of silk	13	20
6205902000	Of wool or fine animal hair	13	20
6206200000	Of wool or fine animal hair	13	20

6207191000	Of man-made fibres	13	20
6207199000	Other	13	20
6207210000	Of cotton	13	20
6207221000	Of synthetic fibres	13	20
6207222000	Of artificial fibres	13	20
6207290000	Of other textile materials	13	20
6207991000	Of silk	13	20
6207992000	Of wool or fine animal hair	13	20
6207993010	Of synthetic fibres	13	20
6207993020	Of artificial fibres	13	20
6207999000	Other	13	20
6208111000	Of synthetic fibres	13	20
6208112000	Of artificial fibres	13	20
6208191000	Of silk	13	20
6208192000	Of cotton	13	20
6208199000	Other	13	20
6208221000	Of synthetic fibres	13	20
6208222000	Of artificial fibres	13	20
6208290000	Of other textile materials	13	20
6208922000	Of artificial fibres	13	20
6208991000	Of silk	13	20
6208992000	Of wool or fine animal hair	13	20
6208999000	Other	13	20
6209202000	Accessories	13	20
6209302000	Accessories	13	20
6209901010	Of wool or fine animal hair	13	20
6209902000	Accessories	13	20
6210101000	Of fabrics of heading 56.02	13	20
6210102000	Of fabrics of heading 56.03	13	20
6210201000	Of fabrics of heading 59.03	13	20
6210202000	Of fabrics of heading 59.06	13	20
6210203000	Of fabrics of heading 59.07	13	20
6210301000	Of fabrics of heading 59.03	13	20
6210302000	Of fabrics of heading 59.06	13	20
6210303000	Of fabrics of heading 59.07	13	20
6210402000	Of fabrics of heading 59.06	13	20
6210502000	Of fabrics of heading 59.06	13	20
6210503000	Of fabrics of heading 59.07	13	20
6211121000	Of man-made fibres	13	20
6211209000	Other	13	20
6211321000	Judo, taekwondo and other oriental martial arts uniforms	13	20
6211332000	Of artificial fibres	13	20
6211391000	Of wool or fine animal hair	13	20
6211410000	Of wool or fine animal hair	13	20
6211421000	Judo, taekwondo and other oriental martial arts uniforms	13	20

6212201000	Of cotton	13	20
6212202000	Of man-made fibres	13	20
6212300000	Corselettes	13	20
6212900000	Other	13	20
6213200000	Of cotton	8	20
6213900000	Of other textile materials	8	20
6214300000	Of synthetic fibres	8	20
6215100000	Of silk or silk waste	8	20
6215200000	Of man-made fibres	8	20
6215900000	Of other textile materials	8	20
6217100000	Accessories	13	20
6217900000	Parts	13	20
6301100000	Electric blankets	10	20
6301200000	Blankets (othet than electric blankets) and travelling rugs, of wool or fine animal hair	10	20
6301300000	Blankets (other than electric blankets) and travelling rugs, of cotton	10	20
6301400000	Blankets (other than electric blankets) and travelling rugs, of synthetic fibers	10	20
6301900000	Other blankets and travelling rugs	10	20
6302101000	Of cotton	13	20
6302109000	Other	13	20
6302210000	Of cotton	13	20
6302220000	Of man-made fibres	13	20
6302290000	Of other textile materials	13	20
6302310000	Of cotton	13	20
6302320000	Of man-made fibres	13	20
6302390000	Of other textile materials	13	20
6302400000	Table linen, knitted or crocheted	13	20
6302510000	Of cotton	13	20
6302530000	Of man-made fibres	13	20
6302590000	Of other textile materials	13	20
6302600000	Toilet linen and kitchen linen, of terry towelling or similar terry fabrics, of cotton	13	20
6302910000	Of cotton	13	20
6302930000	Of man-made fibres	13	20
6302990000	Of other textile materials	13	20
6303120000	Of synthetic fibres	13	20
6303191000	Of cotton	13	20
6303199000	Other	13	20
6303910000	Of cotton	13	20
6303920000	Of synthetic fibres	13	20
6303990000	Of other textile materials	13	20
6304110000	Knitted or crocheted	13	20
6304910000	Knitted or crocheted	13	20

6304920000	Not knitted or crocheted, of cotton	13	20
6304930000	Not knitted or crocheted, of synthetic fibres	13	20
6304990000	Not knitted or crocheted, of other textile materials	13	20
6305100000	Of jute or of other textile bast fibres of heading 53.03	8	20
6305200000	Of cotton	8	20
6305320000	Flexible intermediate bulk containers	8	20
6305330000	Other, of polyethylene or polypropylene strip or the like	8	20
6305390000	Other	8	20
6305900000	Of other textile materials	8	20
6306120000	Of synthetic fibres	13	20
6306190000	Of other textile materials	13	20
6306220000	Of synthetic fibres	13	20
6306290000	Of other textile materials	13	20
6306300000	Sails	13	20
6306401000	Of cotton	13	20
6306409000	Of other textile materials	13	20
6306910000	Of cotton	13	20
6306991000	Of synthetic fibres	13	20
6306999000	Other	13	20
6307100000	Floor-cloths, dish-cloths, dusters and similar cleaning cloths	10	20
6307200000	Life-jackets and life-belts	10	20
6307901000	Footwear lace	10	20
6307902000	Cloth wrappers	10	20
6307903000	Dress patterns	10	20
6307909000	Other	10	20
6308000000	Sets consisting of woven fabric and yarn, whether or not with accessories, for making up into rugs, tapestries, embroidered table cloths or serviettes, or similar textile articles, put up in packings for retail sale.	13	20
6309000000	Worn clothing and other worn articles.	8	20
6310100000	Sorted	8	20
6310900000	Other	8	20
6401100000	Footwear incorporating a protective metal toe-cap	8	20
6401921000	Ski - boots	8	20
6401929010	Of rubber	8	20
6401929090	Other	8	20
6401991010	Of rubber	8	20
6401991090	Other	8	20
6401999000	Other	8	20
6402120000	Ski-boots, cross-country ski footwear and snowboard boots	13	20
6402190000	Other	13	20
6402200000	Footwear with upper straps or thongs assembled to the sole by means of plugs	13	20
6402911000	Footwear, protective against cold	13	20

6402912000	Tennis shoes, basketball shoes, gym shoes, training shoes and the like	13	20
6402919000	Other	13	20
6402991000	Sandals or similar footwear, produced in one piece by moulding	13	20
6402992000	Tennis shoes, basketball shoes, gym shoes, training shoes and the like	13	20
6402999000	Other	13	20
6403120000	Ski-boots, cross-country ski footwear and snowboard boots	13	20
6403190000	Other	13	20
6403200000	Footwear with outer soles of leather, and uppers which consist of leather straps across the instep and around the big toe	13	20
6403400000	Other footwear, incorporating a protective metal toe-cap	13	20
6403511000	Dress shoes	13	20
6403519000	Other	13	20
6403591000	Dress shoes	13	20
6403599000	Other	13	20
6403911000	Dress shoes	13	20
6403912000	Mountaineering footwear	13	20
6403913000	Lace-boots	13	20
6403914000	Tennis shoes, basketball shoes, gym shoes, training shoes and the like	13	20
6403919000	Other	13	20
6403991000	Dress shoes	13	20
6403992000	Mountaineering footwear	13	20
6403993000	Lace-boots	13	20
6403994000	Tennis shoes, basketball shoes, gym shoes, training shoes and the like	13	20
6403999000	Other	13	20
6404110000	Sports footwear; tennis shoes, basketball shoes, gym shoes, training shoes and the like	13	20
6404191000	Slippers	13	20
6404199000	Other	13	20
6404201000	Slippers	13	20
6404209000	Other	13	20
6405100000	With uppers of leather or composition leather	13	20
6405200000	With uppers of texile materials	13	20
6406101000	Uppers	8	20
6406102000	Parts	8	20
6406201000	Outer soles	8	20
6406202000	Heels	8	20
6406910000	Of wood	8	20
6406991000	Removable in-soles	8	20
6406992000	Heel cushion	8	20

6406993000	Gaiters	8	20
6406994000	Leggings	8	20
6406999000	Other	8	20
6501000000	Hat-forms, hat bodies and hoods of felt, neither blocked to shape nor with made brims; plateaux and manchons (including slit manchons), of felt.	8	20
6502000000	Hat-shapes, plaited or made by assembling strips of any material, neither blocked to shape, nor with made brims, nor lined, nor trimmed.	8	20
6504000000	Hats and other headgear, plaited or made by assembling strips of any material, whether or not lined or trimmed.	8	20
6505100000	Hair-nets	8	20
6505901010	Of synthetic fibres	8	20
6505901090	Of other fibres	8	20
6505902010	Sports cap	8	20
6505902020	Berets	8	20
6505902090	Other	8	20
6505909000	Other	8	20
6506910000	Of rubber or of plastics	8	20
6506991000	Of leather	8	20
6506992000	Of metal	8	20
6507000000	Head-bands, lining, covers, hat foundations, hat frames, peaks and chinstraps, for headgear.	8	20
6601100000	Garden or similar umbrellas	13	20
6601910000	Having a telescopic shaft	13	20
6601991000	Walking-stick umbrellas	13	20
6601992000	Sun umbrellas	13	20
6601999000	Other	13	20
6602001000	Walking-sticks	8	20
6602002000	Seat-sticks	8	20
6602003000	Whips, riding-crops	8	20
6602009000	Other	8	20
6603200000	Umbrella frames, including frames mounted on shafts (sticks)	13	20
6603900000	Other	13	20
6701000000	Skins and other parts of birds with their feathers or down, feathers, parts of feathers, down and articles thereof (other than goods of heading 05.05 and worked quills and scapes).	8	20
6702901000	Of woven fabrics	8	20
6702902000	Of paper	8	20
6702909000	Other	8	20
6703001090	Other	8	20
6703009000	Other	8	20
6704110000	Complete wigs	8	20

6704191000	Partial wigs	8	20
6704192000	False beards	8	20
6704193000	False eyebrows	8	20
6704194000	False eyelashes	8	20
6704199000	Other	8	20
6704201000	Complete wigs	8	20
6704202000	Partial wigs	8	20
6704203000	False beards	8	20
6704204000	False eyebrows	8	20
6704205000	False eyelashes	8	20
6704209000	Other	8	20
6704900000	Of other materials	8	20
6801000000	Setts, curbstones and flagstones, of natural stone (except slate).	8	20
6802100000	Tiles, cubes and similar articles, whether or not rectangular (including square), the largest surface area of which is capable of being enclosed in a square the side of which is less than 7 cm; artificially coloured granules, chippings and powder	8	20
6802211000	Marble	8	20
6802212000	Travertine	8	20
6802213000	Alabaster	8	20
6802291000	Other calcareous stone	8	20
6802911000	Marble	8	20
6802912000	Travertine	8	20
6802913000	Alabaster	8	20
6802920000	Other calcareous stone	8	20
6804100000	Millstones and grindstones for milling, grinding or pulping	8	20
6804210000	Of agglomerated synthetic or natural diamond	8	20
6804230000	Of natural stone	8	20
6804300000	Hand sharpening or polishing stones	8	20
6805100000	On a base of woven textile fabric only	8	20
6805200000	On a base of paper or paperboard only	8	20
6805300000	On a base of other materials	8	20
6806101000	Slag wool	8	20
6806103000	Ceramic fibre	8	20
6806109000	Other	8	20
6806201000	Exfoliated vermiculite	8	20
6806202000	Expanded clays	8	20
6806204000	Expanded perlite	8	20
6806209000	Other	8	20
6806901000	Fire proofing material	8	20
6806909000	Other	8	20
6807100000	In rolls	8	20
6807900000	Other	8	20

6808000000	Panels, boards, tiles, blocks and similar articles of vegetable fibre, of straw or of shavings, chips, particles, sawdust or other waste, of wood, agglomerated with cement, plaster or other mineral binders.	8	20
6809110000	Faced or reinforced with paper or paperboard only	8	20
6809190000	Other	8	20
6809900000	Other articles	8	20
6810111000	Blocks	8	20
6810112000	Bricks	8	20
6810191000	Tiles	8	20
6810192000	Flagstones	8	20
6810193000	Roofing tiles	8	20
6810199000	Other	8	20
6810910000	Prefabricated structural components for building or civil engineering	8	20
6810991000	Beams and girders	8	20
6810992000	Pile	8	20
6810993000	Electric pole	8	20
6810994000	Railway sleepers	8	20
6810995000	Pipes	8	20
6810999000	Other	8	20
6811401010	For roofs, ceilings, walls or floors	8	20
6811401090	Other	8	20
6811402010	For roofs, ceilings, walls or floors	8	20
6811402090	Other	8	20
6811403000	Tubes, pipes and tube or pipe fittings	8	20
6811409010	For roofs, ceilings, walls or floors	8	20
6811409090	Other	8	20
6811810000	Corrugated sheets	8	20
6811820000	Other sheets, panels, tiles and similar articles	8	20
6811830000	Tubes, pipes and tube or pipe fittings	8	20
6811890000	Other articles	8	20
6812801000	Clothing, clothing accessories, footwear and headgear	8	20
6812802000	Paper, millboard and felt	8	20
6812803000	Compressed asbestos fibre jointing, in sheets or rolls	8	20
6812809000	Other	8	20
6812910000	Clothing, clothing accessories, footwear and headgear	8	20
6812920000	Paper, millboard and felt	8	20
6812930000	Compressed asbestos fibre jointing, in sheets or rolls	8	20
6812990000	Other	8	20
6813201010	For automobiles	8	20
6813201090	Other	8	20
6813202010	For automobiles	8	20
6813202090	Other	8	20
6813209010	For automobiles	8	20

6813209090	Other	8	20
6813810000	Brake linings and pads	8	20
6813891000	Clutch facing	8	20
6813899000	Other	8	20
6814100000	Plates, sheets and strips of agglomerated or reconstituted mica, whether or not on a support	8	20
6814900000	Other	8	20
6815101000	Non-electrical articles of graphite	8	20
6815102000	Carbon fibre	8	20
6815109000	Other	8	20
6815200000	Articles of peat	8	20
6815910000	Containing magnesite, dolomite or chromite	8	20
6901001000	Bricks	8	20
6901002000	Blocks	8	20
6901009010	Slabs and panels	8	20
6901009090	Other	8	20
6902100000	Containing by weight, singly or together, more than 50 % of the elements Mg, Ca or Cr, expressed as MgO, CaO or Cr_2O_3	8	20
6902901000	Based upon silicon carbide or zircon	8	20
6902909000	Other	8	20
6903101000	Retorts	8	20
6903102010	For furnaces for production of semiconductor wafers	3	20
6903102090	Other	8	20
6903103000	Reaction vessels	8	20
6903104000	Muffles	8	20
6903105000	Nozzles	8	20
6903106000	Plugs	8	20
6903107000	Tubes and pipes	8	20
6903108000	Bars and rods	8	20
6903109000	Others	8	20
6903201000	Retorts	8	20
6903202000	Crucibles	8	20
6903203000	Reaction vessels	8	20
6903204000	Muffles	8	20
6903205000	Nozzles	8	20
6903206000	Plugs	8	20
6903207000	Tubes and pipes	8	20
6903208000	Bars and rods	8	20
6903209000	Other	8	20
6903901000	Based upon silicon carbide or zircon	8	20
6903909010	Retorts	8	20
6903909020	Crucibles	8	20
6903909030	Reaction vessels	8	20
6903909040	Muffles	8	20

6903909050	Nozzles	8	20
6903909060	Plugs	8	20
6903909070	Tubes and pipes	8	20
6903909080	Bars and rods	8	20
6903909090	Other	8	20
6904100000	Building bricks	8	20
6904900000	Other	8	20
6905901000	Chimney pots, cowls and chimney liners	8	20
6905902000	Architectural ornaments	8	20
6905909000	Other	8	20
6906001000	Pipes, conduits and guttering	8	20
6906002000	Pipe fittings	8	20
6909110000	Of porcelain or china	8	20
6909120000	Articles having a hardness equivalent to 9 or more on the Mohs scale	8	20
6909190000	Other	8	20
7001001000	Mass	5	20
7001002000	Waste and scrap, cullet	3	20
7002100000	Balls	8	20
7002201000	For the manufacture of quartz wares for semiconductor	3	20
7002209000	Other	8	20
7002311000	For the manufacture of quartz wares for semiconductor	3	20
7002319000	Other	8	20
7002320000	Of other glass having a linear coefficient of expansion not exceeding 5×10-6 per Kelvin within a temperature range of 0℃ to 300℃	8	20
7002390000	Other	8	20
7003121000	Not more than 2 mm in thickness	8	20
7003122000	More than 2 mm but not more than 3 mm in thickness	8	20
7003123000	More than 3 mm but not more than 4 mm in thickness	8	20
7003124000	More than 4 mm but not more than 5 mm in thickness	8	20
7003125000	More than 5 mm but not more than 6 mm in thickness	8	20
7003126000	More than 6 mm but not more than 8 mm in thickness	8	20
7003127000	More than 8 mm in thickness	8	20
7003191000	Not more than 2 mm in thickness	8	20
7003192000	More than 2 mm but not more than 3 mm in thickness	8	20
7003193000	More than 3 mm but not more than 4 mm in thickness	8	20
7003194000	More than 4 mm but not more than 5 mm in thickness	8	20
7003195000	More than 5 mm but not more than 6 mm in thickness	8	20
7003196000	More than 6 mm but not more than 8 mm in thickness	8	20
7003197000	More than 8 mm in thickness	8	20
7003200000	Wired sheets	8	20
7003300000	Profiles	8	20
7004201000	Not more than 2 mm in thickness	8	20
7004202000	More than 2 mm but not more than 3 mm in thickness	8	20

7004203000	More than 3 mm but not more than 4 mm in thickness	8	20
7004204000	More than 4 mm but not more than 5 mm in thickness	8	20
7004205000	More than 5 mm but not more than 6 mm in thickness	8	20
7004206000	More than 6 mm but not more than 8 mm in thickness	8	20
7004207000	More than 8 mm in thickness	8	20
7004901000	Not more than 2 mm in thickness	8	20
7004902000	More than 2 mm but not more than 3 mm in thickness	8	20
7004903000	More than 3 mm but not more than 4 mm in thickness	8	20
7004904000	More than 4 mm but not more than 5 mm in thickness	8	20
7004905000	More than 5 mm but not more than 6 mm in thickness	8	20
7004906000	More than 6 mm but not more than 8 mm in thickness	8	20
7004907000	More than 8 mm in thickness	8	20
7005101010	Not more than 4 mm in thickness	8	20
7005101020	More than 4 mm but not more than 6 mm in thickness	8	20
7005101030	More than 6 mm but not more than 8 mm in thickness	8	20
7005101040	More than 8 mm in thickness	8	20
7005102010	Not more than 4 mm in thickness	8	20
7005102020	More than 4 mm but not more than 6 mm in thickness	8	20
7005102030	More than 6 mm but not more than 8 mm in thickness	8	20
7005102040	More than 8 mm in thickness	8	20
7005109010	Not more than 4 mm in thickness	8	20
7005109020	More than 4 mm but not more than 6 mm in thickness	8	20
7005109030	More than 6 mm but not more than 8 mm in thickness	8	20
7005109040	More than 8 mm in thickness	8	20
7005212000	More than 2 mm but not more than 3 mm in thickness	8	20
7005213000	More than 3 mm but not more than 4 mm in thickness	8	20
7005214000	More than 4 mm but not more than 5 mm in thickness	8	20
7005215000	More than 5 mm but not more than 6 mm in thickness	8	20
7005216000	More than 6 mm but not more than 8 mm in thickness	8	20
7005217010	Not more than 10 mm in thickness	8	20
7005217020	More than 10 mm but not more than 12 mm in thickness	8	20
7005217030	More than 12 mm in thickness	8	20
7005291010	For PDP (plasma display panel)	4	20
7005291020	For blank mask used in the manufacture of semiconductor, or of FPD (flat panel display)	3	20
7005291030	For OLED (organic light emitting display)	4	20
7005291091	Clear and transparent glass	8	20
7005291092	Extra clear low-iron glass	8	20
7005291099	Other	8	20
7005292010	For PDP (plasma display panel)	4	20
7005292020	For blank mask used in the manufacture of semiconductor, or of FPD (flat panel display)	3	20
7005292030	For OLED (organic light emitting display)	4	20
7005292091	Clear and transparent glass	8	20
7005292092	Extra clear low-iron glass	8	20

7005292099	Other	8	20
7005293010	Clear and transparent glass	8	20
7005293020	Extra clear low-iron glass	8	20
7005293090	Other	8	20
7005294010	Clear and transparent glass	8	20
7005294020	Extra clear low-iron glass	8	20
7005294090	Other	8	20
7005295010	Clear and transparent glass	8	20
7005295020	Extra clear low-iron glass	8	20
7005295090	Other	8	20
7005296010	Clear and transparent glass	8	20
7005296020	Extra clear low-iron glass	8	20
7005296090	Other	8	20
7005297010	Clear and transparent glass	8	20
7005297020	Extra clear low-iron glass	8	20
7005297090	Other	8	20
7005298010	Clear and transparent glass	8	20
7005298020	Extra clear low-iron glass	8	20
7005298090	Other	8	20
7005299010	Clear and transparent glass	8	20
7005299020	Extra clear low-iron glass	8	20
7005299090	Other	8	20
7005300000	Wired glass	8	20
7006001000	For PDP (plasma display panel)	4	20
7006002000	For blank mask used in the manufacture of semiconductor, or of FPD (flat panel display)	3	20
7006003000	For OLED (organic light emitting display)	4	20
7006009000	Other	8	20
7007111000	Not more than 8 mm in thickness	8	20
7007112000	More than 8 mm in thickness	8	20
7007191000	Not more than 8 mm in thickness	8	20
7007192000	More than 8 mm in thickness	8	20
7007211000	Not more than 12 mm in total thickness, including film thickness	8	20
7007212000	More than 12 mm in total thickness, including film thickness	8	20
7007291000	Not more than 12 mm in total thickness, including film thickness	8	20
7007292000	More than 12 mm in total thickness, including film thickness	8	20
7008000000	Multiple-walled insulating units of glass.	8	20
7009100000	Rear-view mirrors for vehicles	8	20
7009920000	Framed	8	20
7010200000	Stoppers, lids and other closures	8	20
7011100000	For electric lighting	8	20

7011201000	Color	8	20
7011209000	Other	8	20
7011900000	Other	8	20
7013100000	Of glass-ceramics	8	20
7013220000	Of lead crystal	8	20
7013280000	Other	8	20
7013330000	Of lead crystal	8	20
7013410000	Of lead crystal	8	20
7013420000	Of glass having a linear coefficient of expansion not exceeding 5 x 10-6 per Kelvin within a temperature range of 0°C to 300°C	8	20
7013490000	Other	8	20
7013910000	Of lead crystal	8	20
7014001000	Of sealed beam lamp	8	20
7014009010	Signalling glassware	8	20
7014009020	Optical elements of glass	8	20
7015100000	Glasses for corrective spectacles	8	20
7015901000	For sun glasses	8	20
7015902000	Clock or watch glasses and the like	8	20
7015909000	Other	8	20
7016100000	Glass cubes and other glass smallwares, whether or not on a backing, for mosaics or similar decorative purposes	8	20
7016901000	Paving blocks, slabs, bricks, squares, tiles and other articles of pressed or moulded glass, whether or not wired, of a kind used for building or construction purposes	8	20
7016909010	Leaded lights	8	20
7016909020	Stained glass	8	20
7016909090	Other	8	20
7017100000	Of fused quartz or other fused silica	8	20
7017200000	Of other glass having a linear coefficient of expansion not exceeding 5 x 10-6 per Kelvin within a temperature range of 0°C to 300°C	8	20
7017900000	Other	8	20
7018101000	Beads	8	20
7018102000	Imitation pearls	8	20
7018103000	Imitation precious and semi-precious stones	8	20
7018104000	Imitation coral	8	20
7018200000	Glass microspheres not exceeding 1 mm in diameter	8	20
7018901000	Glass eyes other than prosthetic articles	8	20
7018909000	Other	8	20
7019120000	Rovings	8	20
7019310000	Mats	8	20
7019320000	Thin sheets (voiles)	8	20
7019390000	Other	8	20

7019400000	Woven fabrics of rovings	8	20
7019510000	Of a width not exceeding 30 cm	8	20
7019590000	Other	8	20
7019901000	Glass wool	8	20
7020001012	Quartz crucibles for production of semiconductor wafers	3	20
7020001013	For the manufacture of quartz wares for semiconductor	3	20
7020001019	Other	8	20
7020001090	Other	8	20
7020009000	Other	8	20
7101101000	Unworked	8	20
7101102000	Worked	8	20
7101210000	Unworked	8	20
7101220000	Worked	8	20
7102100000	unsorted	1	20
7102210000	Unworked or simply sawn, cleaved or bruted	1	20
7102290000	Other	5	20
7102310000	Unworked or simply sawn, cleaved or bruted	1	20
7102390000	Other	5	20
7103100000	Unworked or simply sawn or roughly shaped	1	20
7103911000	Industrial	5	20
7103919010	Rubies	5	20
7103919020	Sapphires	5	20
7103919030	Emeralds	5	20
7103991000	Industrial	5	20
7103999010	Opal	5	20
7103999020	Jade	5	20
7103999030	Chalcedony	5	20
7103999040	Rocky crystal	5	20
7103999090	Other	5	20
7104100000	piezo-electric quartz	5	20
7104201000	Diamonds	5	20
7104209000	Other	5	20
7104901010	Diamonds	5	20
7104901020	Synthetic quartz	5	20
7104901090	Other	5	20
7104909010	Diamonds	5	20
7104909090	Other	5	20
7105101000	Natural	5	20
7105102000	Synthetic	5	20
7105901000	Of garnet	5	20
7105909000	Other	5	20
7106100000	Powder	3	20
7106911000	Containing by weight 99.99 % or more of silver	3	20
7106919000	Other	3	20
7106921000	Bars, rods and shapes	3	20

7106922000	Plates, sheets and strips	3	20
7106923000	Wire	3	20
7106929000	Other	3	20
7107001000	Bars, rods and shapes	3	20
7107002000	Plates, sheets and strips	3	20
7107003000	Wire	3	20
7107004000	Tubes, pipes and hollow bars	3	20
7107009000	Other	3	20
7108110000	Powder	3	20
7108121000	Lumps, billets and grains	3	20
7108129000	Other	3	20
7108131010	For use in manufacturing semiconductor	3	20
7108131090	Other	3	20
7108139010	Bars, rods and shapes	3	20
7108139020	Plates, sheets and strips	3	20
7108139090	Other	3	20
7109000000	Base metals or silver, clad with gold, not further worked than semi-manufactured.	3	20
7110110000	Unwrought or in powder form	3	20
7110190000	Other	3	20
7110210000	Unwrought or in powder form	3	20
7110290000	Other	3	20
7110310000	Unwrought or in powder form	3	20
7110390000	Other	3	20
7110410000	Unwrought or in powder form	3	20
7110490000	Other	3	20
7111000000	Base metals, silver or gold, clad with platinum, not further worked than semi-manufactured.	3	20
7112300000	Ash containing precious metal or precious metal compounds	2	20
7112911000	Of residues	2	20
7112919000	Other	3	20
7112921000	Of residues	2	20
7112929000	Other	3	20
7112991000	Of residues	2	20
7112992000	Of waste, paring and scrap of plastics	6.5	20
7112999000	Other	3	20
7113110000	Of silver, whether or not plated or clad with other precious metal	8	20
7113201000	Platinum-clad	8	20
7113202000	Gold-clad	8	20
7113203000	Silver-clad	8	20
7113209000	Other	8	20
7114111000	For table	8	20
7114112000	For toilet	8	20

7114113000	For office and desk	8	20
7114114000	For use by smokers	8	20
7114119000	Other	8	20
7114191000	For table	8	20
7114192000	For toilet	8	20
7114193000	For office and desk	8	20
7114194000	For use by smokers	8	20
7114199000	Other	8	20
7114201000	For table	8	20
7114202000	For toilet	8	20
7114203000	For office and desk	8	20
7114204000	For use by smokers	8	20
7114209000	Other	8	20
7115100000	Catalysts in the form of wire cloth or grill, of platinum	8	20
7115901010	Platinum crucible	8	20
7115901090	Other	8	20
7115909010	Of gold, including metals clad with gold	8	20
7115909020	Of silver, including metals clad with siver	8	20
7115909090	Other	8	20
7116101000	Of natural pearls	8	20
7116102000	Of cultured pearls	8	20
7116201000	Industrial	8	20
7116209010	For personal adornment	8	20
7117110000	Cuff-links and studs	8	20
7117193000	Earing	8	20
7117194000	Brooch	8	20
7117195000	Ring	8	20
7201501000	Alloy pig iron	2	20
7201502000	Spiegeleisen	2	20
7202110000	Containing by weight more than 2 % of carbon.	5	20
7202190000	Other	5	20
7202210000	Containing by weight more than 55 % of silicon	3	20
7202291000	Containing by weight 2 % or more of magnesium	3	20
7202299000	Other	3	20
7202300000	Ferro-silico-manganese	5	20
7202410000	Containing by weight more than 4 % of carbon	3	20
7202490000	Other	3	20
7202500000	Ferro-silico-chromium	3	20
7202600000	Ferro-nickel	3	20
7202700000	Ferro-molybdenum	3	20
7202800000	Ferro-tungsten and ferro-silico-tungsten	3	20
7202910000	Ferro-titanium and ferro-silico-titanium	3	20
7202920000	Ferro-vanadium	3	20
7202930000	Ferro-niobium	3	20
7202991000	Ferro-phosphorus (iron phosphide),containing by weight	3	20

	15 % or more of phosphorus		
7203900000	Other	1	20
7205101000	Shot	5	20
7205109000	Other	5	20
7205210000	Of alloy steel	5	20
7302300000	Switch blades, crossing frogs, point rods and other crossing pieces	8	20
7303001010	Of ductile cast iron	8	20
7303001090	Other	8	20
7303002000	Hollow profiles	8	20
7307110000	Of non-malleable cast iron	8	20
7307190000	Other	8	20
7307229000	Other	8	20
7307230000	Butt welding fittings	8	20
7307290000	Other	8	20
7307910000	Flanges	8	20
7307929000	Other	8	20
7307930000	Butt welding fittings	8	20
7307991000	Threaded, whether or not plated	8	20
7307999000	Other	8	20
7308200000	Towers and lattice masts	8	20
7308300000	Doors, windows and their frames and thresholds for doors	8	20
7308400000	Equipment for scaffolding, shuttering, propping or pitpropping	8	20
7309000000	Reservoirs, tanks, vats and similar containers for any material (other than compressed or liquefied gas), of iron or steel, of a capacity exceeding 300 ℓ , whether or not lined or heat-insulated, but not fitted with mechanical or thermal equipment.	8	20
7310100000	Of a capacity of 50 ℓ or more	8	20
7310210000	Cans which are to be closed by soldering or crimping	8	20
7310290000	Other	8	20
7311001000	Not more than 30 ℓ in capacity	8	20
7311002000	More than 30 ℓ but not more than 100 ℓ in capacity	8	20
7311003000	More than 100 ℓ in capacity	8	20
7315110000	Roller chain	8	20
7315120000	Other chain	8	20
7315190000	Parts	8	20
7315200000	Skid chain	8	20
7315810000	Stud-link	8	20
7315820000	Other, welded link	8	20
7315890000	Other	8	20
7315900000	Other parts	8	20
7316001000	Anchors and grapnels	8	20
7316002000	Parts	8	20

7318110000	Coach screws	8	20
7318120000	Other wood screws	8	20
7318130000	Screw hooks and screw rings	8	20
7318140000	Self-tapping screws	8	20
7318152000	Bolts	8	20
7318153000	Bolts and nuts (in set)	8	20
7318159000	Other	8	20
7318160000	Nuts	8	20
7318190000	Other	8	20
7318210000	Spring washers and other lock washers	8	20
7318220000	Other washers	8	20
7318230000	Rivets	8	20
7318240000	Cotters and cotter-pins	8	20
7318290000	Other	8	20
7319200000	Safety pins	8	20
7319301000	Pin used for measuring or checking semiconductor wafers or device	8	20
7319309000	Other	8	20
7319901010	Sewing needles	8	20
7319901020	Darning needles	8	20
7319901090	Other	8	20
7319909000	Other	8	20
7320101000	Leaf-springs for automobiles	8	20
7320102000	Leaf-springs for railway locomotives and rollingstocks	8	20
7320109000	Other	8	20
7320201000	For automobiles	8	20
7320202000	For shockabsorbers	8	20
7320203000	For buffers on rolling stock couplings	8	20
7320204000	For upholstery	8	20
7320209000	Other	8	20
7320901000	Flat spiral springs	8	20
7320909000	Other springs	8	20
7321110000	For gas fuel or for both gas and other fuels	8	20
7321120000	For liquid fuel	8	20
7321190000	Other, including appliances for solid fuel	8	20
7321810000	For gas fuel or for both gas and other fuels	8	20
7321820000	For liquid fuel	8	20
7321890000	Other, including appliances for solid fuel	8	20
7321900000	Parts	8	20
7322111000	Radiators	8	20
7322112000	Parts	8	20
7322191000	Radiators	8	20
7322192000	Parts	8	20
7322901000	Solar collector and parts thereof	8	20
7322909010	Air heater	8	20

7322909020	Hot air distributor	8	20
7322909030	Parts	8	20
7323100000	Iron or steel wool; pot scourers and scouring or polishing pads, gloves and the like	8	20
7323910000	Of cast iron, not enamelled	8	20
7323920000	Of cast iron, enamelled	8	20
7323930000	Of stainless steel	8	20
7323940000	Of iron (other than cast iron) or steel, enamelled	8	20
7324101000	Sinks	8	20
7324102000	Wash basins	8	20
7324210000	Of cast iron, whether or not enamelled	8	20
7324291000	Of stainless steel	8	20
7324299000	Other	8	20
7324901000	Toilet sets	8	20
7324908000	Other	8	20
7324909000	Parts	8	20
7325100000	Of non-malleable cast iron	8	20
7325910000	Grinding balls and similar articles for mills	8	20
7325991000	Of cast iron	8	20
7325993000	Of alloy steel	8	20
7325999000	Other	8	20
7326110000	Grinding balls and similar articles for mills	8	20
7326190000	Other	8	20
7326200000	Articles of iron or steel wire	8	20
7326901000	Bobbins for textile machinery	8	20
7326909000	Other	8	20
7403120000	Wire-bars	5	20
7403130000	Billets	5	20
7403191000	Slabs	5	20
7403192000	Ingots	5	20
7403199000	Other	5	20
7403210000	Copper-zinc base alloys (brass)	5	20
7403220000	Copper-tin base alloys (bronze)	5	20
7403291010	Copper-nickel base alloys (cupro-nickel)	5	20
7403291020	Copper-nickel-zinc base alloys (nickel silver)	5	20
7403299000	Other	5	20
7405000000	Master alloys of copper.	5	20
7406100000	Powders of non-lamellar structure	8	20
7406201000	Powders of lamellar structure	8	20
7406202000	Flakes	8	20
7407100000	Of refined copper	8	20
7407210000	Of copper-zinc base alloys (brass)	8	20
7407291000	Of copper-tin base alloys (bronze)	8	20
7407292010	Of copper-nickel base alloys (cupro-nickel)	8	20
7407292020	Of copper-nickel-zinc base alloys (nickel silver)	8	20

7407299000	Other	8	20
7408110000	Of which the maximum cross-sectional dimension exceeds 6 mm	8	20
7408210000	Of copper-zinc base alloys (brass)	8	20
7408221000	Of copper-nickel base alloys (cupro-nickel)	8	20
7408222000	Of copper-nickel-zinc base alloys (nickel silver)	8	20
7408291000	Of copper-tin base alloys (bronze)	8	20
7409111000	For use in manufacturing semiconductor	5	20
7409119000	Other	8	20
7409191000	For use in manufacturing semiconductor	5	20
7409211000	For use in manufacturing semiconductor	5	20
7409291000	For use in manufacturing semiconductor	5	20
7409299000	Other	8	20
7409311000	For use in manufacturing semiconductor	5	20
7409391000	For use in manufacturing semiconductor	5	20
7409399000	Other	8	20
7409401010	For use in manufacturing semiconductor	5	20
7409401090	Other	8	20
7409402010	For use in manufacturing semiconductor	5	20
7409402090	Other	8	20
7409901000	For use in manufacturing semiconductor	5	20
7409909000	Other	8	20
7410110000	Of refined copper	8	20
7410120000	Of copper alloys	8	20
7410219000	Other	8	20
7410221000	Suitable for manufacturing printed circuit board	8	20
7410229000	Other	8	20
7411210000	Of copper-zinc base alloys (brass)	8	20
7411221000	Of copper-niskel base alloys (cupro-nickel)	8	20
7411222000	Of copper-nickel-zinc base alloys (nickel silver)	8	20
7411291000	Of copper-tin base alloys (bronze)	8	20
7411299000	Other	8	20
7412100000	Of refined copper	3	20
7413000000	Stranded wire, cable, plaited bands and the like, of copper, not electrically insulated	3	20
7415101000	Plated, rolled or coated with precious metal	8	20
7415109000	Other	8	20
7415210000	Washers (including spring washers)	8	20
7415290000	Other	8	20
7415330000	Screws; bolts and nuts	8	20
7415390000	Other	8	20
7418110000	Pot scourers and scouring or polishing pads, gloves and the like	8	20
7418191000	Table, kitchen articles	8	20
7418192010	Solar collectors of a kind used for domestic purposes,	5	20

	non-electric		
7418192090	Other	8	20
7418199010	Of solar collectors of a kind used for domestic purposes, non-electric	5	20
7418199090	Other	8	20
7418201000	Sanitary ware	8	20
7418202000	Parts	8	20
7419101000	Chain	8	20
7419102000	Parts	8	20
7419991010	Cloth	8	20
7419992000	Copper springs	8	20
7501201010	Containing by weight 88 % or more of nickel	2	20
7501209010	Containing by weight 88 % or more of nickel	2	20
7502200000	Nickel alloys	3	20
7504001000	Powders	5	20
7504002000	Flakes	5	20
7505110000	Of nickel, not alloyed	5	20
7505210000	Of nickel, not alloyed	5	20
7505220000	Of nickel alloys	5	20
7506101000	Plates, sheets and strip	5	20
7506102000	Foil	5	20
7506201000	Plates, sheets and strip	5	20
7506202000	Foil	5	20
7507110000	Of nickel, not alloyed	8	20
7507200000	Tube or pipe fittings	8	20
7508100000	Cloth, grill and netting, of nickel wire	8	20
7508901000	Electro-plating anodes	8	20
7508902010	Of nickel, not alloyed	8	20
7508902020	Of nickel alloys	8	20
7601202000	Billet	3	20
7603100000	Powders of non-lamellar structure	8	20
7603201000	Powders	8	20
7603202000	Flakes	8	20
7604101000	Bars and rods	8	20
7604102010	Hollow profiles	8	20
7604102090	Other	8	20
7604210000	Hollow profiles	8	20
7604291000	Bars and rods	8	20
7604299000	Other profiles	8	20
7605110000	Of which the maximum cross-sectional dimension exceeds 7 mm	8	20
7605190000	Other	8	20
7605210000	Of which the maximum cross-sectional dimension exceeds 7 mm	8	20
7606111000	Containing not less than 99.99 % by weight of aluminium	8	20

7606120000	Of aluminium alloys	8	20
7606911000	Containing not less than 99.99 % by weight of aluminium	8	20
7606919000	Other	8	20
7607111000	Containing not less than 99.99 % by weight of aluminium	8	20
7607119000	Other	8	20
7607191000	Containing not less than 99.99 % by weight of aluminium	8	20
7607201000	Containing not less than 99.99 % by weight of aluminium	8	20
7608100000	Of aluminium, not alloyed	8	20
7608200000	Of aluminium alloys	8	20
7609000000	Aluminium tube or pipe fittings (for example, couplings, elbows, sleeves).	8	20
7610100000	Doors, windows and their frames and thresholds for doors	8	20
7610901000	Structures	8	20
7610908000	Other	8	20
7610909000	Parts	8	20
7611000000	Aluminium reservoirs, tanks, vats and similar containers, for any material (other than compressed or liquefied gas), of a capacity exceeding 300 ℓ, whether or not lined or heat-insulated, but not fitted with mechanical or thermal equipment.	8	20
7612100000	Collapsible tubular containers	8	20
7612901000	Rigid tubular containers	8	20
7612909010	Less than 1 ℓ capacity	8	20
7612909030	Not less than 20 ℓ in capacity	8	20
7613001000	For compressed gas	8	20
7614100000	With steel core	8	20
7615110000	Pot scourers and scouring or polishing pads, gloves and the like	8	20
7615191000	Solar collectors and parts thereof	5	20
7615192000	Table, kitchen articles	8	20
7615193000	Other household articles	8	20
7615199000	Parts	8	20
7615201000	Sanitary ware	8	20
7615202000	Parts	8	20
7616100000	Nails, tacks, staples (other than those of heading 83.05), screws, bolts, nuts, screw hooks, rivets, cotters, cotter-pins, washers and similar articles	8	20
7616910000	Cloth, grill, netting and fencing, of aluminium wire	8	20
7616999010	Aluminium pouch	8	20
7616999020	Aluminium knob	8	20
7801101000	Containing by weight 99.99 % or more of lead	3	20
7801109000	Other	3	20
7801910000	Containing by weight antimony as the principal other element	3	20
7801992010	Lead-tin alloys	3	20

7801992090	Other	3	20
7804111000	Sheets and strip	8	20
7804112000	Foil	8	20
7804190000	Other	8	20
7804201000	Powders	8	20
7804202000	Flakes	8	20
7806001000	Lead containers	8	20
7806002000	Electro-plating anodes	8	20
7806003010	Bars and rods	8	20
7806003020	Profiles	8	20
7806003030	Wire	8	20
7806004010	Tubes and pipes	8	20
7806004020	Tubes or pipe fittings	8	20
7806009000	Other	8	20
7901110000	Containing by weight 99.99 % or more of zinc	3	20
7901120000	Containing by weight less than 99.99 % of zinc	3	20
7901201000	Zinc-aluminium alloy	3	20
7901202000	Zinc-copper alloy	3	20
7901209000	Other	3	20
7903902000	Flakes	8	20
7904001000	Bars and rods	8	20
7904002000	Profiles	8	20
7904003000	Wire	8	20
7905001000	Plates, sheets and strip	8	20
7905002000	Foil	8	20
7907001000	Gutters, roof capping, skylight frames and other fabricated building components	8	20
7907002010	Tubes and pipes	8	20
7907002020	Tube or pipe fittings	8	20
7907009010	Electro-plating anodes	8	20
7907009090	Other	8	20
8001100000	Tin, not alloyed	3	20
8001200000	Tin alloys	3	20
8007001000	Electro-plating anodes	8	20
8007002000	Plates, sheets and strip, of a thickness exceeding 20 mm	8	20
8007003010	Foil	8	20
8007003021	Powders	8	20
8007003022	Flakes	8	20
8007004000	Tubes, pipes and tube or pipe fittings (for example, couplings, elbows, sleeves)	8	20
8007009000	Other	8	20
8101100000	Powders	3	20
8101940000	Unwrought tungsten, including bars and rods obtained simply by sintering	3	20
8101961000	Spiral filament for electric bulbs or electronic bulbs	8	20

8101991010	Bars and rods	8	20
8101991020	Profiles	8	20
8101991030	Plates, sheets and strips	8	20
8101999000	Other	8	20
8102100000	Powders	3	20
8102940000	Unwrought molybdenum, including bars and rods obtained simply by sintering	3	20
8102951000	Bars and rods	8	20
8102952000	Profiles	8	20
8102953000	Plates, sheets and strip	8	20
8102954000	Foil	8	20
8102961000	Spiral filament for electric bulbs or electronic bulbs	8	20
8102969000	Other	8	20
8102990000	Other	8	20
8103201000	Unwrought	3	20
8103202000	Powders	3	20
8103900000	Other	8	20
8104110000	Containing at least 99.8 % by weight of magnesium	3	20
8104190000	Other	3	20
8104301000	Raspings, turnings and granules	8	20
8104302000	Powders	8	20
8104901000	Bars and rods	8	20
8105202000	Cobalt mattes and other intermediate products of cobalt metallurgy	3	20
8105203000	Powders	3	20
8105300000	Waste and scrap	3	20
8106001010	Unwrought bismuth	3	20
8106001020	Waste and scrap	3	20
8106001030	Powders	3	20
8106009000	Other	3	20
8107201000	Unwrought cadmium	3	20
8107202000	Powders	3	20
8107300000	Waste and scrap	3	20
8107900000	Other	3	20
8108201000	Unwrought	3	20
8108202000	Powders	3	20
8108300000	Waste and scrap	3	20
8108901000	Plates and strips	8	20
8108902000	Tubes and pipes	8	20
8109201000	Unwrought	3	20
8109202000	Powders	3	20
8109300000	Waste and scrap	3	20
8109909000	Other	3	20
8110100000	Unwrought antimony; powders	3	20
8110200000	Waste and scrap	3	20

8110900000	Other	3	20
8112120000	Unwrought; powders	3	20
8112130000	Waste and scrap	3	20
8112190000	Other	3	20
8112210000	Unwrought; powders	3	20
8112220000	Waste and scrap	3	20
8112290000	Other	3	20
8112510000	Unwrought; powders	3	20
8112520000	Waste and scrap	3	20
8112590000	Other	3	20
8112921000	Germanium	3	20
8112922000	Vanadium	3	20
8112923000	Gallium	3	20
8112924000	Hafnium	3	20
8112925000	Indium	3	20
8112926000	Niobium(Columbium)	3	20
8112927000	Rhenium	3	20
8112929000	Other	3	20
8112991000	Germanium	3	20
8112992000	Vanadium	3	20
8112993000	Gallium	3	20
8112994000	Hafnium	3	20
8112995000	Indium	3	20
8112996000	Niobium(Columbium)	3	20
8112997000	Rhenium	3	20
8112999000	Other	3	20
8201100000	Spades and shovels	8	20
8201200000	Forks	8	20
8201300000	Mattocks, picks, hoes and rakes	8	20
8201400000	Axes, bill hooks and similar hewing tools	8	20
8201500000	Secateurs and similar one-handed pruners and shears (including poultry shears)	8	20
8201600000	Hedge shears, two-handed pruning shears and similar two-handed shears	8	20
8201901000	Scythes and sickls	8	20
8201902000	Hay knives	8	20
8201903000	Timber wedges	8	20
8201909000	Other	8	20
8202101000	For wood	8	20
8202102000	For metal	8	20
8202109000	Other	8	20
8202200000	Band saw blades	8	20
8202310000	With working part of steel	8	20
8202391000	With working part of tungsten carbide	8	20
8202392010	For machines sawing semiconductor wafer or device into	8	20

	each unit		
8202392090	Other	8	20
8202393000	With working part of other materials	8	20
8202399000	Parts	8	20
8202400000	Chain saw blades	8	20
8202911000	Hack-saw blades	8	20
8202919000	Other	8	20
8202990000	Other	8	20
8203101000	For saw blades	8	20
8203109000	Other	8	20
8203201000	Plier (including cutting pliers)	8	20
8203202000	Pincer	8	20
8203203000	Tweezers	8	20
8203204000	Nail pullers	8	20
8203209000	Other	8	20
8203300000	Metal cutting shears and similar tools	8	20
8203401000	Pipe cutters	8	20
8203402000	Bolt croppers and clippers	8	20
8203403000	Perforating punches	8	20
8203409000	Other	8	20
8204120000	Adjustable	8	20
8204200000	Interchangeable spanner sockets, with or without handles	8	20
8205101000	For drilling	8	20
8205102000	For threading	8	20
8205103000	For tapping	8	20
8205109000	Other	8	20
8205200000	Hammers and sledge hammers	8	20
8205300000	Planes, chisels, gouges and similar cutting tools for working wood	8	20
8205400000	Screwdrivers	8	20
8205510000	Household tools	8	20
8205591000	Glaziers' diamond	8	20
8205592000	Soldering irons	8	20
8205593000	Grease guns	8	20
8205595000	Tools for mining and public works	8	20
8205596000	Tools for cement workers and painters	8	20
8205597000	Watch makers' tools	8	20
8205599000	Other	8	20
8205600000	Blow lamps	8	20
8205701000	Vices	8	20
8205702000	Clamps	8	20
8205709000	Other	8	20
8205801000	Anvils	8	20
8205802000	Portable forges	8	20
8205803000	Hand or pedal-operated grinding wheels with frameworks	8	20

8205809000	Other	8	20
8205900000	Sets of articles of two or more of the foregoing subheadings	8	20
8206000000	Tools of two or more of the headings 82.02 to 82.05, put up in sets for retail sale.	8	20
8207130000	With working part of cermets	8	20
8207191000	With working part of other materials	8	20
8207201000	For drawing	8	20
8207202000	For extruding	8	20
8207301000	For pressing	8	20
8207302000	For stamping	8	20
8207303000	For punching	8	20
8207309000	Other	8	20
8207401000	For tapping	8	20
8207402000	For threading	8	20
8207409000	Other	8	20
8207501010	Of high speed steel	8	20
8207501090	Other	8	20
8207502000	Brace bits	8	20
8207509000	Other	8	20
8207601000	Reamers	8	20
8207602000	Laps	8	20
8207603000	Broaches	8	20
8207609000	Other	8	20
8207702000	Milling cutters	8	20
8207703000	Gear cutting hobs	8	20
8207704000	Rotary files	8	20
8207709000	Other	8	20
8207801000	Tools for lathes	8	20
8207809000	Other	8	20
8207901000	Diamond tools	8	20
8207909000	Other	8	20
8208100000	For metal working	8	20
8208200000	For wood working	8	20
8208300000	For kitchen appliances or for machines used by the food industry	8	20
8208400000	For agricultural, horticultural or forestry machines	8	20
8208900000	Other	8	20
8209001010	Of tungsten carbide, treated with gamma coating	8	20
8209001040	Of cermets	8	20
8209001090	Others	8	20
8209002010	Of tungsten carbide	8	20
8209002040	Of cermets	8	20
8209002090	Other	8	20
8210001000	Mills and grinders	8	20

8210002000	Extractors and pressers	8	20
8210003000	Beaters and mixers	8	20
8210004000	Slicers and cutters	8	20
8210005000	Openers, corkers and sealers	8	20
8210008000	Other domestic food-processing appliances	8	20
8210009000	Parts	8	20
8211100000	Sets of assorted articles	8	20
8211910000	Table knives having fixed blades	8	20
8211920000	Other knives having fixed blades	8	20
8211930000	Knives having other than fixed blades	8	20
8211940000	Blades	8	20
8211950000	Handles of base metal	8	20
8212100000	Razors	8	20
8212200000	Safety razor blades, including razor blade blanks in strips	8	20
8212900000	Other parts	8	20
8213001000	Ordinary scissors	8	20
8213002010	For tailors and dressmakers	8	20
8213002020	For hairdressers	8	20
8213002090	Other	8	20
8213004000	Scissor blades	8	20
8213009000	Other	8	20
8214101000	Pencil sharpeners	8	20
8214109000	Other	8	20
8214200000	Manicure or pedicure sets and instruments (including nail files)	8	20
8214901000	Hair clippers	8	20
8214902000	Butchers' or kitchen cleavers, choppers and mincing knives	8	20
8214909000	Other	8	20
8215100000	Sets of assorted articles containing at least one article plated with precious metal	8	20
8215200000	Other sets of assorted articles	8	20
8215911000	Spoons	8	20
8215912000	Forks	8	20
8215913000	Ladles and skimmers	8	20
8215914000	Fish-knives and butter-knives	8	20
8215915000	Tongs of all kinds	8	20
8215919000	Other	8	20
8215991000	Spoons	8	20
8215992000	Forks	8	20
8215993000	Ladles and skimmers	8	20
8215994000	Fish-knives and butter-knives	8	20
8215995000	Tong of all kinds	8	20
8215999000	Other	8	20
8301100000	Padlocks	8	20

8301200000	Locks of a kind used for motor vehicles	8	20
8301300000	Locks of a kind used for furniture	8	20
8301401010	Digital door locks	8	20
8301401090	Other	8	20
8301409000	Other	8	20
8301500000	Clasps and frames with clasps, incorporating locks	8	20
8301600000	Parts	8	20
8301700000	Keys presented separately	8	20
8302100000	Hinges	8	20
8302200000	Castors	8	20
8302300000	Other mountings, fittings and similar articles suitable for motor vehicles	8	20
8302411000	Suitable for doors or windows	8	20
8302419000	Other	8	20
8302491000	Suitable for trunks, suitcases, or similar travel goods.	8	20
8302499000	Other	8	20
8302500000	Hat-racks, hat-pegs, brackets and similar fixtures	8	20
8303001000	Safes	8	20
8303009000	Other	8	20
8304000000	Filing cabinets, card-index cabinets, paper trays, paper rests, pen trays, office-stamp stands and similar office or desk equipment, of base metal, other than office furniture of heading 94.03.	8	20
8305100000	Fittings for loose-leaf binders of files	8	20
8305200000	Staples in strips	8	20
8305900000	Other, including parts	8	20
8306100000	Bells, gongs and the like	8	20
8306210000	Plated with precious metal	8	20
8306290000	Other	8	20
8306301000	Photograph, picture or similar frames	8	20
8306302000	Mirrors of base metal	8	20
8307100000	Of iron or steel	8	20
8307900000	Of other base metal	8	20
8308101000	Hooks	8	20
8308102000	Eyes and eyelets	8	20
8308200000	Tubular or bifurcated rivets	8	20
8308901000	Clasps and frames with clasps	8	20
8308903000	Beads	8	20
8308904000	Spangles	8	20
8308909000	Other	8	20
8309100000	Crown corks	8	20
8309901000	Easy opener end	8	20
8309909000	Other	8	20
8310000000	Sign-plates, name-plates, address-plates and similar plates, numbers, letters and other symbols, of base metal,	8	20

	excluding those of heading 94.05.		
8311101000	For use in manufacturing semiconductor	8	20
8311109000	Other	8	20
8311201000	For use in manufacturing semiconductor	8	20
8311209000	Other	8	20
8311301000	For use in manufacturing semiconductor	8	20
8311309090	Other	8	20
8311901000	For use in manufacturing semiconductor	8	20
8311909000	Other	8	20
8402110000	Watertube boilers with a steam production exceeding 45t per hour	8	20
8402199000	Other	8	20
8402200000	Super-heated water boilers	8	20
8402901000	Of steam and other vapour generating boilers	8	20
8402902000	Of super-heated water boilers	8	20
8403101000	Central heating boilers, using fuel oil	8	20
8403102000	Central heating boilers, using coal or coke	8	20
8403103000	Central heating boilers, using gas	8	20
8403109000	Other	8	20
8403900000	Parts	8	20
8404101000	Economisers	8	20
8404102000	Super-heaters	8	20
8404103000	Soot recoverers	8	20
8404104000	Gas recoverers	8	20
8404109000	Other	8	20
8404200000	Condensers for steam of other vapour power units	8	20
8404901000	Of condensers for vapour generating boilers	8	20
8404902000	Of condensers for vapour engines and power units	8	20
8404909000	Other	8	20
8405101000	Producer gas generators	8	20
8405102000	Water gas generators	8	20
8405103000	Acetylene gas generators	8	20
8405104000	Oxygen generators	8	20
8405109000	Other	8	20
8405901000	Of producer gas genertord	8	20
8405902000	Of water gas generators	8	20
8405903000	Of acetylene gas generators	8	20
8405904000	Of oxygen generators	8	20
8405909000	Other	8	20
8406103000	Of an output exceeding 2 MW	5	20
8406109000	Other	5	20
8406811000	Of an output exceeding 40 MW but not exceeding 100 MW	5	20
8406812000	Of an output exceeding 100 MW but not exceeding 300 MW	5	20

8406813000	Of an output exceeding 300 MW	5	20
8406820000	Of an output not exceeding 40 MW	5	20
8406901000	Of steam turbines for marine propulsion	8	20
8406909000	Other	8	20
8407210000	Outboard motors	8	20
8407290000	Other	8	20
8407311000	For moter-cycles	8	20
8407319000	Other	8	20
8407321000	For motor-cycles	8	20
8407329000	Other	8	20
8407331000	For motor-cycles	8	20
8407339000	Other	8	20
8407341000	For motor-cycles	8	20
8407909000	Other	8	20
8408101000	With a rating not exceeding 300 kW	8	20
8408102000	With a rating more than 300 kW, not exceeding 2,000 kW	8	20
8408103000	With a rating more than 2,000 kW	8	20
8408201000	Of a cylinder capacity not exceeding 1,000cc	8	20
8408202000	Of a cylinder capacity exceeding 1,000cc but not exceeding 2,000cc	8	20
8408203000	Of a cylinder capacity exceeding 2,000cc but not exceeding 4,000cc	8	20
8408204000	Of a cylinder capacity exceeding 4,000cc but not exceeding 10,000cc	8	20
8408205000	Of a cylinder capacity exceeding 10,000cc	8	20
8408901090	Other	5	20
8408909010	Internal combustion engines for ships	8	20
8408909021	For generating of a power not less than 400 kW (Of a rpm 1,500 or 1,800)	4	20
8408909029	Other	8	20
8408909030	Internal combustion engines for subheading 84.29	8	20
8408909090	Other	8	20
8409100000	For aircraft engines	5	20
8409911000	For vehicles of Chapter 87	8	20
8409912000	For outboat motors	8	20
8409919000	Other	8	20
8409991000	For railway locomotives and rolling stock	5	20
8409992000	For vehicles of Chapter 87	8	20
8409993010	Of internal combustion engines with a rating not exceeding 300 kW	8	20
8409993020	Of internal combustion engins with a rating exceeding 300 kW, but not exceeding 2,000 kW	8	20
8409993030	Of internal combustion engines with a rating exceeding 2,000 kW	8	20
8409999010	For generating	8	20

8409999090	Other	8	20
8410119000	Other	8	20
8410901090	Other	8	20
8410909090	Other	8	20
8411111000	For aircraft	3	20
8411119010	For marine	8	20
8411119090	Other	8	20
8411121000	For aircraft	3	20
8411129010	For marine	8	20
8411129090	Other	8	20
8411211000	For aircraft	3	20
8411219010	For marine	8	20
8411219090	Other	8	20
8411221000	For aircraft	3	20
8411229010	For marine	8	20
8411229090	Other	8	20
8411811000	For aircraft	3	20
8411819010	For marine	8	20
8411819090	Other	8	20
8411821000	For aircraft	3	20
8411829010	For marine	8	20
8411829090	Other	8	20
8411911000	For aircraft	3	20
8411919000	Other	8	20
8411991000	For aircraft	3	20
8411999000	Other	8	20
8412101010	Ram-jet or pulsejct engines	5	20
8412101090	Other	5	20
8412109000	Other	8	20
8412211000	Hydraulic cylinder	8	20
8412219000	Other	8	20
8412290000	Other	8	20
8412310000	Linear acting (cylinders)	8	20
8412390000	Other	8	20
8412800000	Other	8	20
8412901010	Ram-jet or pulse-jet engines	5	20
8412901090	Other	5	20
8412909000	Other	8	20
8413110000	Pumps for dispensing fuel or lubricants, of the type used in filling-stations or in garages	8	20
8413190000	Other	8	20
8413200000	Hand pumps, other than those of subheading 8413.11 or 8413. 19	8	20
8413301000	For aircraft	8	20
8413302000	For railway locomotive	8	20

8413303000	For marine	8	20
8413304000	For vehicles falling within Chapter 87	8	20
8413309000	Other	8	20
8413400000	Concrete pumps	8	20
8413504000	Pumps to be used with swimming pools	8	20
8413509010	Plunger pumps	8	20
8413509020	Pistion pumps	8	20
8413509030	Diaphram pumps	8	20
8413509090	Other	8	20
8413604000	Pumps to be used with swimming pools	8	20
8413609010	Gear pumps	8	20
8413609020	Vane pumps	8	20
8413609030	Screw pumps	8	20
8413609090	Other	8	20
8413703000	Pumps to be used with swimming pools	8	20
8413709010	Turbine pumps	8	20
8413709020	Volute pumps	8	20
8413709090	Other	8	20
8413811000	Pumps to be used with swimming pools	8	20
8413819000	Other	8	20
8413820000	Liquid elevators	8	20
8413911000	Of pumps for dispensing fuel or lubricants	8	20
8413912000	Of internal combustion engine	8	20
8413913000	Of reciprocating pumps	8	20
8413914000	Of contrifugal pumps	8	20
8413915000	Of rotary pumps	8	20
8413919000	Other	8	20
8413920000	Of liquid elevators	8	20
8414101000	For aircrafts	8	20
8414109010	For machines and mechanical appliances for making semiconductor devices(other than those of an ultimate vacuum not exceeding 9×10^{-8}Torr)	3	20
8414109090	Other	8	20
8414200000	Hand- or foot-operated air pumps	8	20
8414400000	Air compressors mounted on a wheeled chassis for towing	8	20
8414511000	For aircrafts	8	20
8414519000	Other	8	20
8414591000	For aircrafts	8	20
8414601000	For aircrafts	8	20
8414609000	Other	8	20
8414801000	Hoods having a maximum horizontal side exceeding 120 cm	8	20
8414809110	For aircrafts	8	20
8414809210	Of a power requirement less than 74.6 kW	8	20
8414809220	Of a power requirement not less than 74.6 kW, less than	8	20

	373 kW		
8414809230	Of a power not less than 373 kW	8	20
8414809900	Other	8	20
8414901000	Of fans and hoods	8	20
8414909010	Of compressors used in refrigerating equipment	8	20
8414909020	Of air or gas compressors (excluding for refrigerating equipment)	8	20
8414909090	Other	8	20
8415101011	Of a power less than 11 kW	8	20
8415101012	Of a power not less than 11 kW	8	20
8415101021	Of a power less than 11 kW	8	20
8415101022	Of a power not less than 11 kW	8	20
8415102010	Of a power less than 11 kW	8	20
8415102020	Of a power not less than 11 kW	8	20
8415200000	Of a kind used for persons, in motor vehicles	8	20
8415810000	Incorporating a refrigerating unit and a valve for reversal of the cooling/heat cycle (reversible heat pumps)	8	20
8415820000	Other, incorporating a refrigerating unit	8	20
8415830000	Not incorporating a refrigerating unit	8	20
8415900000	Parts	8	20
8416101000	Of the maximum consumption capacity of fuel not more than 200 ℓ per hour	8	20
8416102000	Of the maximum consumption capacity of fuel exceeding 200 ℓ, but less than 1,500 ℓ per hour	8	20
8416103000	Of the maximum consumption capacity of fuel not less than 1,500 ℓ per hour	8	20
8416201000	Furnace burners for pulverised solid fuel	8	20
8416202000	Furnace burners for gas	8	20
8416300000	Mechanical stokers, including their mechanical grates, mechanical ash dischargers and similar appliances	8	20
8416901000	Of furnace burners	8	20
8416909000	Other	8	20
8417101010	For iron-ores	8	20
8417101090	Other	8	20
8417102010	For iron or steel	8	20
8417102090	Other	8	20
8417200000	Bakery ovens, including biscuit ovens	8	20
8417801010	For cements	8	20
8417801020	For glasses	8	20
8417801030	For ceramics	8	20
8417801090	Other	8	20
8417802000	Laboratory type	8	20
8417809000	Other	8	20
8417900000	Parts	8	20
8418101010	Of a capacity not exceeding 200 ℓ.	8	20

8418101030	Of a capacity exceeding 400 ℓ	8	20
8418109000	Other	8	20
8418211000	Of a capacity less than 200 ℓ	8	20
8418212000	Of a capacity not less than 200 ℓ, but less than 400 ℓ	8	20
8418213000	Of a capacity not less than 400 ℓ	8	20
8418291000	Absorption-type, electrical	8	20
8418299000	Other	8	20
8418300000	Freezers of the chest type, not exceeding 800 ℓ capacity	8	20
8418400000	Freezers of the upright type, not exceeding 900 ℓ capacity	8	20
8418509000	Other	8	20
8418610000	Heat pumps other than air conditioning machines of heading 84.15	8	20
8418691000	Blood storage refrigerators	8	20
8418692010	Ice-cream making machines	8	20
8418692020	Ice-cuber	8	20
8418692030	Water cooler	8	20
8418692090	Other	8	20
8418693000	Heat pumps	8	20
8418910000	Furniture designed to receive refrigerating or freezing equipment	8	20
8418991000	Of house hold type refrigerators	8	20
8418999000	Other	8	20
8419110000	Instantaneous gas water heaters	8	20
8419310000	For agricultural products	8	20
8419320000	For wood, paper pulp, paper or paperboard	8	20
8419391000	Spin dryers for machines and mechanical appliances for making semiconductor devices	3	20
8419399000	Other	8	20
8419400000	Distilling or rectifying plant	8	20
8419501000	For aircrafts	8	20
8419509000	Other	8	20
8419600000	Machinery for liquefying air or other gases	8	20
8419810000	For making hot drinks or for cooking or heating food	8	20
8419891000	Polymerization autoclaves for man-made fibre making	8	20
8419899010	Heating plant and machinery	8	20
8419899020	Cooling plant and machinery	8	20
8419899030	Evaporating plant and machinery	8	20
8419899040	Condensing plant and machinery	8	20
8419899050	Sollar-collectors and equipments	8	20
8419899060	Constant high or low temperature chambers	8	20
8419899070	Constant temperature and humidity chambers	8	20
8419899080	Air-conditioner	8	20
8419899090	Other	8	20
8419901000	Of polymerization autoclaves for man-made fibre making	8	20

8419909010	Of instantaneous or storage water heaters	8	20
8427102000	Of non counter balance type	8	20
8427109000	Other	8	20
8427201010	With a loading capacity not more than 3 metric tons	8	20
8427201020	With a loading capacity more than 3 metric tons	8	20
8427209000	Other	8	20
8427901000	Hand pallet trucks	8	20
8427909000	Other	8	20
8431200000	Of machinery of heading 84.27	8	20
8435101000	Presses for the extraction of fruit juice	8	20
8435102000	Crushers for the extraction of fruit juice	8	20
8435103000	Homogenisers for the preparation of fruit juice	8	20
8435109000	Other	8	20
8435900000	Parts	8	20
8436101000	Feed cutter	8	20
8436102000	Feed grinder, mill or crusher	8	20
8436103000	Feed mixer	8	20
8436109000	Other	8	20
8436211000	Incubators	8	20
8436219000	Other	8	20
8436290000	Other	8	20
8436800000	Other machinery	8	20
8436910000	Of poultry-keeping machinery or poultry incubators and brooders	8	20
8436990000	Other	8	20
8437101000	Forage-grass seed selectors	8	20
8437109000	Other	8	20
8437801000	Machinery used in the milling industry	8	20
8437802000	Machinery for the working of cereals or dried leguminous vegetables	8	20
8437901000	Of machines for cleaning sorting or grading seed, grain or dried leguninous vegetables	8	20
8437909000	Other	8	20
8438109000	Other	8	20
8438200000	Machinery for the manufacture of confectionery, cocoa or chocolate	8	20
8438300000	Machinery for sugar manufacture	8	20
8438400000	Brewery machinery	8	20
8438501000	Machinery used in meat preparation	8	20
8438509000	Other	8	20
8438600000	Machinery for the preparation of fruits, nuts or vegetables	8	20
8438801000	Machines for preparing fish, shell fish, etc	8	20
8438809000	Other	8	20
8438900000	Parts	8	20
8439101000	Grinders	8	20

8439102000	Cutters	8	20
8439103000	Strainers	8	20
8439104000	Press-pate machines	8	20
8439105000	Beaters	8	20
8439109000	Other	8	20
8439201000	Machines for forming paper	8	20
8439202000	Paper making machine	8	20
8439209000	Other	8	20
8439301000	Reeling machines	8	20
8439302000	Machines for working surface	8	20
8439303000	Machines for impregnating paper or paperboard	8	20
8439309000	Other	8	20
8439910000	Of machinery for making pulp of fibrous cellulosic material	8	20
8439990000	Other	8	20
8440101000	Book-sewing machines	8	20
8440102000	Leaf-folding machines for book-binding	8	20
8440109000	Other	8	20
8440901000	Of book-sewing machines	8	20
8440909000	Other	8	20
8441100000	Cutting machines	8	20
8441201000	Machines for making bags or sacks	8	20
8441202000	Machines for making envelopes	8	20
8441300000	Machines for making cartons, boxes, cases, tubes, drums or similar containers, other than by moulding	8	20
8441400000	Machines for moulding articles in paper pulp, paper or paperboard	8	20
8441801000	Paper or paperboard trimming machines	8	20
8441809000	Other	8	20
8441900000	Parts	8	20
8442301000	Machinery and apparatus for type-founding	8	20
8442302000	Special moulding presses	8	20
8442303000	Acid etching machines	8	20
8442304000	Phototype-setting and composing machines	8	20
8442305000	Machinery,apparatus and equipment for type-setting or composing by other processes,with or without founding device	8	20
8442309000	Other	8	20
8442401000	Of machinery and apparatus for type-setting	8	20
8442402000	Of machinery and apparatus for type-founding	8	20
8442409000	Other	8	20
8442500000	Plates, cylinders and other printing components; plates, cylinders and lithographic stones, prepared for printing purposes (for example, planed, grained or polished)	8	20
8443110000	Offset printing machinery, reel fed	8	20

8443120000	Offset printing machinery, sheet-fed, office type (using sheets with one side not exceeding 22 cm and the other side not exceeding 36 cm in the unfolded state)	8	20
8443130000	Other offset printing machinery	8	20
8443140000	Letterpress printing machinery, reel fed, excluding flexographic printing	8	20
8443150000	Letterpress printing machinery, other than reel fed, excluding flexographic printing	8	20
8443160000	Flexographic printing machinery	8	20
8443170000	Gravure printing machinery	8	20
8443191000	Textile printing machines	8	20
8443192000	Other printing machines of a type used for printing a repetitive design, repetitve words or overall colour on textiles, leather, wallpaper, wrapping paper, linoleum or other materials	8	20
8443199000	Other	8	20
8443313020	Operating by reproducing the original image via an intermediate onto the copy (indirect process)	8	20
8443314000	Ink-jet printing machines, other than subheading 8443.31.10	8	20
8443324020	Operating by reproducing the original image via an intermediate onto the copy (indirect process)	8	20
8443325090	Other	8	20
8443391090	Other	8	20
8443392020	Operating by reproducing the original image via an intermediate onto the copy (indirect process)	8	20
8443393020	Of the contact type	8	20
8443394000	Thermo-copying apparatus	8	20
8443399000	Other	8	20
8443911010	Automatic feeders	8	20
8443911020	Folders, gummers, preforators and staplers	8	20
8443911030	Serial numbering machines	8	20
8443911090	Other	8	20
8443919000	Other	8	20
8443995000	Of subheading 8443.31.4000, 8443.32.5010, 8443.32.5090, 8443.39.1010 or 8443.39.1090	8	20
8443999000	Other	8	20
8444001000	Machines for extruding man-made textiles	5	20
8444002000	Machines for drawing man-made textiles	5	20
8444003000	Machines for texturing man-made textiles	5	20
8444004000	Machines for cutting man-made textiles	5	20
8444009000	Other	5	20
8445110000	Carding machines	5	20
8445120000	Combing machines	5	20
8445130000	Drawing or roving machines	5	20

8445191000	Blowing and mixing machines	5	20
8445192000	Lap machines	5	20
8445193000	Cotton gin	8	20
8445199000	Other	5	20
8445201010	Fine spinning frames	5	20
8445201090	Other	5	20
8445202010	Fine spinning frames	5	20
8445202090	Other	5	20
8445203000	For silk	5	20
8445209000	Other	5	20
8445301000	For filament yarns	5	20
8445302000	For spun yarns	5	20
8445309000	Other	5	20
8445401000	Cones winders	5	20
8445402000	Cheeses winders	5	20
8445409000	Other	5	20
8445901000	Warping machines	8	20
8445902000	Warp sizing machines	8	20
8445903000	Drawing-in machines	8	20
8445904000	Warp tying-in machines	8	20
8445909000	Other	8	20
8446100000	For weaving fabrics of a width not exceeding 30 cm	8	20
8446211000	For cotton	8	20
8446212000	For wool	8	20
8446213000	For silk	8	20
8446219000	Other	8	20
8446290000	Other	8	20
8446301010	For cotton	8	20
8446301020	For silk	8	20
8446301030	For towel	8	20
8446301090	Other	8	20
8446302010	For cotton	8	20
8446302020	For silk	8	20
8446302030	For towel	8	20
8446302090	Other	8	20
8446303010	For cotton	8	20
8446303020	For silk	8	20
8446303030	For towel	8	20
8446303090	Other	8	20
8446309010	For cotton	8	20
8446309020	For silk	8	20
8446309030	For towel	8	20
8446309090	Other	8	20
8447111000	Stocking knitting machines	8	20
8447119000	Other	8	20

8447120000	With cylinder diameter exceeding 165 mm	8	20
8447201010	Hand-knitting machines (including semi- automatic flat knitting machines)	8	20
8447201020	Automatic flat knitting machines	8	20
8447201090	Other	8	20
8447202010	Raschel knitting machines	8	20
8447202020	Tricot knitting machines	8	20
8447202090	Other	8	20
8447209000	Other	8	20
8447901000	Lace machines	8	20
8447902010	Automatic embroidery machines	8	20
8447902090	Other	8	20
8447903000	Machines for making knotted net	8	20
8447909000	Other	8	20
8448111000	Dobbies	8	20
8448112000	Jacquards	8	20
8448113000	Card punching machines	8	20
8448119000	Other	8	20
8448191000	Warp beam stands or creels	8	20
8448192000	Automatic stop motions	8	20
8448193000	Warp tyers	8	20
8448199010	Auxiliary machines for making yarn (excluding cotton gin)	5	20
8448199090	Other	8	20
8448201000	Extruding nipples	5	20
8448209000	Other	5	20
8448310000	Card clothing	8	20
8448321000	For carding machine(excluding garnet wires)	5	20
8448329000	Other	8	20
8448331000	Spindle flyers	5	20
8448339010	Spindle	8	20
8448339020	Spinning ring	8	20
8448339030	Ring travellers	8	20
8448391000	Warp beams	8	20
8448399000	Other	8	20
8448420000	Reeds for looms, healds and heald-frames	8	20
8448491000	Shuttles	8	20
8448499000	Other	8	20
8448511000	Hoisery needles	8	20
8448512000	Needles for embroidery machines	8	20
8448513000	Needles for lace machines	8	20
8448519000	Other	8	20
8448590000	Other	8	20
8449001010	Machinery for making felt hats	8	20
8449001090	Other	8	20
8449002000	Bolcks for making hats	8	20

8449009000	Parts	8	20
8450110000	Fully-automatic machines	8	20
8450120000	Other machines, with built-in centrifugal drier	8	20
8450190000	Other	8	20
8450200000	Machines, each of a dry linen capacity exceeding 10 kg	8	20
8450900000	Parts	8	20
8451100000	Dry-cleaning machines	8	20
8451210000	Each of a dry linen capacity not exceeding 10 kg	8	20
8451290000	Other	8	20
8451301000	Steam presses	8	20
8451309000	Other	8	20
8451401000	Washing machines	8	20
8451402000	Bleaching machines	8	20
8451403000	Dyeing machines	8	20
8451501000	Reeling unreeling machines	8	20
8451502000	Cutting machines	8	20
8451509000	Other	8	20
8451801000	Heat treating machines	8	20
8451802000	Stentering machines	8	20
8451803000	Mercerising machines	8	20
8451809010	Shrinking machines	8	20
8451809020	Coating or impregnating machines	8	20
8451809030	Raising machines	8	20
8451809040	Padding machines	8	20
8451809090	Other	8	20
8451901000	Of dry cleaning machines	8	20
8451902000	Of drying machines	8	20
8451909000	Other	8	20
8452101010	For straight stitch	8	20
8452101020	For zigzag stitch	8	20
8452101030	Of free arm type	8	20
8452101090	Other	8	20
8452102000	Of manual type	8	20
8452211000	For manufacturing shoes	8	20
8452212000	For sewing sacks	8	20
8452213000	For sewing leather or other thick stuffs	8	20
8452214000	For sewing furs	8	20
8452219000	Other	8	20
8452291000	For manufacturing shoes	8	20
8452292000	For sewing sacks	8	20
8452293000	For sewing leather or other thicks stuffs	8	20
8452294000	For sewing furs	8	20
8452299000	Other	8	20
8452300000	Sewing machine needles	8	20
8452400000	Furniture, bases and covers for sewing machines and parts	8	20

	thereof		
8452900000	Other parts of sewing machines	8	20
8453101000	Machinery for preparing hides, skins or leather	8	20
8453102000	Machinery for tanning hides, skins or leather	8	20
8453103000	Machinery for working hides, skins or leather	8	20
8453201000	Machinery for making footwear	8	20
8453202000	Machinery for repairing footwear	8	20
8453800000	Other machinery	8	20
8453900000	Parts	8	20
8454100000	Converters	8	20
8454200000	Ingot moulds and ladles	8	20
8454301010	Die-casting machines	8	20
8454301090	Other	8	20
8454309000	Other	8	20
8454901000	Of converters	8	20
8454909000	Other	8	20
8455100000	Tube mills	8	20
8455210000	Hot or combination hot and cold	8	20
8455220000	Cold	8	20
8455301000	Of casting	8	20
8455302000	Of forging	8	20
8455309000	Other	8	20
8455900000	Other parts	8	20
8456103000	Operated by laser processes	8	20
8456109000	Other	8	20
8456301010	Wire cut electric discharge machine	8	20
8456301090	Other	8	20
8456309000	Other	8	20
8456900000	Other	8	20
8457101000	Of vertical type	8	20
8457102000	Of horizontal type	8	20
8457103000	Of double column type	8	20
8457109000	Other	8	20
8457200000	Unit construction machines (single station)	8	20
8457300000	Multi-station transfer machines	8	20
8458110000	Numerically controlled	8	20
8458190000	Other	8	20
8458910000	Numerically controlled	8	20
8458990000	Other	8	20
8459100000	Way-type unit head machines	8	20
8459210000	Numerically controlled	8	20
8459291000	Radial drilling machines	8	20
8459292000	Upright drilling machines	8	20
8459293000	Multi-spindle drilling machines	8	20
8459299000	Other	8	20

8459310000	Numerically controlled	8	20
8459390000	Other	8	20
8459401000	Jig boring machines	8	20
8459402000	Horizontal boring machines	8	20
8459409000	Other	8	20
8459510000	Numerically controlled	8	20
8459590000	Other	8	20
8459611000	Bed type milling machines	8	20
8459612000	Planing milling machines	8	20
8459619000	Other	8	20
8459691000	Bed type milling machines	8	20
8459692000	Planing milling machines	8	20
8459693000	Universal tool milling machines	8	20
8459694000	Profile milling machines	8	20
8459699000	Other	8	20
8459701000	Tapping machines	8	20
8459709000	Other threading machines	8	20
8460110000	Numerically controlled	8	20
8460190000	Other	8	20
8460211000	Cylindrical grinders	8	20
8460212000	Internal grinders	8	20
8460213000	Centerless grinders	8	20
8460214000	Profile grinders	8	20
8460291000	Cylindrical grinders	8	20
8460292000	Internal grinders	8	20
8460293000	Centerless grinders	8	20
8460294000	Profile grinders	8	20
8460299000	Other	8	20
8460310000	Numerically controlled	8	20
8460390000	Other	8	20
8460401000	Honing machines	8	20
8460402000	Lapping machines	8	20
8460900000	Other	8	20
8461200000	Shaping or slotting machines	8	20
8461300000	Broaching machines	8	20
8461401010	Numerically controlled	8	20
8461401090	Other	8	20
8461402000	Gear grinding or gear finishing machines	8	20
8461500000	Sawing or cutting-off machines	8	20
8461900000	Other	8	20
8462101000	Air hammer	8	20
8462109000	Other	8	20
8462210000	Numerically controlled	8	20
8462290000	Other	8	20
8462310000	Numerically controlled	8	20

8462390000	Other	8	20
8462411000	Punching machines (including combined shearing machines)	8	20
8462412000	Notching machines	8	20
8462491000	Punching machines (including combined shearing machines)	8	20
8462492000	Notching machines	8	20
8462911000	Of the maximum pressure not more than 100 metric tons	8	20
8462912000	Of the maximum pressure more than 100 metric tons, but not more than 300 metric tons	8	20
8462913000	Of the maximum pressure more than 300 metric tons, but not more than 1000 metric tons	8	20
8462914000	Of the maximum pressure more than 1000 metric tons	8	20
8462991010	Of the maximum pressure not more than 30 metric tons	8	20
8462991020	Of the maximum pressure more than 30 metric tons, but not more than 100 metric tons	8	20
8462991030	Of the maximum pressure more than 100 metric tons, but not more than 300 metric tons	8	20
8462991040	Of the maximum pressure more than 300 metric tons, but not more than 600 metric tons	8	20
8462991050	Of the maximum pressure more than 600 metric tons, but not more than 1,500 metric tons	8	20
8462991090	Other	8	20
8462999000	Other	8	20
8463100000	Draw-benches for bars, tubes, profiles, wire or the like	8	20
8463200000	Thread rolling machines	8	20
8463300000	Machines for working wire	8	20
8463900000	Other	8	20
8464100000	Sawing machines	8	20
8464201000	For working optical or spectacle glass	8	20
8464202000	For working other glass	8	20
8464209000	Other	8	20
8464901000	Machine-tools for cold working glass	8	20
8464902000	Machine-tools for working concrete	8	20
8464903000	Machine-tools for working ceramics	8	20
8464909000	Other	8	20
8465101000	For working wood	8	20
8465109000	Other	8	20
8465911000	For working wood	8	20
8465919000	Other	8	20
8465921000	For working wood	8	20
8465929000	Other	8	20
8465931000	For working wood	8	20
8465939000	Other	8	20
8465941000	For working wood	8	20

8465949000	Other	8	20
8465951000	For working wood	8	20
8465959000	Other	8	20
8465961000	For working wood	8	20
8465969000	Other	8	20
8465991000	For working wood	8	20
8465999000	Other	8	20
8466100000	Tool holders and self-opening dieheads	8	20
8466201000	For aircrafts	8	20
8466209000	Other	8	20
8466300000	Dividing heads and other special attachments for machine-tools	8	20
8466910000	For machines of heading 84.64	8	20
8466920000	For machines of heading 84.65	8	20
8466930000	For machines of headings 84.56 to 84.61	8	20
8466940000	For machines of heading 84.62 or 84.63	8	20
8467111000	Rock drillers	8	20
8467112000	Screw drivers	8	20
8467114000	Impact wrench	8	20
8467115000	Drill	8	20
8467119000	Other	8	20
8467191000	Rock drillers	8	20
8467210000	Drills of all kinds	8	20
8467220000	Saws	8	20
8467290000	Other	8	20
8467810000	Chain saws	8	20
8467891020	Of subheading 8479.89.9010, 8479.89.9030 or 8479.89.9091	8	20
8467891090	Other	8	20
8467899000	Other	8	20
8467910000	Of chain saws	8	20
8467920000	Of pneumatic tools	8	20
8467990000	Other	8	20
8468100000	Hand-held blow pipes	8	20
8468201000	Gas welding machines	8	20
8468202000	Gas automatic cutting machines	8	20
8468209000	Other	8	20
8468800000	Other machinery and apparatus	8	20
8468900000	Parts	8	20
8469001020	Automatic typewriters	8	20
8469002000	Other typewriters, electric	8	20
8469003000	Other typewriters, non-electric	8	20
8472100000	Duplicating machines	8	20
8472301000	Letters sorting machines	8	20
8472302000	Machines for cancelling postage stamps	8	20

8472309000	Other	8	20
8472901050	Coin-counting or wrapping machines	8	20
8472901090	Other	8	20
8472902000	Automatic sheet making machines for duplicating and printing	8	20
8472903000	Ticket-issuing machines	8	20
8472904000	Pencil-sharpening machines	8	20
8472905000	Paper shredders	8	20
8472906000	Addressing machines and address plate embossing machines	8	20
8472909000	Other	8	20
8473109000	Other	8	20
8473409000	Other	8	20
8475100000	Machines for assembling electric or electronic lamps, tubes or valves or flashbulbs, in glass envelopes	8	20
8475210000	Machines for making optical fibres and preforms thereof	8	20
8475291000	For the manufacture of plate glass	8	20
8475292000	For the manufacture of glass-bottle	8	20
8475299000	Other	8	20
8475901000	Of machines for the manufacture of plate glass	8	20
8475909000	Other	8	20
8476210000	Incorporating heating or refrigerating devices	8	20
8476290000	Other	8	20
8476811000	For selling foods	8	20
8476819000	Other	8	20
8476891000	For selling foods	8	20
8476893000	For selling cigarettes	8	20
8476894000	For money-changing	8	20
8476899000	Other	8	20
8476900000	Parts	8	20
8477101000	For rubber-industry	8	20
8477102000	For plastic-industry	8	20
8477201000	For rubber-industry	8	20
8477202000	For plastic-industry	8	20
8477300000	Blow moulding machines	8	20
8477400000	Vacuum moulding machines and other thermoforming machines	8	20
8477510000	For moulding or retreading pneumatic tyres or for moulding or otherwise forming inner tubes	8	20
8477590000	Other	8	20
8477800000	Other machinery	8	20
8477900000	Parts	8	20
8478100000	Machinery	8	20
8478900000	Parts	8	20
8479200000	Machinery for the extraction or preparation of animal or	8	20

	fixed vegetable fats or oils		
8479300000	Presses for the manufacture of particle board or fibre building board of wood or other ligneous materials and other machinery for treating wood or cork	8	20
8479400000	Rope or cable-making machines	8	20
8479501000	Of subheading 8479.81, 8479.82, 8479.89.9010, 8479.89.9030, 8479.89.9040, 8479.89.9060 or 8479.89.9091	8	20
8479502000	Of Subheading 8479.89.9080	8	20
8479509000	Other	8	20
8479600000	Evaporative air coolers	8	20
8479811000	Metal scouring machines	8	20
8479812010	For the purpose of semiconductor manufacturing	3	20
8479812090	Other	8	20
8479813000	Winding machines	8	20
8479814000	Insulating or protective material covering machines	8	20
8479819000	Other	8	20
8479821000	Mixers	8	20
8479822000	Crushers and grinders	8	20
8479824000	Agitators	8	20
8479829000	Other	8	20
8479891010	Air purifiers (having funtions of humidifying and dehumidifying)	8	20
8479891090	Other	8	20
8479899010	Presses or extruding machines	8	20
8479899020	Machines and appliances for ships or fishing industry	8	20
8479899030	Eyeletting or tubular rivetting machines	8	20
8479899040	Automatic magnetic tape assembling machines	8	20
8479899050	Coating machines	8	20
8479899060	Auto-door operators	8	20
8479899080	Automatic winding machines for fishing	8	20
8479899091	For vehicles of Chapter 87	8	20
8479899092	Surface mount machines for electronic parts	8	20
8479899099	Other	8	20
8479901010	Of air coolers (including parts of carcoolers)	8	20
8479901020	Of machines and mechanical appliances of the household type	8	20
8479901030	Of vehicles of Chapter 87	8	20
8479902000	Of those specified in subheading 8479.89.9080	8	20
8479903000	Of machines and mechanical appliances for making semi-con ductor devices	8	20
8479909010	Of machinery for public works, building or the like	8	20
8479909020	Of machinery for the extraction or preparation of animal or fixed vegetable fats or oils	8	20
8479909030	Of rope or cable-making machines	8	20
8479909040	Of machines and appliances for treating metal	8	20

8479909050	Of mixing, kneading, crushing, grinding, screening, sifting, homogenising, emulsifying or stirring machines	8	20
8479909060	Of presses or extruding machines	8	20
8479909070	Of machines and appliances of ships or fishing industry	8	20
8479909080	Of automatic magnetic tape assembling machines	8	20
8479909090	Other	8	20
8480100000	Moulding boxes for metal foundry	8	20
8480200000	Mould bases	8	20
8480300000	Moulding patterns	8	20
8480410000	Injection or compression types	8	20
8480490000	Other	8	20
8480500000	Moulds for glass	8	20
8480600000	Moulds for mineral materials	8	20
8480710000	Injection or compression types	8	20
8480790000	Other	8	20
8481100000	Pressure-reducing valves	8	20
8481201000	Valves for oleohydraulic transmissions	8	20
8481202000	Valves for pneumatic transmissions	8	20
8481300000	Check (nonreturn) valves	8	20
8481400000	Safety or relief valves	8	20
8481801010	Electric operated	8	20
8481801090	Other	8	20
8481802000	Taps, cocks and traps	8	20
8481809000	Other	8	20
8481909000	Other	8	20
8482101000	Of the inside diameter exceeding 100 mm	8	20
8482102000	Of the inside diameter not exceeding 100 mm	13	20
8482200000	Tapered roller bearings, including cone and tapered roller assemblies	8	20
8482300000	Spherical roller bearings	8	20
8482400000	Needle roller bearings	8	20
8482500000	Other cylindrical roller bearings	8	20
8482800000	Other, including combined ball/roller bearings	8	20
8482990000	Other	8	20
8483101000	For aircrafts	3	20
8483109010	For vehicles of Chapter 87	8	20
8483109090	Other	8	20
8483201000	For aircrafts	3	20
8483209000	Other	8	20
8483301000	For aircrafts	3	20
8483309000	Other	8	20
8483401010	Roller screws	3	20
8483401090	Other	3	20
8483409010	Gear	8	20
8483409020	Gear boxes	8	20

8483409030	Automatic transmissions	8	20
8483409041	For vehicles of Chapter 87	8	20
8483409049	Other	8	20
8483409090	Other	8	20
8483501000	For aircrafts	8	20
8483509000	Other	8	20
8483601000	For aircrafts	3	20
8483609000	Other	8	20
8483901000	For aircrafts	3	20
8483909000	Other	8	20
8484101000	For vehicles of Chapter 87	8	20
8484109000	Other	8	20
8484200000	Mechanical seals	8	20
8484900000	Other	8	20
8486103090	Other	8	20
8486104019	Other	8	20
8486104029	Other	8	20
8486109000	Other	8	20
8486202290	Other	8	20
8486205190	Other	8	20
8486205990	Other	8	20
8486208190	Other	8	20
8486208490	Other	8	20
8486209390	Other	8	20
8486209900	Other	8	20
8486303010	Operated by laser or other light or photon beam processes	8	20
8486303020	Operated by ultrasonic processes	8	20
8486303030	Operated by electro-discharge processes	8	20
8486303041	Dry etcher	8	20
8486303049	Other	8	20
8486304010	Grinding or polishing machines	8	20
8486304090	Other	8	20
8486305010	Coating machines	8	20
8486305020	Coating and developing machines	8	20
8486305031	Operated by physical method	8	20
8486305032	Operated by chemical method	8	20
8486305039	Other	8	20
8486306010	Seal, Short, Spacer or Liquid crystal dispenser	8	20
8486306020	Scribing machines	8	20
8486306030	Panel assembler	8	20
8486306090	Other	8	20
8486307000	Centrifuges, including centrifugal dryers	8	20
8486308000	Mechanical appliances for projecting, dispersing or spraying liquids or powders	8	20

8486309020	Robots for making flat panel displays	8	20
8486309090	Other	8	20
8486401040	Machines and apparatus for etching, cleaning or stripping mask and reticle	8	20
8486401090	Other	8	20
8486402020	Machines for inserting or removing semiconductor devices	8	20
8486402039	Other	8	20
8486402040	Machines to attach solder ball on semiconductor circuit board or ceramic board	3	20
8486402050	Apparatus designed to bond or datach wafer on ceramic block in polish wafers	8	20
8486402092	Machine-tools (including presses) for working metal by bending, folding, straightening, flattening, other than semiconductor leads, whether or not numerically controlled	8	20
8486402093	Machines for forming connections(bump) on an entire wafer before dicing	8	20
8486402099	Other	8	20
8486901020	Of subheading 8486.10.3090, 8486.10.4019, 8486.10.4029 or 8486.10.9000	8	20
8486902020	Of subheading 8486.220290, 8486.20.5190, 8486.20.5990, 8486.20.8190, 8486.20.8490, 8486.20.9390 or 8486.20.9900	8	20
8486903020	Of subheading 8486.30.3010, 8486.30.3020, 8486.30.3030, 8486.30.3041, 8486.30.3049, 8486.30.4010, 8486.30.4090, 8486.30.6020, 8486.30.7000, 8486.30.8000, 8486.30.9020 or 8486.30.9090	8	20
8486903030	Of subheading 8486.30.5010, 8486.30.5020, 8486.30.5031, 8486.30.5032, 8486.30.5039, 8486.30.6010, 8486.30.6030, or 8486.30.6090	8	20
8486904020	Of subheading 8486.40.1040, 8486.40.1090, 8486.420020, 8486.420039, 8486.420040, 8486.420050, 8486.420061, 8486.420062, 8486.420063, 8486.420092, 8486.420093, 8486.420099 or 8486.40.9000	8	20
8487100000	Ships' or boats' propellers and blades therefor	8	20
8487909010	Oil seal rings	8	20
8487909090	Other	8	20
8501101000	DC motors	8	20
8501103000	Universal AC/DC motors	8	20
8501201000	Of an output exceeding 37.5 W, but not exceeding 100 W	8	20
8501202000	Of an output exceeding 100 W, but not exceeding 750 W	8	20
8501203000	Of an output exceeding 750 W	8	20
8501311010	Of an output not exceeding 100 W	8	20
8501312000	DC generators	8	20
8501321000	DC motors	8	20
8501322000	DC generators	8	20

8501331000	DC motors	8	20
8501332000	DC generatrors	8	20
8501341000	DC motors	8	20
8501342000	DC generators	8	20
8501401000	Of an output not exceeding 100 W	8	20
8501402000	Of an output exceeding 100 W but not exceeding 750 W	8	20
8501403000	Of an output exceeding 750 W but not exceeding 75 kW	8	20
8501404000	Of an output exceeding 75 kW	8	20
8501510000	Of an output not exceeding 750 W	8	20
8501532000	Of an output exceeding 375 kW but not exceeding 1500 kW	8	20
8501534000	Of an output exceeding 1500 kW	8	20
8501611000	Of an output not exceeding 750 VA	8	20
8501612000	Of an output exceeding 750 VA but not exceeding 75 kVA	8	20
8501620000	Of an output exceeding 75 kVA but not exceeding 375 kVA	8	20
8501639000	Other	8	20
8502111000	Of an output not exceeding 750 VA	8	20
8502112000	Of an output exceeding 750 VA but not exceeding 75 kVA	8	20
8502120000	Of an output exceeding 75 kVA but not exceeding 375 kVA	8	20
8502131090	Other	8	20
8502201000	Of an output not exceeding 75 kVA	8	20
8502202000	Of an output exceeding 75 kVA but not exceeding 375 kVA	8	20
8502203090	Other	8	20
8502311000	Of an output not exceeding 75 kVA	8	20
8502312000	Of an output exceeding 75 kVA but not exceeding 375 kVA	8	20
8502313000	Of an output exceeding 375 kVA but not exceeding 750 kVA	8	20
8502314000	Of an output exceeding 750 kVA	8	20
8502391000	Of an output not exceeding 75 kVA	8	20
8502392000	Of an output exceeding 75 kVA but not exceeding 375 kVA	8	20
8502393000	Of an output exceeding 375 kVA but not exceeding 750 kVA	8	20
8502394000	Of an output exceeding 750 kVA	8	20
8502400000	Electric rotary converters	8	20
8503001000	Of motors	8	20
8503002000	Of generators and of generating sets	8	20
8503003000	Of rotary converters	8	20
8504101010	Rated at not more than 1 A	8	20

8504102000	Rated at more than 20 A but not more than 60 A	8	20
8504103000	Rated at more than 60 A	8	20
8504211000	Instrument transformers	8	20
8504219010	Having a power handling capacity not exceeding 100 kVA	8	20
8504221000	Instrument transformers	8	20
8504229010	Having a power handling capacity exceeding 650 kVA but not exceeding 1,000 kVA	8	20
8504229020	Having a power handling capacity exceeding 1,000 kVA but not exceeding 5,000 kVA	8	20
8504229030	Having a power handling capacity exceeding 5,000 kVA but not exceeding 10,000 kVA	8	20
8504230000	Having a power handling capacity exceeding 10,000 kVA	8	20
8504312000	Voltage regulators	8	20
8504319010	Having a power handling capacity not exceeding 100 VA	8	20
8504319020	Having a power handling capacity exceeding 100 VA but not exceeding 500 VA	8	20
8504319040	Having a power handling capacity exceeding 500 VA but not exceeding 1 kVA	8	20
8504321000	Instrument transformers	8	20
8504322000	Voltage regulators	8	20
8504329010	Having a power handling capacity exceeding 1 kVA but not exceeding 5 kVA	8	20
8504329020	Having a power handling capacity exceeding 5 kVA but not exceeding 16 kVA	8	20
8504331000	Instrument transformers	8	20
8504332000	Voltage regulators	8	20
8504339010	Having a power handling capacity exceeding 16 kVA but not exceeding 30 kVA	8	20
8504339020	Having a power handling capacity exceeding 30 kVA but not exceeding 100 kVA	8	20
8504339040	Having a power handling capacity exceeding 100 kVA but not exceeding 500 kVA	8	20
8504341000	Instrument transformers	8	20
8504342000	Voltage regulators	8	20
8504349010	Having a power handling capacity exceeding 500 kVA but not exceeding 2,000 kVA	8	20
8504349030	Having a power handling capacity exceeding 2,000 kVA	8	20
8504401090	Other	8	20
8504402019	Other	8	20
8504402099	Other	8	20
8504403090	Other	8	20
8504404090	Other	8	20
8504405090	Other	8	20
8504501090	Other	8	20
8504509090	Other	8	20

8504909000	Other	8	20
8505111000	Of alnico	8	20
8505119000	Other	8	20
8505191000	Of iron oxide	8	20
8505200000	Electro-magnetic couplings, clutches and brakes	8	20
8505902000	Electro-magnetic or permanent magnet chucks, clamps, vices and similar work holders	8	20
8505903000	Electro-magnetic lifting heads	8	20
8506102000	Alkali manganese batteries	13	20
8506109000	Other	8	20
8506300000	Mercuric oxide	8	20
8506400000	Silver oxide	8	20
8506500000	Lithium	8	20
8506600000	Air-Zinc	8	20
8506801000	Zinc oxide	8	20
8506809000	Other	8	20
8506900000	Parts	8	20
8507100000	Lead-acid, of a kind used for starting piston engines	8	20
8507200000	Other lead-acid accumulators	8	20
8507300000	Nickel-cadmium	8	20
8507400000	Nickel-iron	8	20
8507801000	Nikel metal hydride	8	20
8507802000	Lithium Ion	8	20
8507803000	Lithium polymer	8	20
8507809000	Other	8	20
8507901000	Seperators	8	20
8507909000	Other	8	20
8508110000	Of a power not exceeding 1,500 W and having a dust bag or other receptacle capacity not exceeding 20 ℓ	8	20
8508191000	Of a kind used for domestic purposes	8	20
8508199000	Other	8	20
8508701000	Of subheading 8508.11.0000 or 8508.19.1000	8	20
8508702000	Of subheading 8508.19.9000 or 8508.60.0000	8	20
8509801000	Coffee grinders	8	20
8509802000	Ice grinders	8	20
8509803000	Floor polishers	8	20
8509804000	Kitchen waste disposers	8	20
8509900000	Parts	8	20
8510100000	Shavers	8	20
8510200000	Hair clippers	8	20
8510300000	Hair-removing appliances	8	20
8510901000	Of shavers	8	20
8510902000	Of hair clippers	8	20
8510903000	Of hair-removing appliances	8	20
8511101000	For aircrafts	3	20

8511109000	Other	8	20
8511201000	For aircrafts	3	20
8511209000	Other	8	20
8511301000	For aircrafts	3	20
8511309000	Other	8	20
8511401000	For aircrafts	3	20
8511409000	Other	8	20
8511501000	For aircrafts	3	20
8511509000	Other	8	20
8511801000	For aircraft	3	20
8511809000	Other	8	20
8511901000	For aircraft	3	20
8511909000	Other	8	20
8512100000	Lighting or visual signalling equipment of a kind used on bicycles	8	20
8512201000	Lighting equipment	8	20
8512202000	Signalling equipment	8	20
8512400000	Windscreen wipers, defrosters and demisters	8	20
8512900000	Parts	8	20
8513101000	Safety lamps of a kind used in mining	8	20
8513102000	Flashlights	8	20
8513109000	Other	8	20
8513900000	Parts	8	20
8514101000	For laboratory	8	20
8514102000	For metal industrys	8	20
8514103000	For food industrys	8	20
8514109000	Other	8	20
8514201000	For laboratory	8	20
8514202000	For metal industrys	8	20
8514203000	For food industrys	8	20
8514209000	Other	8	20
8514409000	Other	8	20
8514909000	Other	8	20
8515110000	Soldering irons and guns	8	20
8515190000	Other	8	20
8515211010	Of robot type	8	20
8515211090	Other	8	20
8515212010	Of robot type	8	20
8515212090	Other	8	20
8515213010	Of robot type	8	20
8515213090	Other	8	20
8515219010	Of robots type	8	20
8515219090	Other	8	20
8515291000	Spot welders	8	20
8515292000	Seam welders	8	20

8515293000	Butt welders	8	20
8515299000	Other	8	20
8515311010	Of robot type	8	20
8515311090	Other	8	20
8515319010	Of robot type	8	20
8515319090	Other	8	20
8515391000	AC arc welding machines and apparatus	8	20
8515399000	Other	8	20
8515801000	Ultrasonic machines	8	20
8515802000	Electron beam machines	8	20
8515803000	Laser operated machines	8	20
8515809000	Other	8	20
8515901000	Of welding machines	8	20
8515909000	Other	8	20
8516210000	Storage heating radiators	8	20
8516290000	Other	8	20
8516310000	Hair dryers	8	20
8516320000	Other hair-dressing apparatus	8	20
8516330000	Hand-drying apparatus	8	20
8516400000	Electric smoothing irons	8	20
8516500000	Microwave ovens	8	20
8516601000	Electrical ovens	8	20
8516602000	Electric rice cookers(including with constant warming function)	8	20
8516609000	Other	8	20
8516710000	Coffee or tea makers	8	20
8516720000	Toasters	8	20
8516791000	Electric jar	8	20
8516799000	Other	8	20
8516800000	Electric heating resistors	8	20
8516900000	Parts	8	20
8517691100	HF (high frequency), MF (medium frequency) or LF(low frequency) receiving apparatus	8	20
8517691219	Other	8	20
8517691290	Other	8	20
8517691900	Other	8	20
8517704019	Other	8	20
8517704090	Other	8	20
8518210000	Single loudspeakers, mounted in their enclosures	8	20
8518220000	Multiple loudspeakers, mounted in the same enclosure	8	20
8518299000	Other	8	20
8518309000	Other	8	20
8518400000	Audio-frequency electric amplifiers	8	20
8518500000	Electric sound amplifier sets	8	20
8518909000	Other	8	20

8519201000	Coin- or disc-operated record-players, not incorporating a sound recording device	8	20
8519209000	Other, not incorporating a sound recording device	8	20
8519301000	With automatic record changing mechanism	8	20
8519309000	Other	8	20
8519811000	Transcribing machines, not incorporating a sound recording device	8	20
8519812100	Cassette-players, as defined in Subheading Notes 1 to Chapter 85	8	20
8519812210	For vehicles	8	20
8519812220	Of portable type, other than as defined in Subheading Notes 1 to Chapter 85	8	20
8519812290	Other	8	20
8519812310	For vehicles	8	20
8519812320	Of portable type	8	20
8519812390	Other	8	20
8519812900	Other	8	20
8519813000	Dictating machines not capable of operating without an external source of power	8	20
8519814111	For vehicles	8	20
8519814112	Of portable type	8	20
8519814119	Other	8	20
8519814190	Other	8	20
8519814210	For vehicles	8	20
8519814220	Of portable type	8	20
8519814290	Other	8	20
8519814310	Of reel type	8	20
8519814390	Other	8	20
8519815010	Of reel type	8	20
8519815020	Of disc type	8	20
8519815030	Cassette-type	8	20
8519815090	Other	8	20
8519819000	Other sound recording apparatus, whether or not incorporating a sound reproducing device	8	20
8519891010	Without loudspeaker	8	20
8519891090	Other	8	20
8519892000	Transcribing machines, not incorporating a sound recording device	8	20
8519893000	Decks, whether or not incorporating a sound reproducing device	8	20
8519899010	Other sound reproducing apparatus, not incorporating a sound recording device	8	20
8521101000	Of a width exceeding 12.7 mm	8	20
8522100000	Pick-up cartridges	8	20
8522901010	For audio recording	8	20

8522901020	For video recording	8	20
8522901090	Other	8	20
8522902000	Laser pick-up	8	20
8522909090	Other	8	20
8523210000	Cards incorporating a magnetic stripe, whether or not recording	8	20
8523292211	Those recorded video	8	20
8523292219	Other	8	20
8523292221	Those recorded video	8	20
8523292229	Other	8	20
8523292231	Those recorded video	13.0% or 34won/min (at standard speed)	20
8523292239	Other	8	20
8523292991	Those recorded video	8	20
8523292999	Other	8	20
8523402120	For reproducing sound only	8	20
8523402139	Other	8	20
8523402991	Those recorded video	8	20
8523402999	Other	8	20
8523512910	Those recorded video	8	20
8523512990	Other	8	20
8523529000	Other and parts thereof	8	20
8523592910	Those recorded video	8	20
8523592990	Other	8	20
8523802100	Gramophone records	8	20
8523802910	Those recorded video	8	20
8523802990	Other	8	20
8525501000	Radio-broadcasting apparatus	8	20
8525509000	Other	8	20
8525801010	For video tape recorder	8	20
8525801020	For monitor television	8	20
8525801090	Other	8	20
8526101000	For aircrafts	8	20
8526109000	Other	8	20
8526911010	For aircrafts	8	20
8526911090	Other	8	20
8526912010	For aircrafts	8	20
8526912090	Other	8	20
8526913010	For aircrafts	8	20
8526913020	For vehicles	8	20
8526913090	Other	8	20
8526914000	Loran receivers	8	20
8526919010	For aircrafts	8	20

8526919020	For vehicles	8	20
8526919090	Other	8	20
8526920000	Radio remote control apparatus	8	20
8527120000	Pocket-size radio cassette-players	8	20
8527131000	Of Cassette-type	8	20
8527132000	Of disc type	8	20
8527133000	Combined with Cassette-type and disc type	8	20
8527139000	Other	8	20
8527190000	Other	8	20
8527211000	Of Cassette-type	8	20
8527213000	Combined with Cassette-type and disc type	8	20
8527219000	Other	8	20
8527290000	Other	8	20
8527911010	Of Cassette-type	8	20
8527911020	Of disc type	8	20
8527911030	Combined with Cassette-type and disc type	8	20
8527911090	Other	8	20
8527919000	Other	8	20
8527920000	Not combined with sound recording or reproducing apparatus but combined with a clock	8	20
8527990000	Other	8	20
8528491010	Television monitors specially manufactured for medical purpose	8	20
8528491090	Other	8	20
8528492010	Television monitors specially manufactured for medical purpose	8	20
8528492090	Other	8	20
8528591010	Television monitors specially manufactured for medical purpose	8	20
8528591090	Other	8	20
8528592010	Television monitors specially manufactured for medical purpose	8	20
8528592090	Other	8	20
8528711010	Colour	8	20
8528711020	Black and white or other monochrome	8	20
8528712010	Supporting reception of broadcasting of which vertical resolution is more than or equal to 720lines	8	20
8528712090	Other	8	20
8528719010	Colour	8	20
8528719020	Black and white or other monochrome	8	20
8528721010	Of analog	8	20
8528721020	Of digital	8	20
8528722010	Of analog	8	20
8528722020	Of digital	8	20
8528723010	Of analog	8	20

8528723020	Of digital	8	20
8528724010	Of analog	8	20
8528724020	Of digital	8	20
8528729000	Other	8	20
8528731000	Of the length of fluorescent screen of braun tube under 37 cm in diagnal line	8	20
8528732000	Of the length of fluorescent screen of braun tube not less than 37 cm but under 45.72 cm in diagnal line	8	20
8528733000	Of the length of fluorescent screen of braun tube not less than 45.72 cm in diagnal line	8	20
8528739000	Other	8	20
8529101000	For radar apparatus	8	20
8529109100	For radio navigational aid or radio remote control apparatus	8	20
8529109210	For receiving from satellites	8	20
8529109290	Other	8	20
8529901000	Of radar apparatus	8	20
8529909100	Of radio navigational aid or radio remote control apparatus	8	20
8529909200	Of transmission apparatus for radio-broadcasting ortelevision	8	20
8529909400	Of radio-broadcast receivers	8	20
8529909500	Of television cameras	8	20
8529909610	Tuner for colour	8	20
8529909620	Tuner for black and white or monochrome	8	20
8529909630	Screen for video projector	8	20
8529909641	For plasma display panel type	8	20
8529909649	Other	8	20
8529909650	Other parts for black and white or monochrome	8	20
8529909990	Other	8	20
8530101010	For ground equipment	8	20
8530101090	Other	8	20
8530109000	Other	8	20
8530800000	Other equipment	8	20
8530900000	Parts	8	20
8531101000	Burglar alarms	8	20
8531102000	Fire alarms	8	20
8531103000	Gas alarms	8	20
8531104000	Electric bells	8	20
8531105000	Sirens	8	20
8531109000	Other sound or signalling apparatus	8	20
8531801010	Of mobile telephones for cellular networks	8	20
8531801090	Other	8	20
8535211000	Rated at less than 7.25 kV	8	20
8535212000	Rated at 7.25 kV and more but less than 75.5 kV	8	20

8535291000	Rated at less than 200 kV	8	20
8535292000	Rated at 200 kV and more	8	20
8535301000	Rated at less than 7.25 kV	8	20
8535302000	Rated at 7.25 kV and more but less than 72.5 kV	8	20
8535303000	Rated at 72.5 kV and more but less than 200 kV	8	20
8535304000	Rated at 200 kV and more	8	20
8535400000	Lightning arresters, voltage limiters and surge suppressors	8	20
8535901000	Connector	8	20
8535902000	Electrical terminal	8	20
8535909000	Other	8	20
8536109000	Other	8	20
8536200000	Automatic circuit breakers	8	20
8536300000	Other apparatus for protecting electrical circuits	8	20
8536410000	For a voltage not exceeding 60 V	8	20
8536490000	Other	8	20
8536501000	Rotary type	8	20
8536504000	Of magnet switches (including magnretic contactors)	8	20
8536610000	Lamp-holders	8	20
8536699000	Other	8	20
8536701000	Of plastics	6.5	20
8536702000	Of ceramic wares for laboratory, chemical or other technical uses	8	20
8536703090	Other	8	20
8537101000	Switch boards	8	20
8537102000	Automatic control panels	8	20
8537202000	Automatic control panels	8	20
8537209000	Other	8	20
8538100000	Boards, panels, consoles, desks, cabinets and other bases for the goods of heading 85.37, not equipped with their apparatus	8	20
8538901000	Of switches	8	20
8538902000	Of automatic circuit breakers	8	20
8538903000	Of relays	8	20
8538904000	Of automatic control panels	8	20
8539100000	Sealed beam lamp units	8	20
8539210000	Tungsten halogen	8	20
8539221000	Incandescent lamps	8	20
8539222000	Decoration lamps	8	20
8539223000	Beam lamps	8	20
8539224000	Attracting fish lamps	8	20
8539290000	Other	8	20
8539310000	Fluorescent, hot cathode	8	20
8539321000	Mercury lamps	8	20
8539322000	Sodium vapout lamps	8	20
8539323000	Metal halide lamps	8	20

8539391000	Cold cathode fluorescent lamp(CCFL)	8	20
8539399000	Other	8	20
8539410000	Arc lamps	8	20
8539491010	Of machines and mechanical appliances for making semiconductor devices	3	20
8539491090	Other	8	20
8539492000	Infra-red lamps	8	20
8539902000	Of discharge lamps	8	20
8539909000	Other	8	20
8540110000	Colour	8	20
8540120000	Black and white or other monochrome	8	20
8540201000	Television camera tubes	8	20
8540209000	Other	8	20
8540400000	Data/graphic display tubes, colour, with a phosphor dot screen pitch smaller than 0.4 mm	8	20
8540500000	Data/graphic display tubes, black and white or other monochrome	8	20
8540609000	Other	8	20
8540720000	Klystrons	8	20
8540790000	Other	8	20
8540810000	Receiver or amplifier valves and tubes	8	20
8540891000	Thermionic valves and tubes for transmitters	8	20
8540892000	Discharge tubes	8	20
8540893000	Digitron	8	20
8540899000	Other	8	20
8540911000	Deflection coils	8	20
8540912000	Electronic guns	8	20
8540913000	Shadow mask	8	20
8540919000	Other	8	20
8540990000	Other	8	20
8543100000	Particle accelerators	8	20
8543200000	Signal generators	8	20
8543300000	Machines and apparatus for electroplating, electrolysis or electrophoresis	8	20
8543701000	Electric fence energisers	8	20
8543702010	Medicated water electrolysis apparatus	8	20
8543702020	Electical beauty appliances	8	20
8543702030	Audio mixers	8	20
8543702040	Equalizers	8	20
8543702050	Ozon generator	8	20
8543702090	Other	8	20
8543709010	High frequency amplifiers	8	20
8543709020	Detectors, including optical sensor	8	20
8544111000	Insulating lacquer or enamel insulated	8	20
8544119000	Other	8	20

8544190000	Other	8	20
8544200000	Co-axial cable and other co-axial electric conductors	8	20
8544300000	Ignition wiring sets and other wiring sets of a kind used invehicles, aircraft or ships	8	20
8544421090	Other	8	20
8544422090	Other	8	20
8544491012	For a voltage exceeding 80V but not exceeding 1,000 V	8	20
8544491090	Other	8	20
8544492012	For a voltage exceeding 80 V but not exceeding 1,000 V	8	20
8544492090	Other	8	20
8544499012	For a voltage exceeding 80 V but not exceeding 1,000 V	8	20
8544499090	Other	8	20
8544601010	Plastic insulated wire	8	20
8544601090	Other	8	20
8544602010	Plastic insulated wire	8	20
8544602090	Other	8	20
8544603090	Other	8	20
8545110000	Of a kind used for furnaces	5	20
8545190000	Other	5	20
8545200000	Brushes	8	20
8545901000	Carbons rod	8	20
8545909000	Other	8	20
8546101000	Rated at not more than 1,000 V	8	20
8546102000	Rated at more than 1,000 V	8	20
8546201000	Rated at not more than 1,000 V	8	20
8546202000	Rated at more than 1,000 V but not more than 10 kV	8	20
8546203000	Rated at more than 10 kV but not more than 100 kV	8	20
8546204000	Rated at more than 100 kV but not more than 300 kV	8	20
8546205000	Rated at more than 300 kV	8	20
8546901000	Artificial plastic insulators	8	20
8546909000	Other	8	20
8547100000	Insulating fittings of ceramics	8	20
8547200000	Insulating fittings of plastics	8	20
8547900000	Other	8	20
8548101000	Of subheading 3824.90	6.5	20
8548106010	Of subheading 8107.30	3	20
8548106020	Of subheading 8111.00	3	20
8548107000	Of subheading 8506.10, 8506.30, 8506.40, 8506.50, 8506.60 or 8506.80	8	20
8548109000	Other	8	20
8548909000	Other	8	20
8601100000	Powered from an external source of electricity	5	20
8601200000	Powered by electric accumulators	5	20
8603101000	Coaches	5	20
8603102000	Vans and trucks	5	20

8603901000	Coaches	5	20
8603902000	Vans and trucks	5	20
8604001000	Workshops	5	20
8604002000	Cranes	5	20
8604003000	Testing coaches	5	20
8604004000	Track inspection vehicles	5	20
8604009000	Other	5	20
8605001010	Sleeping cars	5	20
8605001090	Other	5	20
8605002000	Luggage vans	5	20
8605003000	Travelling post office coaches	5	20
8605004000	Hospital coaches	5	20
8605009000	Other	5	20
8607110000	Driving bogies and bissel-bogies	5	20
8607120000	Other bogies and bissel-bogies	5	20
8607191000	Axles	5	20
8607192000	Wheels	5	20
8607193000	Pair of axle and wheel	5	20
8607199000	Other	5	20
8607210000	Air brakes and parts thereof	5	20
8607290000	Other	5	20
8607301000	Hooks	5	20
8607302000	Coupling device	5	20
8607303000	Buffers	5	20
8607309000	Other	5	20
8607910000	Of locomotives	5	20
8607990000	Other	5	20
8608001000	Railway or tramway track fixtures and fittings	8	20
8608002000	Mechanical signalling, safety or traffic control equipment	8	20
8608009000	Parts	8	20
8701100000	Pedestrian controlled tractors	8	20
8701202000	Used	8	20
8701901010	New	8	20
8701901020	Used	8	20
8701909900	Other	8	20
8702101010	New	10	20
8702101020	Used	10	20
8702102010	New	10	20
8702102020	Used	10	20
8702103010	New	10	20
8702103020	Used	10	20
8702901010	New	10	20
8702901020	Used	10	20
8702902010	New	10	20
8702902020	Used	10	20

8702903010	New	10	20
8702903020	Used	10	20
8703101000	For travelling on snow	8	20
8703102000	Golf cars	8	20
8703109000	Other	8	20
8703217000	New	8	20
8703218000	Used	8	20
8703227000	New	8	20
8703228000	Used	8	20
8703231010	New	8	20
8703231020	Used	8	20
8703239010	New	8	20
8703239020	Used	8	20
8703241010	New	8	20
8703241020	Used	8	20
8703249010	New	8	20
8703249020	Used	8	20
8703317000	New	8	20
8703318000	Used	8	20
8703321010	New	8	20
8703321020	Used	8	20
8703329010	New	8	20
8703329020	Used	8	20
8703337000	New	8	20
8703338000	Used	8	20
8703907000	Electric vehicle	8	20
8703909000	Other	8	20
8704211010	New	10	20
8704211020	Used	10	20
8704219010	Freezer and refrigerator vehicles	10	20
8704219020	Tank lorries	10	20
8704219090	Other	10	20
8704221011	New	10	20
8704221012	Used	10	20
8704221091	New	10	20
8704221092	Used	10	20
8704229010	Freezer and refrigerator vehicles	10	20
8704229020	Tank lorries	10	20
8704229090	Other	10	20
8704231010	New	10	20
8704231020	Used	10	20
8704239010	Freezer and refrigerator vehicles	10	20
8704239020	Tank lorries	10	20
8704239090	Other	10	20
8704311010	New	10	20

8704311020	Used	10	20
8704319010	Freezer and refrigerator vehicles	10	20
8704319020	Tank lorries	10	20
8704319090	Other	10	20
8704321010	New	10	20
8704321020	Used	10	20
8704329010	Freezer and refrigerator vehicles	10	20
8704329020	Tank lorries	10	20
8704329090	Other	10	20
8704901010	New	10	20
8704901020	Used	10	20
8704909010	Freezer and refrigerator vehicles	10	20
8704909020	Tank lorries	10	20
8704909090	Other	10	20
8705101000	Of telescopic boom type	8	20
8705102000	Of latticed boom type	8	20
8705109000	Other	8	20
8705200000	Mobile drilling derricks	8	20
8705300000	Fire fighting vehicles	8	20
8705400000	Concrete-mixer lorries	8	20
8705901010	Agicultural spraying lorries	8	20
8705901090	Other	8	20
8705909010	Breakdown lorries	8	20
8705909020	Road sweeper lorries	8	20
8705909030	Mobile workshops	8	20
8705909040	Mobile broadcast vans	8	20
8705909050	Mobile clinics	8	20
8705909060	Telegraphy, radiotelegraphy and radiotelephony transmitting and receiving vans and radar vehicles	8	20
8705909070	Snow-ploughs and snow-blowers	8	20
8705909090	Other	8	20
8706001010	Of those specified in subheading 8701.20 or 8701.90.10	8	20
8706001090	Other	8	20
8706002000	For the motor vehicles falling within heading 87.02	8	20
8706003000	For the motor vehicles falling within heading 87.03	8	20
8706004000	For the motor vehicles falling within heading 87.04	8	20
8706005000	For the motor vehicles falling within heading 87.05	8	20
8707100000	For the vehicles of heading 87.03	8	20
8707901010	Of those specified in subheading 8701.20 or 8701.90.10	8	20
8707901090	Other	8	20
8707902000	For the motor vehicles falling within heading 87.02	8	20
8707903000	For the motor vehicles falling within heading 87.04	8	20
8707904000	For the motor vehicles falling within heading 87.05	8	20
8708100000	Bumpers and parts thereof	8	20
8708210000	Safety seat belts	8	20

8708290000	Other	8	20
8708301000	Mounted brake linings	8	20
8708302000	Brake boosers	8	20
8708303000	Electronic control brakes	8	20
8708309000	Other	8	20
8708400000	Gear boxes and parts thereof	8	20
8708501000	Drive-axles with differential, whether or not provided with other transmission components and parts thereof	8	20
8708502000	Non-driving axles and parts thereof	8	20
8708700000	Road wheels and parts and accessories thereof	8	20
8708800000	Suspension systems and parts thereof (including shock-absorbers)	8	20
8708920000	Silencers (mufflers) and exhaust pipes; parts thereof	8	20
8708930000	Clutches and parts thereof	8	20
8708940000	Steering wheels, steering columns and steering boxes; parts thereof	8	20
8708951000	Air bags	8	20
8708959000	Other	8	20
8708991010	For the motor vehicles falling within heading 87.01	8	20
8708991020	For the motor vehicles falling within heading 87.02	8	20
8708991030	For the motor vehicles falling within heading 87.03	8	20
8708991040	For the motor vehicles falling within heading 87.04	8	20
8708991050	For the motor vehicles falling within heading 87.05	8	20
8708999000	Other	8	20
8709110000	Electrical	8	20
8709190000	Other	8	20
8709900000	Parts	8	20
8711101000	Motor cycles	8	20
8711102000	Mopeds	8	20
8711103000	Side-cars	8	20
8711109000	Other	8	20
8711201000	Motor cycles	8	20
8711202000	Side-cars	8	20
8711209000	Other	8	20
8711301000	Motor cycles	8	20
8711302000	Side-cars	8	20
8711309000	Other	8	20
8711401000	Motor cycles	8	20
8711402000	Side-cars	8	20
8711409000	Other	8	20
8711501000	Motor cycles	8	20
8711502000	Side-cars	8	20
8711509000	Other	8	20
8711901000	Motor cycles	8	20
8711902000	Side-cars	8	20

8711909000	Other	8	20
8712001000	Racing bicycles	8	20
8712009010	For transportation of goods	8	20
8712009020	Tricycles	8	20
8712009090	Other	8	20
8714110000	Saddles	8	20
8714190000	Other	8	20
8714911000	Frames	8	20
8714912000	Forks	8	20
8714919000	Other parts	8	20
8714921000	Wheel Rims	8	20
8714922000	Spokes	8	20
8714931000	Hubs, other than coaster braking hubs and hub brakes	8	20
8714932000	Free-wheel sprocket-wheels	8	20
8714941000	Coaster braking hubs and hub brakes	8	20
8714942000	Other brakes	8	20
8714949000	Parts thereof	8	20
8714950000	Saddles	8	20
8714961000	Pedals	8	20
8714962000	Crankgear	8	20
8714969000	Parts thereof	8	20
8714990000	Other	8	20
8715000000	Baby carriages and parts thereof.	8	20
8716100000	Trailers and semi-trailers of the caravan type, for housing or camping	8	20
8716200000	Self-loading or self-unloading trailers and semi-trailers for agricultural purposes	8	20
8716310000	Tanker trailers and tanker semi-trailers	8	20
8716390000	Other	8	20
8716400000	Other trailers and semi-trailers	8	20
8716801000	Hand-carts	8	20
8716802000	Carts drawn by ox or horse	8	20
8716803000	Sledges	8	20
8716901000	Of trailers and semi-trailers	8	20
8716909000	Other	8	20
8801009010	Balloons and dirigibles	8	20
8805101090	Other	5	20
8805102090	Other	5	20
8805109090	Other	5	20
8805211090	Other	5	20
8805212090	Other	5	20
8805291090	Other	5	20
8805292090	Other	5	20
8903910000	Sailboats, with or without auxiliary motor	8	20
8903920000	Motorboats, other than outboard motorboats	8	20

8903991000	Outboard motorboats	8	20
8903999000	Other	8	20
8904001000	Tugs	5	20
8904002000	Pusher craft	5	20
8904009000	Other	5	20
8905100000	Dredgers	5	20
8905201000	Drilling ships platforms	5	20
8905202000	Production plat forms	5	20
8905209000	Other	5	20
8905901000	Light-vessels	5	20
8905902000	Fire-floats	5	20
8905903000	Floating cranes	5	20
8905904000	Generating vessels	5	20
8905905000	Salvage ships	5	20
8905906000	Work-shop vessels	5	20
8905907000	Drilling ships	5	20
8905908000	Floating docks	5	20
8905909000	Other	5	20
8907100000	Inflatable rafts	5	20
8907901000	Rafts (other than subheading 8907.10)	5	20
8907902000	Tanks	5	20
8907903000	Coffer-dams	5	20
8907904000	Landing-stages	5	20
8907905000	Buoys	5	20
8907906000	Beacons	5	20
9001101000	Optical fibres	8	20
9001102000	Optical fibre bundles	8	20
9001103000	Optical fibre cables	8	20
9001200000	Sheets and plates of polarising material	8	20
9001300000	Contact lenses	8	20
9001409000	Other	8	20
9001501000	For correcting visions	8	20
9001509000	Other	8	20
9001901000	Prisms	8	20
9001903000	Other lenses	8	20
9001909000	Other	8	20
9002111000	For photographic cameras.	8	20
9002119010	For movie cameras and VTR(video tape recorder) cameras	8	20
9002119020	For projectors	8	20
9002191000	For microscopes	8	20
9002192000	For astronomical telescopes	8	20
9002201000	For photographic cameras	8	20
9002209000	Other	8	20
9002901000	For photographic cameras	8	20
9002909010	Of machines and mechanical appliances for making	3	20

	semiconductor devices		
9002909090	Other	8	20
9003110000	Of plastics	8	20
9003191000	Made of or combined with precious metals	8	20
9003199000	Other	8	20
9003900000	Parts	8	20
9004101000	Made of or combined with precious metals	8	20
9004109000	Other	8	20
9004901010	Made of, or combined with, precious metals	8	20
9004909010	Made of, or combined with, precious metals	8	20
9005100000	Binoculars	8	20
9005801000	Monoculars	8	20
9005802010	Reflecting telescopes	8	20
9005802020	Astronomical refracting telescopes	8	20
9005802030	Transit instruments, equatorial or zenith telescopes and altazimuths	8	20
9005802090	Other	8	20
9005809000	Other	8	20
9005900000	Parts and accessories (including mountings)	8	20
9006100000	Cameras of a kind used for preparing printing plates or cylinders	8	20
9006301000	For subaqueous photography	8	20
9006302000	Air survey cameras	8	20
9006303000	For medical or surgical examination of internal organs	8	20
9006304000	Comparision cameras for forensic and criminological purposes	8	20
9006401000	Instant polaroid cameras	8	20
9006402000	Instant sticker cameras	8	20
9006409000	Others	8	20
9006511000	Photographic cameras for special use	8	20
9006519000	Other	8	20
9006521000	Photographic cameras for special use	8	20
9006529010	Cameras of a kind used for recording documents on microfilm, microfiche or other microforms	8	20
9006529090	Other	8	20
9006531000	Photographic cameras for special use	8	20
9006539010	Single use/disposable cameras	8	20
9006539020	Cameras of a kind used for recording documents on microfilm, microfiche or other microforms	8	20
9006539090	Other	8	20
9006591000	Photographic cameras for special use	8	20
9006599010	Cameras of a kind used for recording documents on microfilm, microfiche or other microforms	8	20
9006599090	Other	8	20
9006610000	Discharge lamp("electronic") flashlight apparatus	8	20

9006691000	Flashbulbs, flashcubes and the like	8	20
9006699000	Other	8	20
9006910000	For cameras	8	20
9006990000	Other	8	20
9007110000	For film of less than 16 mm width or for double-8 mm film	8	20
9007191000	For film of less 30 mm width	8	20
9007199000	Other	8	20
9007201000	For film of less than 16 mm width	8	20
9007209010	For film of less than 20 mm width	8	20
9007209020	For film of not less than 20 mm width	8	20
9007910000	For cameras	8	20
9007920000	For projectors	8	20
9008100000	Slide projectors	8	20
9008200000	Microfilm, microfiche or other microform readers, whether or not capable of producing copies	8	20
9008300000	Other image projectors	8	20
9008401000	For the preparation of printing plates	8	20
9008402000	For microfilm	8	20
9008409000	Other	8	20
9008900000	Parts and accessories	8	20
9010101000	For photo-engraving	8	20
9010102000	For microfilm	8	20
9010109090	Other	8	20
9010509000	Other	8	20
9010600000	Projection screens	8	20
9010909000	Other	8	20
9011109000	Other	8	20
9011201090	Other	8	20
9011209000	Other	8	20
9011801000	Polarising microscopes	8	20
9011802000	Metallurgical microscopes	8	20
9011803000	Phase contrast and interference microscopes	8	20
9011804000	Biological microscopes	8	20
9011805000	Comparison microsecopes	8	20
9011809000	Other	8	20
9011909000	Other	8	20
9012101090	Other	8	20
9012102000	Diffraction apparatus	8	20
9012909000	Other	8	20
9013100000	Telescopic sights for fitting to arms; periscopes; telescopes designed to form parts of machines, appliances, instruments or apparatus of this Chapter or Section XVI	8	20
9013200000	Lasers, other than laser diodes	8	20
9013801110	For opto-elecrionic watchs	8	20
9013801130	For televisions	8	20

9013801140	For monitor	8	20
9013801190	Other	8	20
9013801910	For opto-elecrionic watchs	8	20
9013801930	For televisions	8	20
9013801990	Other	8	20
9013802000	Magnifiers, loupes, thread counters	8	20
9013803000	Door viewers (door eyes)	8	20
9013909000	Other	8	20
9014101010	For aircrafts	8	20
9014101090	Other	8	20
9014102010	For aircrafts	8	20
9014102090	Other	8	20
9014109000	Other	8	20
9014200000	Instruments and appliances for aeronautical or space navigation (other then compasses)	8	20
9014901000	For aircrafts	8	20
9014909000	Other	8	20
9015100000	Rangefinders	8	20
9015200000	Theodolites and tachymeters (tacheometers)	8	20
9015300000	Levels	8	20
9015400000	Photogrammetrical surveying instruments and appliances	8	20
9015801000	For use in the field.	8	20
9015802000	For hydrographic use	8	20
9015803000	For oceanographic use	8	20
9015804000	For hydrological use	8	20
9015805000	For meteorological use	8	20
9015809000	Other	8	20
9015900000	Parts and accessories	8	20
9016001000	Direct reading balances	8	20
9016002000	Electronic balances	8	20
9016008000	Other	8	20
9016009000	Parts or accessories	8	20
9017109000	Other	8	20
9017201090	Other	8	20
9017202090	Other	8	20
9017203000	Mathematical calculating instruments	8	20
9017209000	Other	8	20
9017301000	Micrometers	8	20
9017302000	Dialgauges	8	20
9017303000	Vernier callipers	8	20
9017309000	Other	8	20
9017801000	Divided scales, measuring rod and tapes	8	20
9017809090	Other	8	20
9017909090	Other	8	20
9018119000	Parts and accessories	8	20

9018191000	Electro-encephalographs	8	20
9018192000	Audiometers and similar apparatus	8	20
9018197000	Patient monitoring system	8	20
9018198000	Other	8	20
9018201000	Ultra-violet or infra-red ray apparatus	8	20
9018209000	Parts and accessories	8	20
9018310000	Syringes, with or without needles	8	20
9018321000	Needles for injections	8	20
9018322000	Needles for sutures	8	20
9018329000	Other	8	20
9018419000	Parts and accessories	8	20
9018492000	Dental units	8	20
9018499000	Parts and accessories	8	20
9018501000	Ophthalmic instruments and appliances	8	20
9018901000	Pregnancy diagnostic apparatus	8	20
9018909020	Gynaecological or obstetrical instruments	8	20
9018909040	Artificial kidney apparatus	8	20
9018909050	Dialyzers for artificial kidney apparatus	8	20
9018909060	Veterinary instrument and appliances	8	20
9020001000	Gas masks	8	20
9020008000	Other breathing appliances	8	20
9022130000	Other, for dental uses	8	20
9022141020	Angiography units	8	20
9022141090	Other	8	20
9022142000	For verterinary use	8	20
9022191000	For physical or chemical testing	8	20
9022192000	For industrial use	8	20
9022199000	Other	8	20
9022211010	Gamma cameras	8	20
9022211020	Linear accelerators	8	20
9022211030	Cobalt 60 therapy units	8	20
9022211090	Other	8	20
9022212000	For verterinary use	8	20
9022291000	For physical or chemical testing	8	20
9022292000	For industrial use	8	20
9022299000	Other	8	20
9022300000	X-ray tubes	8	20
9022901010	X-ray generators	8	20
9022901030	X-ray high tension generators	8	20
9022901090	Other	8	20
9023001000	Models of human or animal anatomies	8	20
9023009000	Other	8	20
9024101000	Hardness testing machines	8	20
9024102000	Tensile testing machines	8	20
9024103000	Compression testing machines	8	20

9024104000	Fatigue testing machines	8	20
9024105000	Universal type testing machines	8	20
9024106000	Machines and appliances for testing adhesive strength or shear force of ball or wire of printed circuits board, semiconductor device and electronic integrated circuit	8	20
9024109000	Other	8	20
9024801010	Testing machines to detect changes in the dimensions of textile	8	20
9024801020	Abrasion testing machines	8	20
9024801090	Other	8	20
9024809010	Elasticity meters	8	20
9024809020	Plastimeters	8	20
9024809090	Other	8	20
9024901000	Sensor (devices sensing a specific quantity of change, whether or not combined with equipment which convert measured signal into electrical signal)	8	20
9024909000	Other	8	20
9025119000	Other	8	20
9025192010	Optical pyrometers	8	20
9025801000	Hydrometers and similar floating instruments	8	20
9025802010	Mercury barometer	8	20
9025802090	Other	8	20
9025803010	Psychrometers	8	20
9025803020	Hair hygrometers	8	20
9025803090	Other	8	20
9025809000	Other	8	20
9025901900	Other sensor	8	20
9025909000	Other	8	20
9027100000	Gas or smoke analysis apparatus	8	20
9027802050	Exposure meters	8	20
9027901000	Microtomes	8	20
9027909110	Gas sensor	8	20
9027909122	Of smoke	8	20
9027909991	For gas or smoke analysis apparatus and microtomes	8	20
9028101010	Of digital type	8	20
9028101090	Other	8	20
9028102000	Calibrating meters	8	20
9028201010	Of digital type	8	20
9028201090	Other	8	20
9028202000	Calibrating meters	8	20
9028301010	Not less than 50 A	8	20
9028301020	Less than 50 A	8	20
9028302000	Calibrating meters	8	20
9028900000	Parts and accessories	8	20
9029101000	Revolution counters	8	20

9029102000	Production counters	8	20
9029103000	Taximeters	8	20
9029104000	Mileometers	8	20
9029105000	Counters for indicating the working hours of machines	8	20
9029109000	Other	8	20
9029201010	Chronometric system	8	20
9029201090	Other	8	20
9029202000	Stroboscopes	8	20
9029901200	Rotation sensor	8	20
9029901900	Other sensor	8	20
9029909000	Other	8	20
9030201090	Other	8	20
9030202010	Of cathode-ray	8	20
9030202090	Other	8	20
9030320000	Multimeters with a recording device	8	20
9030331000	Voltmeters	8	20
9030332000	Ammeters	8	20
9030333000	Circuit testers	8	20
9030334000	Registance meters	8	20
9030335000	Galvanometer	8	20
9030336000	Frequency measuring apparatus	8	20
9030339000	Other	8	20
9030391000	Voltmeters	8	20
9030392000	Ammeters	8	20
9030393000	Circuit testers	8	20
9030394000	Registance meters	8	20
9030395000	Galvanometer	8	20
9030840000	Other, with a recording device	8	20
9030901100	Electromagnetic sensor	8	20
9030901200	Radiation ray sensor	8	20
9030901900	Other sensor	8	20
9030909090	Other	8	20
9031100000	Machines for balancing mechanical parts	8	20
9031200000	Test benches	8	20
9031491000	Optical surface testers	8	20
9031492000	Optical goniometers or angle gauges	8	20
9031493000	Focimeters	8	20
9031494090	Other	8	20
9031499090	Other	8	20
9031801000	Ultrasonic fish finders	8	20
9031802000	Load-cells	8	20
9031809010	Equipment for testing the characteristics of internal combustion engines	8	20
9031809020	Gear testing machines	8	20
9031809030	Planimeters	8	20

9031809040	Spherometers	8	20
9031809050	Apparatus for checking textile materials	8	20
9031809060	Ultra-sonic thickness measuring instruments	8	20
9031809070	Instruments for detecting faults cracks or other defects	8	20
9031809080	Dynamometers	8	20
9031809099	Other	8	20
9031901190	Other	8	20
9031901299	Other	8	20
9031909090	Other	8	20
9032101010	For refrigerators	8	20
9032101020	For aircraft	5	20
9032101090	Other	8	20
9032102000	Of fixed type	8	20
9032200000	Manostats	8	20
9032811010	For aircraft	5	20
9032811090	Other	8	20
9032812010	For aircraft	5	20
9032812091	Of machines and mechanical appliances for making semiconductor devices	3	20
9032812099	Other	8	20
9032819010	For aircraft	5	20
9032819090	Other	8	20
9032891010	For aircraft	5	20
9032891090	Other	8	20
9032892010	For aircraft	5	20
9032892090	Other	8	20
9032893010	For aircraft	5	20
9032893090	Other	8	20
9032899010	For aircraft	5	20
9032899090	Other	8	20
9032901000	For aircraft	5	20
9033000000	Parts and accessories (not specified or included elsewhere in this Chapter) for machines, appliances, instruments or apparatus of Chapter 90.	8	20
9101110000	With mechanical display only	8	20
9101191000	With opto-electronic display only	8	20
9101199000	Other	8	20
9101210000	With automatic winding	8	20
9101290000	Other	8	20
9101910000	Electrically operated	8	20
9101990000	Other	8	20
9102111000	For the blind	8	20
9102112000	With dials bands or similar of precious metal or of metal clad with precious metal	8	20
9102119010	Battery or accumulator operated	8	20

9102119090	Other	8	20
9102121000	Battery or accumulator operated	8	20
9102129010	For the blind	8	20
9102129020	With dials bands or similar of precious metal or of metal clad with precious metal	8	20
9102129090	Other	8	20
9102191000	Battery or accumulator operated	8	20
9102199010	For the blind	8	20
9102199020	With dials bands or similar of precious metal or of metal clad with precious metal	8	20
9102199090	Other	8	20
9102211000	For the blind	8	20
9102212000	With dials bands or similar of precious metal or of metal clad with precious metal	8	20
9102219000	Other	8	20
9102291000	For the blind	8	20
9102292000	With dials bands or similar of precious metal or of metal clad with precious metal.	8	20
9102299000	Other	8	20
9102911000	Stop-watches	8	20
9102912000	For the blind	8	20
9102919010	Battery or accumulator powered	8	20
9102919090	Other	8	20
9102991000	Stop-watches	8	20
9102992000	For the blind	8	20
9102999000	Other	8	20
9103101000	Travel clocks	8	20
9103109000	Other	8	20
9103901000	Travel clocks	8	20
9103909000	Other	8	20
9104001000	For vehicles	8	20
9104002000	For aircraft	8	20
9104004000	For vessels	8	20
9104009000	Other	8	20
9105110000	Electrically operated	8	20
9105190000	Other	8	20
9105210000	Electrically operated	8	20
9105290000	Other	8	20
9105910000	Electrically operated	8	20
9105990000	Other	8	20
9106100000	Time-registers; time-recorders	8	20
9106901000	Watchmen's telltales	8	20
9106902000	Timers	8	20
9106903000	Parking meters	8	20
9106909000	Other	8	20

9107001000	With synchronous motor	8	20
9107009000	Other	8	20
9108110000	With mechanical display only or with a device to which a mechanical display can be incorporated	5	20
9108120000	With opto-electronic display only	5	20
9108190000	Other	5	20
9108200000	With automatic winding	5	20
9108900000	Other	5	20
9109110000	Of alarm clocks	8	20
9109190000	Other	8	20
9109900000	Other	8	20
9110111000	Battery or accumulator powered	8	20
9110112000	With automatic winding	8	20
9110119000	Other	8	20
9110121000	Battery or accumulator powered.	8	20
9110122000	With automatic winding	8	20
9110129000	Other	8	20
9110191000	Battery or accumulator powered	8	20
9110192000	With automatic winding	8	20
9110199000	Other	8	20
9110901000	Battery or accumulator powered	8	20
9110909000	Other	8	20
9111100000	Cases of precious metal or of metal clad with precious metal	8	20
9111200000	Cases of base metal, whether or not gold-or silver-plated	8	20
9111800000	Other cases	8	20
9111901000	Of precious metal or metal clad with precious metal	8	20
9111909000	Other	8	20
9112200000	Cases	8	20
9112900000	Parts	8	20
9113100000	Of precious metal or of metal clad with precious metal	8	20
9113200000	Of base metal, whether or not gold-or silver-plated	8	20
9113901000	Of plastics	8	20
9113902000	Of leather or composition leather	8	20
9113909000	Other	8	20
9114100000	Springs, including hair-springs	8	20
9114200000	Jewels	8	20
9114300000	Dials	8	20
9114400000	Plates and bridges	8	20
9201101000	Of automatic	8	20
9201109000	Other	8	20
9201200000	Grand pianos	8	20
9201901000	Harpsichords	8	20
9201909000	Other	8	20
9202101000	Violins	8	20

9202102000	Violoncellos	8	20
9202109000	Other	8	20
9202902000	Harps	8	20
9202903000	Mandolines	8	20
9202904000	Banjo	8	20
9202909000	Other	8	20
9205101000	Trumpets	8	20
9205102000	Trombones	8	20
9205109000	Other	8	20
9205901010	Flutes	8	20
9205901020	Clarinets	8	20
9205901030	Saxophones	8	20
9205901040	Recoder	8	20
9205901090	Other	8	20
9205902010	Pipe organs	8	20
9205902020	Reed organs	8	20
9205902090	Other	8	20
9205903010	Accordions	8	20
9205903020	Melodicas	8	20
9205903090	Other	8	20
9205904000	Mouth organs	8	20
9205909000	Other	8	20
9206001000	Drums	8	20
9206002000	Xylophones	8	20
9206003000	Cymbals	8	20
9206004000	Castanets	8	20
9206005000	Maracas	8	20
9206006000	Tambourine	8	20
9206009000	Other	8	20
9207101000	Organs (including synthesizers)	8	20
9207103000	Pianos	8	20
9207109000	Other	8	20
9207901000	Guitars	8	20
9207902000	Accordions	8	20
9207903000	Rythm box	8	20
9207909000	Other	8	20
9208100000	Musical boxes	8	20
9208901000	Fair ground organs	8	20
9208902000	Mechanical street organs	8	20
9208903000	Mechanical singing birds	8	20
9208904000	Musical saws	8	20
9208909000	Other	8	20
9209301000	Of metal wire	8	20
9209309000	Other	8	20
9209920000	Parts and accessories for the musical instruments of	8	20

	heading 92.02		
9209940000	Parts and accessories for the musical instruments of heading 92.07	8	20
9209991000	For musical movements	8	20
9209992000	Metronomes, tuning forks and pitch pipes of all kinds	8	20
9209993000	Mechanisms for musical boxes	8	20
9303100000	Muzzle-loading firearms	8	20
9303201011	Pump-action	8	20
9303201012	Semi-automatic	8	20
9303201019	Other	8	20
9303201020	Shotguns, multiple barrel, including combination guns	8	20
9303201090	Other	8	20
9303209011	Pump-action	8	20
9303209012	Semi-automatic	8	20
9303209019	Other	8	20
9303209020	Shotguns, multiple barrel, including combination guns	8	20
9303209090	Other	8	20
9303301010	Single-shot	8	20
9303301020	Semi-automatic	8	20
9303301090	Other	8	20
9303309010	Single-shot	8	20
9303309020	Semi-automatic	8	20
9303309090	Other	8	20
9303900000	Other	8	20
9304001000	Air guns	8	20
9304009000	Other	8	20
9305109010	Firing mechanisms	8	20
9305109020	Frames and receivers	8	20
9305109030	Barrels	8	20
9305109040	Pistons, locking lugs and gas buffers	8	20
9305109050	Magazines and parts thereof	8	20
9305109060	Silencers (sound moderators) and parts thereof	8	20
9305109070	Butts, grips and plates	8	20
9305109080	Slides(for pistols) and cylinders (for revolvers)	8	20
9305109090	Other	8	20
9305210000	Shotgun barrels	8	20
9305291000	Firing mechanisms	8	20
9305292000	Frames and receivers	8	20
9305293000	Rifle barrels	8	20
9305294000	Pistons, locking lugs and gas buffers	8	20
9305295000	Magazines and parts thereof	8	20
9305296000	Silencers (sound moderators) and parts thereof	8	20
9305297000	Flash eliminators and parts thereof	8	20
9305298000	Breeches, bolts (gunlocks) and bolt carriers	8	20
9305299000	Other	8	20

9305990000	Other	8	20
9401200000	Seats of a kind used for motor vehicles	8	20
9401901000	Of wooden	8	20
9401902000	Of metal	8	20
9403401000	Dinner tables	8	20
9403409000	Other	8	20
9403900000	Parts	8	20
9404210000	Of cellular rubber or plastics, whether or not covered	8	20
9404300000	Sleeping bags	8	20
9405101000	Of filament lamps	8	20
9405102000	Of fluorescent lamps	8	20
9405201000	Of filament lamps	8	20
9405209000	Other	8	20
9405301000	Of filament lamps	8	20
9405309000	Other	8	20
9405401000	Of anti-explosive type	8	20
9405402000	Of flood type	8	20
9405403000	Of street type	8	20
9405409000	Other	8	20
9405500000	Non-electrical lamps and lighting fittings	8	20
9405601000	Of neon tubes	8	20
9405602000	Of filament lamps	8	20
9405603000	Of fluorescent lamps	8	20
9405609000	Other	8	20
9405911000	Of chandeliers	8	20
9405919000	Other	8	20
9405921000	Of chandeliers	8	20
9405929000	Other	8	20
9405991000	Of chandeliers	8	20
9405999000	Other	8	20
9406009010	Of plastic	8	20
9406009020	Of iron or steel	8	20
9406009030	Of aluminium	8	20
9406009090	Other	8	20
9503002110	Of textiles	8	20
9503002130	Of plastics	8	20
9503002190	Other	8	20
9503002910	Garments and accessories therefor, footwear and headgear	8	20
9503003411	Of textile materials	8	20
9503003419	Other	8	20
9503003491	Of textile material	8	20
9503003493	Of plastics	8	20
9503003494	Of metal	8	20
9503003499	Other	8	20
9503003500	Toy musical instruments and apparatus	8	20

9503003700	Other toys, put up in sets or outfits	8	20
9503003800	Other toys and models, incorporating a motor	8	20
9503003911	Balloons, toy balls, kites and the like	8	20
9503003919	Other	8	20
9505100000	Articles for Christmas festivities	8	20
9505900000	Other	8	20
9506110000	Skis	8	20
9506120000	Ski-fastenings (ski-bindings)	8	20
9506190000	Other	8	20
9506210000	Sailboards	8	20
9506290000	Other	8	20
9506310000	Clubs, complete	8	20
9506320000	Balls	8	20
9506399000	Other	8	20
9506401000	Table-tennis tables	8	20
9506402000	Table-tennis rackets	8	20
9506403000	Table-tennis balls	8	20
9506409000	Other	8	20
9506510000	Lawn-tennis rackets, whether or not strung	8	20
9506591000	Badminton rackets	8	20
9506599000	Other	8	20
9506610000	Lawn-tennis balls	8	20
9506621000	Soccer balls	8	20
9506622000	Basket balls	8	20
9506623000	Volley balls	8	20
9506624000	Hand balls	8	20
9506625000	American footballs	8	20
9506629000	Other	8	20
9506691000	Badminton shuttlecock	8	20
9506692000	Baseballs	8	20
9506699000	Other	8	20
9506700000	Ice skates and roller skates, including skating boots with skates attached	8	20
9506910000	Articles and equipment for general physical exercise, gymnastics or athletics	8	20
9506990000	Other	8	20
9507101000	Of glass fibre	8	20
9507109000	Other	8	20
9507200000	Fish-hooks, whether or not snelled	8	20
9507901000	Fish landing nets and other fishing tackles	8	20
9507909000	Other	8	20
9508100000	Travelling circuses and travelling menageries	8	20
9508900000	Other	8	20
9601100000	Worked ivory and articles of ivory	8	20
9601901090	Other	8	20

9601902000	Of horn	8	20
9601903000	Of bone	8	20
9601904000	Of coral	8	20
9601909090	Other	8	20
9602001000	Gelatin capsules	8	20
9602009010	Worked vegetable carving material (for example, corozo) and articles of vegetable carving material	8	20
9602009020	Worked jet (and mineral substitutes for jet), amber, meerschaum agglomerated amber and agglomerated meerschaum, and articles of those substances	8	20
9602009090	Other	8	20
9603100000	Brooms and brushes, consisting of twigs or other vegetable materials bound together, with or without handles	8	20
9603210000	Tooth brushes, including dental-plate brushes	8	20
9603290000	Other	8	20
9603300000	Artists' brushes, writing brushes and similar brushes for the application of cosmetics	8	20
9603400000	Paint, distemper, varnish or similar brushes (other than brushes of subheading 9603.30); paint pads and rollers	8	20
9603500000	Other brushes constituting parts of machines, appliances or vehicles	8	20
9603900000	Other	8	20
9604000000	Hand sieves and hand riddles.	8	20
9605000000	Travel sets for personal toilet, sewing or shoe or clothes cleaning.	8	20
9606100000	Press-fasteners, snap-fasteners and press-studs and parts therefor	8	20
9606210000	Of plastics, not covered with textile material	8	20
9606220000	Of base metal, not covered with textile material	8	20
9606291000	Of shell-fish shell	8	20
9606299000	Other	8	20
9606300000	Button moulds and other parts of buttons; button blanks	8	20
9607110000	Fitted with chain scoops of base metal	8	20
9607191000	Of plastic	8	20
9607199000	Other	8	20
9607201000	Of base metal	8	20
9607209000	Other	8	20
9608100000	Ball point pens	8	20
9608200000	Felt tipped and other porous-tipped pens and markers	8	20
9608310000	Indian ink drawing pens	8	20
9608391000	Fountainpens	8	20
9608399000	Other	8	20
9608401000	Propelling Pencils	8	20
9608402010	Of mechanical type	8	20

9608402090	Other	8	20
9608500000	Sets of articles from two or more of the foregoing subheadings	8	20
9608600000	Refills for ball point pens, comprising the ball point and ink-reservoir	8	20
9608911000	Pen nibs	8	20
9608912000	Nib points	8	20
9608991000	Parts	8	20
9608999000	Other	8	20
9609101000	Pencils	8	20
9609103000	Crayons	8	20
9609200000	Pencil leads, black or coloured	8	20
9609902000	Pastels	8	20
9609903010	For writing	8	20
9609903090	Other	8	20
9609909000	Other	8	20
9610001000	Slates	8	20
9610002000	Black boards	8	20
9610009000	Other	8	20
9611001000	Stamps	8	20
9611002000	Hand printing sets	8	20
9611009000	Other	8	20
9612101000	For typewriter	8	20
9612102000	For EDPS machines	8	20
9612109000	Other	8	20
9612200000	Ink-pads	8	20
9613100000	Pocket lighters, gas fuelled, non-refillable	8	20
9613200000	Pocket lighters, gas fuelled, refillable	8	20
9613800000	Other lighters	8	20
9613901000	Piezo-electric ignition units	8	20
9613909000	Other	8	20
9614001000	Pipes and pipe bowls	8	20
9614009000	Other	8	20
9615111000	Combs	8	20
9615119000	Other	8	20
9615191000	Combs	8	20
9615199000	Other	8	20
9615901000	Hair-pins	8	20
9615909000	Other	8	20
9616100000	Scent sprays and similar toilet sprays, and mounts and heads therefor	8	20
9616200000	Powder-puffs and pads for the application of cosmetics or toilet preparations	8	20
9617001000	Vacuum flasks	8	20
9617002000	Vacuum lunch-boxes	8	20

9617008000	Other	8	20
9617009000	Parts	8	20
9618001000	Tailors' dummies	8	20
9618002000	Automata	8	20
9618009000	Other	8	20
8419909020	Of making hot drinks or for cooking or heating food machinery and equipment	8	20
8419909030	Of air-conditioning machinery, plant and equipment	8	20
8419909090	Other	8	20
8420101000	For paper making	8	20
8420102000	For textile fabrics	8	20
8420103000	For leather	8	20
8420104000	For rubber or plastic	8	20
8420109000	Other	8	20
8420910000	Cylinders	8	20
8420990000	Other	8	20
8421110000	Cream separators	8	20
8421120000	Clothes-dryers	8	20
8421192000	For food industry use	8	20
8421193000	For petro-chemical industry use	8	20
8421211000	Of the household type	8	20
8421219010	Filtering or purifying machinery and apparatus to be used with swimming pools	8	20
8421219020	Filtering or purifying machinery and apparatus for making semiconductor devices	3	20
8421220000	For filtering or purifying beverages other than water	8	20
8421231000	For internal combustion engines for vehicles of Chapter 87	8	20
8421232000	For aircrafts	8	20
8421239000	Other	8	20
8421291000	For dairy industry	8	20
8421292000	For the treatment of harmful waste water	8	20
8421294000	For aircrafts	8	20
8421299000	Other	8	20
8421311000	For internal combustion engines for vehicles of Chapter 87	8	20
8421312000	For aircrafts	8	20
8421319000	Other	8	20
8421391000	For the household type	8	20
8421392000	For purifying exhaust gas for vehicles of Chapter 87	8	20
8421399010	For the treatment of harmful exhaust gas	8	20
8421399030	For aircrafts	8	20
8421399090	Other	8	20
8421910000	Of centrifuges, including centrifugal dryers	8	20
8421991000	For purifying exhaust gas for vehicles of Chapter 87	8	20
8421999010	Of filtering or purifying machinery and apparatus, for internal combustion	8	20

8421999020	Filter for purifing machinery	8	20
8421999090	Other	8	20
8422110000	Of the household type	8	20
8422190000	Other	8	20
8422200000	Machinery for cleaning or drying bottles or other containers	8	20
8422301000	Machinery for filling bottles or other containers	8	20
8422302000	Machinery for closing or sealing bottles or other containers	8	20
8422303000	Machinery for capsuling or labelling bottles or other containers	8	20
8422304000	Machinery for aerating beverages	8	20
8422309000	Other	8	20
8422404000	Heat shrink wrapping machinery	8	20
8422409010	Automatic wrapping machinery, including binding and tying machines	8	20
8422409020	Automatic pack tiers	8	20
8422409030	Vacuum packers	8	20
8422409090	Other	8	20
8422901000	Of dish washing machines	8	20
8422902000	Of other packing or wrapping machinery	8	20
8422909000	Other	8	20
8423100000	Personal weighing machines, including baby scales; household scales	8	20
8423201000	Conveyer scale	8	20
8423202000	Feed meter or feed weighers	8	20
8423209000	Other	8	20
8423300000	Constant weight scales and scales for discharging a predetermined weight of material into a bag or container, including hopper scales	8	20
8423810000	Having a maximum weighing capacity not exceeding 30 kg	8	20
8423820000	Having a maximum weighing capacity exceeding 30 kg but not exceeding 5,000 kg	8	20
8423891000	Truck scale	8	20
8423899000	Other	8	20
8423901010	Weights in the accuracy class	8	20
8423901090	Other	8	20
8423909000	Parts of weighing machinery	8	20
8424100000	Fire extinguishers, whether or not charged	8	20
8424201000	Spray guns	8	20
8424202010	Of robot type	8	20
8424202090	Other	8	20
8424209000	Other	8	20
8424301000	Steam or sand blasting machines	8	20

8424302000	High-pressure steam cleaners	8	20
8424309000	Other	8	20
8424811000	Self-propelled sprayers	8	20
8424812000	Other sprayers	8	20
8424819000	Other	8	20
8424899000	Other	8	20
8424901000	Of fire extinguishers	8	20
8424902000	Of spray guns	8	20
8424903000	Of sprayers	8	20
8424909090	Other	8	20
8427101000	Of counter balance type	8	20
8427102000	Of non counter balance type	8	20
8427109000	Other	8	20
8427201010	With a loading capacity not more than 3 metric tons	8	20
8427201020	With a loading capacity more than 3 metric tons	8	20
8427209000	Other	8	20
8427901000	Hand pallet trucks	8	20
8427909000	Other	8	20
8431200000	Of machinery of heading 84.27	8	20
8435101000	Presses for the extraction of fruit juice	8	20
8435102000	Crushers for the extraction of fruit juice	8	20
8435103000	Homogenisers for the preparation of fruit juice	8	20
8435109000	Other	8	20
8435900000	Parts	8	20
8436101000	Feed cutter	8	20
8436102000	Feed grinder, mill or crusher	8	20
8436103000	Feed mixer	8	20
8436109000	Other	8	20
8436211000	Incubators	8	20
8436219000	Other	8	20
8436290000	Other	8	20
8436800000	Other machinery	8	20
8436910000	Of poultry-keeping machinery or poultry incubators and brooders	8	20
8436990000	Other	8	20
8437101000	Forage-grass seed selectors	8	20
8437109000	Other	8	20
8437801000	Machinery used in the milling industry	8	20
8437802000	Machinery for the working of cereals or dried leguminous vegetables	8	20
8437901000	Of machines for cleaning sorting or grading seed, grain or dried leguninous vegetables	8	20
8437909000	Other	8	20
8438109000	Other	8	20
8438200000	Machinery for the manufacture of confectionery, cocoa or	8	20

		chocolate		
	8438300000	Machinery for sugar manufacture	8	20
	8438400000	Brewery machinery	8	20
	8438501000	Machinery used in meat preparation	8	20
	8438509000	Other	8	20
	8438600000	Machinery for the preparation of fruits, nuts or vegetables	8	20
	8438801000	Machines for preparing fish, shell fish, etc	8	20
	8438809000	Other	8	20
	8438900000	Parts	8	20
	8439101000	Grinders	8	20
	8439102000	Cutters	8	20
	8439103000	Strainers	8	20
	8439104000	Press-pate machines	8	20
	8439105000	Beaters	8	20
	8439109000	Other	8	20
	8439201000	Machines for forming paper	8	20
	8439202000	Paper making machine	8	20
	8439209000	Other	8	20
	8439301000	Reeling machines	8	20
	8439302000	Machines for working surface	8	20
	8439303000	Machines for impregnating paper or paperboard	8	20
	8439309000	Other	8	20
	8439910000	Of machinery for making pulp of fibrous cellulosic material	8	20
	8439990000	Other	8	20
	8440101000	Book-sewing machines	8	20
	8440102000	Leaf-folding machines for book-binding	8	20
	8440109000	Other	8	20
	8440901000	Of book-sewing machines	8	20
	8440909000	Other	8	20
	8441100000	Cutting machines	8	20
	8441201000	Machines for making bags or sacks	8	20
	8441202000	Machines for making envelopes	8	20
	8441300000	Machines for making cartons, boxes, cases, tubes, drums or similar containers, other than by moulding	8	20
	8441400000	Machines for moulding articles in paper pulp, paper or paperboard	8	20
	8441801000	Paper or paperboard trimming machines	8	20
	8441809000	Other	8	20
	8441900000	Parts	8	20
	8442301000	Machinery and apparatus for type-founding	8	20
	8442302000	Special moulding presses	8	20
	8442303000	Acid etching machines	8	20
	8442304000	Phototype-setting and composing machines	8	20
	8442305000	Machinery,apparatus and equipment for type-setting or	8	20

	composing by other processes,with or without founding device		
8442309000	Other	8	20
8442401000	Of machinery and apparatus for type-setting	8	20
8442402000	Of machinery and apparatus for type-founding	8	20
8442409000	Other	8	20
8442500000	Plates, cylinders and other printing components; plates, cylinders and lithographic stones, prepared for printing purposes (for example, planed, grained or polished)	8	20
8443110000	Offset printing machinery, reel fed	8	20
8443120000	Offset printing machinery, sheet-fed, office type (using sheets with one side not exceeding 22 cm and the other side not exceeding 36 cm in the unfolded state)	8	20
8443130000	Other offset printing machinery	8	20
8443140000	Letterpress printing machinery, reel fed, excluding flexographic printing	8	20
8443150000	Letterpress printing machinery, other than reel fed, excluding flexographic printing	8	20
8443160000	Flexographic printing machinery	8	20
8443170000	Gravure printing machinery	8	20
8443191000	Textile printing machines	8	20
8443192000	Other printing machines of a type used for printing a repetitive design, repetitve words or overall colour on textiles, leather, wallpaper, wrapping paper, linoleum or other materials	8	20
8443199000	Other	8	20
8443313020	Operating by reproducing the original image via an intermediate onto the copy (indirect process)	8	20
8443314000	Ink-jet printing machines, other than subheading 8443.31.10	8	20
8443324020	Operating by reproducing the original image via an intermediate onto the copy (indirect process)	8	20
8443325090	Other	8	20
8443391090	Other	8	20
8443392020	Operating by reproducing the original image via an intermediate onto the copy (indirect process)	8	20
8443393020	Of the contact type	8	20
8443394000	Thermo-copying apparatus	8	20
8443399000	Other	8	20
8443911010	Automatic feeders	8	20
8443911020	Folders, gummers, preforators and staplers	8	20
8443911030	Serial numbering machines	8	20
8443911090	Other	8	20
8443919000	Other	8	20
8443995000	Of subheading 8443.31.4000, 8443.32.5010, 8443.32.5090,	8	20

	8443.39.1010 or 8443.39.1090		
8443999000	Other	8	20
8444001000	Machines for extruding man-made textiles	5	20
8444002000	Machines for drawing man-made textiles	5	20
8444003000	Machines for texturing man-made textiles	5	20
8444004000	Machines for cutting man-made textiles	5	20
8444009000	Other	5	20
8445110000	Carding machines	5	20
8445120000	Combing machines	5	20
8445130000	Drawing or roving machines	5	20
8445191000	Blowing and mixing machines	5	20
8445192000	Lap machines	5	20
8445193000	Cotton gin	8	20
8445199000	Other	5	20
8445201010	Fine spinning frames	5	20
8445201090	Other	5	20
8445202010	Fine spinning frames	5	20
8445202090	Other	5	20
8445203000	For silk	5	20
8445209000	Other	5	20
8445301000	For filament yarns	5	20
8445302000	For spun yarns	5	20
8445309000	Other	5	20
8445401000	Cones winders	5	20
8445402000	Cheeses winders	5	20
8445409000	Other	5	20
8445901000	Warping machines	8	20
8445902000	Warp sizing machines	8	20
8445903000	Drawing-in machines	8	20
8445904000	Warp tying-in machines	8	20
8445909000	Other	8	20
8446100000	For weaving fabrics of a width not exceeding 30 cm	8	20
8446211000	For cotton	8	20
8446212000	For wool	8	20
8446213000	For silk	8	20
8446219000	Other	8	20
8446290000	Other	8	20
8446301010	For cotton	8	20
8446301020	For silk	8	20
8446301030	For towel	8	20
8446301090	Other	8	20
8446302010	For cotton	8	20
8446302020	For silk	8	20
8446302030	For towel	8	20
8446302090	Other	8	20

8446303010	For cotton	8	20
8446303020	For silk	8	20
8446303030	For towel	8	20
8446303090	Other	8	20
8446309010	For cotton	8	20
8446309020	For silk	8	20
8446309030	For towel	8	20
8446309090	Other	8	20
8447111000	Stocking knitting machines	8	20
8447119000	Other	8	20
8447120000	With cylinder diameter exceeding 165 mm	8	20
8447201010	Hand-knitting machines (including semi- automatic flat knitting machines)	8	20
8447201020	Automatic flat knitting machines	8	20
8447201090	Other	8	20
8447202010	Raschel knitting machines	8	20
8447202020	Tricot knitting machines	8	20
8447202090	Other	8	20
8447209000	Other	8	20
8447901000	Lace machines	8	20
8447902010	Automatic embroidery machines	8	20
8447902090	Other	8	20
8447903000	Machines for making knotted net	8	20
8447909000	Other	8	20
8448111000	Dobbies	8	20
8448112000	Jacquards	8	20
8448113000	Card punching machines	8	20
8448119000	Other	8	20
8448191000	Warp beam stands or creels	8	20
8448192000	Automatic stop motions	8	20
8448193000	Warp tyers	8	20
8448199010	Auxiliary machines for making yarn (excluding cotton gin)	5	20
8448199090	Other	8	20
8448201000	Extruding nipples	5	20
8448209000	Other	5	20
8448310000	Card clothing	8	20
8448321000	For carding machine(excluding garnet wires)	5	20
8448329000	Other	8	20
8448331000	Spindle flyers	5	20
8448339010	Spindle	8	20
8448339020	Spinning ring	8	20
8448339030	Ring travellers	8	20
8448391000	Warp beams	8	20
8448399000	Other	8	20
8448420000	Reeds for looms, healds and heald-frames	8	20

8448491000	Shuttles	8	20
8448499000	Other	8	20
8448511000	Hoisery needles	8	20
8448512000	Needles for embroidery machines	8	20
8448513000	Needles for lace machines	8	20
8448519000	Other	8	20
8448590000	Other	8	20
8449001010	Machinery for making felt hats	8	20
8449001090	Other	8	20
8449002000	Bolcks for making hats	8	20
8449009000	Parts	8	20
8450110000	Fully-automatic machines	8	20
8450120000	Other machines, with built-in centrifugal drier	8	20
8450190000	Other	8	20
8450200000	Machines, each of a dry linen capacity exceeding 10 kg	8	20
8450900000	Parts	8	20
8451100000	Dry-cleaning machines	8	20
8451210000	Each of a dry linen capacity not exceeding 10 kg	8	20
8451290000	Other	8	20
8451301000	Steam presses	8	20
8451309000	Other	8	20
8451401000	Washing machines	8	20
8451402000	Bleaching machines	8	20
8451403000	Dyeing machines	8	20
8451501000	Reeling unreeling machines	8	20
8451502000	Cutting machines	8	20
8451509000	Other	8	20
8451801000	Heat treating machines	8	20
8451802000	Stentering machines	8	20
8451803000	Mercerising machines	8	20
8451809010	Shrinking machines	8	20
8451809020	Coating or impregnating machines	8	20
8451809030	Raising machines	8	20
8451809040	Padding machines	8	20
8451809090	Other	8	20
8451901000	Of dry cleaning machines	8	20
8451902000	Of drying machines	8	20
8451909000	Other	8	20
8452101010	For straight stitch	8	20
8452101020	For zigzag stitch	8	20
8452101030	Of free arm type	8	20
8452101090	Other	8	20
8452102000	Of manual type	8	20
8452211000	For manufacturing shoes	8	20
8452212000	For sewing sacks	8	20

8452213000	For sewing leather or other thick stuffs	8	20
8452214000	For sewing furs	8	20
8452219000	Other	8	20
8452291000	For manufacturing shoes	8	20
8452292000	For sewing sacks	8	20
8452293000	For sewing leather or other thicks stuffs	8	20
8452294000	For sewing furs	8	20
8452299000	Other	8	20
8452300000	Sewing machine needles	8	20
8452400000	Furniture, bases and covers for sewing machines and parts thereof	8	20
8452900000	Other parts of sewing machines	8	20
8453101000	Machinery for preparing hides, skins or leather	8	20
8453102000	Machinery for tanning hides, skins or leather	8	20
8453103000	Machinery for working hides, skins or leather	8	20
8453201000	Machinery for making footwear	8	20
8453202000	Machinery for repairing footwear	8	20
8453800000	Other machinery	8	20
8453900000	Parts	8	20
8454100000	Converters	8	20
8454200000	Ingot moulds and ladles	8	20
8454301010	Die-casting machines	8	20
8454301090	Other	8	20
8454309000	Other	8	20
8454901000	Of converters	8	20
8454909000	Other	8	20
8455100000	Tube mills	8	20
8455210000	Hot or combination hot and cold	8	20
8455220000	Cold	8	20
8455301000	Of casting	8	20
8455302000	Of forging	8	20
8455309000	Other	8	20
8455900000	Other parts	8	20
8456103000	Operated by laser processes	8	20
8456109000	Other	8	20
8456301010	Wire cut electric discharge machine	8	20
8456301090	Other	8	20
8456309000	Other	8	20
8456900000	Other	8	20
8457101000	Of vertical type	8	20
8457102000	Of horizontal type	8	20
8457103000	Of double column type	8	20
8457109000	Other	8	20
8457200000	Unit construction machines (single station)	8	20
8457300000	Multi-station transfer machines	8	20

8458110000	Numerically controlled	8	20
8458190000	Other	8	20
8458910000	Numerically controlled	8	20
8458990000	Other	8	20
8459100000	Way-type unit head machines	8	20
8459210000	Numerically controlled	8	20
8459291000	Radial drilling machines	8	20
8459292000	Upright drilling machines	8	20
8459293000	Multi-spindle drilling machines	8	20
8459299000	Other	8	20
8459310000	Numerically controlled	8	20
8459390000	Other	8	20
8459401000	Jig boring machines	8	20
8459402000	Horizontal boring machines	8	20
8459409000	Other	8	20
8459510000	Numerically controlled	8	20
8459590000	Other	8	20
8459611000	Bed type milling machines	8	20
8459612000	Planing milling machines	8	20
8459619000	Other	8	20
8459691000	Bed type milling machines	8	20
8459692000	Planing milling machines	8	20
8459693000	Universal tool milling machines	8	20
8459694000	Profile milling machines	8	20
8459699000	Other	8	20
8459701000	Tapping machines	8	20
8459709000	Other threading machines	8	20
8460110000	Numerically controlled	8	20
8460190000	Other	8	20
8460211000	Cylindrical grinders	8	20
8460212000	Internal grinders	8	20
8460213000	Centerless grinders	8	20
8460214000	Profile grinders	8	20
8460291000	Cylindrical grinders	8	20
8460292000	Internal grinders	8	20
8460293000	Centerless grinders	8	20
8460294000	Profile grinders	8	20
8460299000	Other	8	20
8460310000	Numerically controlled	8	20
8460390000	Other	8	20
8460401000	Honing machines	8	20
8460402000	Lapping machines	8	20
8460900000	Other	8	20
8461200000	Shaping or slotting machines	8	20
8461300000	Broaching machines	8	20

8461401010	Numerically controlled	8	20
8461401090	Other	8	20
8461402000	Gear grinding or gear finishing machines	8	20
8461500000	Sawing or cutting-off machines	8	20
8461900000	Other	8	20
8462101000	Air hammer	8	20
8462109000	Other	8	20
8462210000	Numerically controlled	8	20
8462290000	Other	8	20
8462310000	Numerically controlled	8	20
8462390000	Other	8	20
8462411000	Punching machines (including combined shearing machines)	8	20
8462412000	Notching machines	8	20
8462491000	Punching machines (including combined shearing machines)	8	20
8462492000	Notching machines	8	20
8462911000	Of the maximum pressure not more than 100 metric tons	8	20
8462912000	Of the maximum pressure more than 100 metric tons, but not more than 300 metric tons	8	20
8462913000	Of the maximum pressure more than 300 metric tons, but not more than 1000 metric tons	8	20
8462914000	Of the maximum pressure more than 1000 metric tons	8	20
8462991010	Of the maximum pressure not more than 30 metric tons	8	20
8462991020	Of the maximum pressure more than 30 metric tons, but not more than 100 metric tons	8	20
8462991030	Of the maximum pressure more than 100 metric tons, but not more than 300 metric tons	8	20
8462991040	Of the maximum pressure more than 300 metric tons, but not more than 600 metric tons	8	20
8462991050	Of the maximum pressure more than 600 metric tons, but not more than 1,500 metric tons	8	20
8462991090	Other	8	20
8462999000	Other	8	20
8463100000	Draw-benches for bars, tubes, profiles, wire or the like	8	20
8463200000	Thread rolling machines	8	20
8463300000	Machines for working wire	8	20
8463900000	Other	8	20
8464100000	Sawing machines	8	20
8464201000	For working optical or spectacle glass	8	20
8464202000	For working other glass	8	20
8464209000	Other	8	20
8464901000	Machine-tools for cold working glass	8	20
8464902000	Machine-tools for working concrete	8	20
8464903000	Machine-tools for working ceramics	8	20

8464909000	Other	8	20
8465101000	For working wood	8	20
8465109000	Other	8	20
8465911000	For working wood	8	20
8465919000	Other	8	20
8465921000	For working wood	8	20
8465929000	Other	8	20
8465931000	For working wood	8	20
8465939000	Other	8	20
8465941000	For working wood	8	20
8465949000	Other	8	20
8465951000	For working wood	8	20
8465959000	Other	8	20
8465961000	For working wood	8	20
8465969000	Other	8	20
8465991000	For working wood	8	20
8465999000	Other	8	20
8466100000	Tool holders and self-opening dieheads	8	20
8466201000	For aircrafts	8	20
8466209000	Other	8	20
8466300000	Dividing heads and other special attachments for machine-tools	8	20
8466910000	For machines of heading 84.64	8	20
8466920000	For machines of heading 84.65	8	20
8466930000	For machines of headings 84.56 to 84.61	8	20
8466940000	For machines of heading 84.62 or 84.63	8	20
8467111000	Rock drillers	8	20
8467112000	Screw drivers	8	20
8467114000	Impact wrench	8	20
8467115000	Drill	8	20
8467119000	Other	8	20
8467191000	Rock drillers	8	20
8467210000	Drills of all kinds	8	20
8467220000	Saws	8	20
8467290000	Other	8	20
8467810000	Chain saws	8	20
8467891020	Of subheading 8479.89.9010, 8479.89.9030 or 8479.89.9091	8	20
8467891090	Other	8	20
8467899000	Other	8	20
8467910000	Of chain saws	8	20
8467920000	Of pneumatic tools	8	20
8467990000	Other	8	20
8468100000	Hand-held blow pipes	8	20
8468201000	Gas welding machines	8	20

8468202000	Gas automatic cutting machines	8	20
8468209000	Other	8	20
8468800000	Other machinery and apparatus	8	20
8468900000	Parts	8	20
8469001020	Automatic typewriters	8	20
8469002000	Other typewriters, electric	8	20
8469003000	Other typewriters, non-electric	8	20
8472100000	Duplicating machines	8	20
8472301000	Letters sorting machines	8	20
8472302000	Machines for cancelling postage stamps	8	20
8472309000	Other	8	20
8472901050	Coin-counting or wrapping machines	8	20
8472901090	Other	8	20
8472902000	Automatic sheet making machines for duplicating and printing	8	20
8472903000	Ticket-issuing machines	8	20
8472904000	Pencil-sharpening machines	8	20
8472905000	Paper shredders	8	20
8472906000	Addressing machines and address plate embossing machines	8	20
8472909000	Other	8	20
8473109000	Other	8	20
8473409000	Other	8	20
8475100000	Machines for assembling electric or electronic lamps, tubes or valves or flashbulbs, in glass envelopes	8	20
8475210000	Machines for making optical fibres and preforms thereof	8	20
8475291000	For the manufacture of plate glass	8	20
8475292000	For the manufacture of glass-bottle	8	20
8475299000	Other	8	20
8475901000	Of machines for the manufacture of plate glass	8	20
8475909000	Other	8	20
8476210000	Incorporating heating or refrigerating devices	8	20
8476290000	Other	8	20
8476811000	For selling foods	8	20
8476819000	Other	8	20
8476891000	For selling foods	8	20
8476893000	For selling cigarettes	8	20
8476894000	For money-changing	8	20
8476899000	Other	8	20
8476900000	Parts	8	20
8477101000	For rubber-industry	8	20
8477102000	For plastic-industry	8	20
8477201000	For rubber-industry	8	20
8477202000	For plastic-industry	8	20
8477300000	Blow moulding machines	8	20

8477400000	Vacuum moulding machines and other thermoforming machines	8	20
8477510000	For moulding or retreading pneumatic tyres or for moulding or otherwise forming inner tubes	8	20
8477590000	Other	8	20
8477800000	Other machinery	8	20
8477900000	Parts	8	20
8478100000	Machinery	8	20
8478900000	Parts	8	20
8479200000	Machinery for the extraction or preparation of animal or fixed vegetable fats or oils	8	20
8479300000	Presses for the manufacture of particle board or fibre building board of wood or other ligneous materials and other machinery for treating wood or cork	8	20
8479400000	Rope or cable-making machines	8	20
8479501000	Of subheading 8479.81, 8479.82, 8479.89.9010, 8479.89.9030, 8479.89.9040, 8479.89.9060 or 8479.89.9091	8	20
8479502000	Of Subheading 8479.89.9080	8	20
8479509000	Other	8	20
8479600000	Evaporative air coolers	8	20
8479811000	Metal scouring machines	8	20
8479812010	For the purpose of semiconductor manufacturing	3	20
8479812090	Other	8	20
8479813000	Winding machines	8	20
8479814000	Insulating or protective material covering machines	8	20
8479819000	Other	8	20
8479821000	Mixers	8	20
8479822000	Crushers and grinders	8	20
8479824000	Agitators	8	20
8479829000	Other	8	20
8479891010	Air purifiers (having funtions of humidifying and dehumidifying)	8	20
8479891090	Other	8	20
8479899010	Presses or extruding machines	8	20
8479899020	Machines and appliances for ships or fishing industry	8	20
8479899030	Eyeletting or tubular rivetting machines	8	20
8479899040	Automatic magnetic tape assembling machines	8	20
8479899050	Coating machines	8	20
8479899060	Auto-door operators	8	20
8479899080	Automatic winding machines for fishing	8	20
8479899091	For vehicles of Chapter 87	8	20
8479899092	Surface mount machines for electronic parts	8	20
8479899099	Other	8	20
8479901010	Of air coolers (including parts of carcoolers)	8	20
8479901020	Of machines and mechanical appliances of the household	8	20

	type		
8479901030	Of vehicles of Chapter 87	8	20
8479902000	Of those specified in subheading 8479.89.9080	8	20
8479903000	Of machines and mechanical appliances for making semi-con ductor devices	8	20
8479909010	Of machinery for public works, building or the like	8	20
8479909020	Of machinery for the extraction or preparation of animal or fixed vegetable fats or oils	8	20
8479909030	Of rope or cable-making machines	8	20
8479909040	Of machines and appliances for treating metal	8	20
8479909050	Of mixing, kneading, crushing, grinding, screening, sifting, homogenising, emulsifying or stirring machines	8	20
8479909060	Of presses or extruding machines	8	20
8479909070	Of machines and appliances of ships or fishing industry	8	20
8479909080	Of automatic magnetic tape assembling machines	8	20
8479909090	Other	8	20
8480100000	Moulding boxes for metal foundry	8	20
8480200000	Mould bases	8	20
8480300000	Moulding patterns	8	20
8480410000	Injection or compression types	8	20
8480490000	Other	8	20
8480500000	Moulds for glass	8	20
8480600000	Moulds for mineral materials	8	20
8480710000	Injection or compression types	8	20
8480790000	Other	8	20
8481100000	Pressure-reducing valves	8	20
8481201000	Valves for oleohydraulic transmissions	8	20
8481202000	Valves for pneumatic transmissions	8	20
8481300000	Check (nonreturn) valves	8	20
8481400000	Safety or relief valves	8	20
8481801010	Electric operated	8	20
8481801090	Other	8	20
8481802000	Taps, cocks and traps	8	20
8481809000	Other	8	20
8481909000	Other	8	20
8482101000	Of the inside diameter exceeding 100 mm	8	20
8482102000	Of the inside diameter not exceeding 100 mm	13	20
8482200000	Tapered roller bearings, including cone and tapered roller assemblies	8	20
8482300000	Spherical roller bearings	8	20
8482400000	Needle roller bearings	8	20
8482500000	Other cylindrical roller bearings	8	20
8482800000	Other, including combined ball/roller bearings	8	20
8482990000	Other	8	20
8483101000	For aircrafts	3	20

8483109010	For vehicles of Chapter 87	8	20
8483109090	Other	8	20
8483201000	For aircrafts	3	20
8483209000	Other	8	20
8483301000	For aircrafts	3	20
8483309000	Other	8	20
8483401010	Roller screws	3	20
8483401090	Other	3	20
8483409010	Gear	8	20
8483409020	Gear boxes	8	20
8483409030	Automatic transmissions	8	20
8483409041	For vehicles of Chapter 87	8	20
8483409049	Other	8	20
8483409090	Other	8	20
8483501000	For aircrafts	8	20
8483509000	Other	8	20
8483601000	For aircrafts	3	20
8483609000	Other	8	20
8483901000	For aircrafts	3	20
8483909000	Other	8	20
8484101000	For vehicles of Chapter 87	8	20
8484109000	Other	8	20
8484200000	Mechanical seals	8	20
8484900000	Other	8	20
8486103090	Other	8	20
8486104019	Other	8	20
8486104029	Other	8	20
8486109000	Other	8	20
8486202290	Other	8	20
8486205190	Other	8	20
8486205990	Other	8	20
8486208190	Other	8	20
8486208490	Other	8	20
8486209390	Other	8	20
8486209900	Other	8	20
8486303010	Operated by laser or other light or photon beam processes	8	20
8486303020	Operated by ultrasonic processes	8	20
8486303030	Operated by electro-discharge processes	8	20
8486303041	Dry etcher	8	20
8486303049	Other	8	20
8486304010	Grinding or polishing machines	8	20
8486304090	Other	8	20
8486305010	Coating machines	8	20
8486305020	Coating and developing machines	8	20

8486305031	Operated by physical method	8	20
8486305032	Operated by chemical method	8	20
8486305039	Other	8	20
8486306010	Seal, Short, Spacer or Liquid crystal dispenser	8	20
8486306020	Scribing machines	8	20
8486306030	Panel assembler	8	20
8486306090	Other	8	20
8486307000	Centrifuges, including centrifugal dryers	8	20
8486308000	Mechanical appliances for projecting, dispersing or spraying liquids or powders	8	20
8486309020	Robots for making flat panel displays	8	20
8486309090	Other	8	20
8486401040	Machines and apparatus for etching, cleaning or stripping mask and reticle	8	20
8486401090	Other	8	20
8486402020	Machines for inserting or removing semiconductor devices	8	20
8486402039	Other	8	20
8486402040	Machines to attach solder ball on semiconductor circuit board or ceramic board	3	20
8486402050	Apparatus designed to bond or datach wafer on ceramic block in polish wafers	8	20
8486402092	Machine-tools (including presses) for working metal by bending, folding, straightening, flattening, other than semiconductor leads, whether or not numerically controlled	8	20
8486402093	Machines for forming connections(bump) on an entire wafer before dicing	8	20
8486402099	Other	8	20
8486901020	Of subheading 8486.10.3090, 8486.10.4019, 8486.10.4029 or 8486.10.9000	8	20
8486902020	Of subheading 8486.220290, 8486.20.5190, 8486.20.5990, 8486.20.8190, 8486.20.8490, 8486.20.9390 or 8486.20.9900	8	20
8486903020	Of subheading 8486.30.3010, 8486.30.3020, 8486.30.3030, 8486.30.3041, 8486.30.3049, 8486.30.4010, 8486.30.4090, 8486.30.6020, 8486.30.7000, 8486.30.8000, 8486.30.9020 or 8486.30.9090	8	20
8486903030	Of subheading 8486.30.5010, 8486.30.5020, 8486.30.5031, 8486.30.5032, 8486.30.5039, 8486.30.6010, 8486.30.6030, or 8486.30.6090	8	20
8486904020	Of subheading 8486.40.1040, 8486.40.1090, 8486.420020, 8486.420039, 8486.420040, 8486.420050, 8486.420061, 8486.420062, 8486.420063, 8486.420092, 8486.420093, 8486.420099 or 8486.40.9000	8	20
8487100000	Ships' or boats' propellers and blades therefor	8	20
8487909010	Oil seal rings	8	20

8487909090	Other	8	20
8501101000	DC motors	8	20
8501103000	Universal AC/DC motors	8	20
8501201000	Of an output exceeding 37.5 W, but not exceeding 100 W	8	20
8501202000	Of an output exceeding 100 W, but not exceeding 750 W	8	20
8501203000	Of an output exceeding 750 W	8	20
8501311010	Of an output not exceeding 100 W	8	20
8501312000	DC generators	8	20
8501321000	DC motors	8	20
8501322000	DC generators	8	20
8501331000	DC motors	8	20
8501332000	DC generatrors	8	20
8501341000	DC motors	8	20
8501342000	DC generators	8	20
8501401000	Of an output not exceeding 100 W	8	20
8501402000	Of an output exceeding 100 W but not exceeding 750 W	8	20
8501403000	Of an output exceeding 750 W but not exceeding 75 kW	8	20
8501404000	Of an output exceeding 75 kW	8	20
8501510000	Of an output not exceeding 750 W	8	20
8501532000	Of an output exceeding 375 kW but not exceeding 1500 kW	8	20
8501534000	Of an output exceeding 1500 kW	8	20
8501611000	Of an output not exceeding 750 VA	8	20
8501612000	Of an output exceeding 750 VA but not exceeding 75 kVA	8	20
8501620000	Of an output exceeding 75 kVA but not exceeding 375 kVA	8	20
8501639000	Other	8	20
8502111000	Of an output not exceeding 750 VA	8	20
8502112000	Of an output exceeding 750 VA but not exceeding 75 kVA	8	20
8502120000	Of an output exceeding 75 kVA but not exceeding 375 kVA	8	20
8502131090	Other	8	20
8502201000	Of an output not exceeding 75 kVA	8	20
8502202000	Of an output exceeding 75 kVA but not exceeding 375 kVA	8	20
8502203090	Other	8	20
8502311000	Of an output not exceeding 75 kVA	8	20
8502312000	Of an output exceeding 75 kVA but not exceeding 375 kVA	8	20
8502313000	Of an output exceeding 375 kVA but not exceeding 750 kVA	8	20
8502314000	Of an output exceeding 750 kVA	8	20
8502391000	Of an output not exceeding 75 kVA	8	20

8502392000	Of an output exceeding 75 kVA but not exceeding 375 kVA	8	20
8502393000	Of an output exceeding 375 kVA but not exceeding 750 kVA	8	20
8502394000	Of an output exceeding 750 kVA	8	20
8502400000	Electric rotary converters	8	20
8503001000	Of motors	8	20
8503002000	Of generators and of generating sets	8	20
8503003000	Of rotary converters	8	20
8504101010	Rated at not more than 1 A	8	20
8504102000	Rated at more than 20 A but not more than 60 A	8	20
8504103000	Rated at more than 60 A	8	20
8504211000	Instrument transformers	8	20
8504219010	Having a power handling capacity not exceeding 100 kVA	8	20
8504221000	Instrument transformers	8	20
8504229010	Having a power handling capacity exceeding 650 kVA but not exceeding 1,000 kVA	8	20
8504229020	Having a power handling capacity exceeding 1,000 kVA but not exceeding 5,000 kVA	8	20
8504229030	Having a power handling capacity exceeding 5,000 kVA but not exceeding 10,000 kVA	8	20
8504230000	Having a power handling capacity exceeding 10,000 kVA	8	20
8504312000	Voltage regulators	8	20
8504319010	Having a power handling capacity not exceeding 100 VA	8	20
8504319020	Having a power handling capacity exceeding 100 VA but not exceeding 500 VA	8	20
8504319040	Having a power handling capacity exceeding 500 VA but not exceeding 1 kVA	8	20
8504321000	Instrument transformers	8	20
8504322000	Voltage regulators	8	20
8504329010	Having a power handling capacity exceeding 1 kVA but not exceeding 5 kVA	8	20
8504329020	Having a power handling capacity exceeding 5 kVA but not exceeding 16 kVA	8	20
8504331000	Instrument transformers	8	20
8504332000	Voltage regulators	8	20
8504339010	Having a power handling capacity exceeding 16 kVA but not exceeding 30 kVA	8	20
8504339020	Having a power handling capacity exceeding 30 kVA but not exceeding 100 kVA	8	20
8504339040	Having a power handling capacity exceeding 100 kVA but not exceeding 500 kVA	8	20
8504341000	Instrument transformers	8	20
8504342000	Voltage regulators	8	20
8504349010	Having a power handling capacity exceeding 500 kVA but	8	20

	not exceeding 2,000 kVA		
8504349030	Having a power handling capacity exceeding 2,000 kVA	8	20
8504401090	Other	8	20
8504402019	Other	8	20
8504402099	Other	8	20
8504403090	Other	8	20
8504404090	Other	8	20
8504405090	Other	8	20
8504501090	Other	8	20
8504509090	Other	8	20
8504909000	Other	8	20
8505111000	Of alnico	8	20
8505119000	Other	8	20
8505191000	Of iron oxide	8	20
8505200000	Electro-magnetic couplings, clutches and brakes	8	20
8505902000	Electro-magnetic or permanent magnet chucks, clamps, vices and similar work holders	8	20
8505903000	Electro-magnetic lifting heads	8	20
8506102000	Alkali manganese batteries	13	20
8506109000	Other	8	20
8506300000	Mercuric oxide	8	20
8506400000	Silver oxide	8	20
8506500000	Lithium	8	20
8506600000	Air-Zinc	8	20
8506801000	Zinc oxide	8	20
8506809000	Other	8	20
8506900000	Parts	8	20
8507100000	Lead-acid, of a kind used for starting piston engines	8	20
8507200000	Other lead-acid accumulators	8	20
8507300000	Nickel-cadmium	8	20
8507400000	Nickel-iron	8	20
8507801000	Nikel metal hydride	8	20
8507802000	Lithium Ion	8	20
8507803000	Lithium polymer	8	20
8507809000	Other	8	20
8507901000	Seperators	8	20
8507909000	Other	8	20
8508110000	Of a power not exceeding 1,500 W and having a dust bag or other receptacle capacity not exceeding 20 ℓ	8	20
8508191000	Of a kind used for domestic purposes	8	20
8508199000	Other	8	20
8508701000	Of subheading 8508.11.0000 or 8508.19.1000	8	20
8508702000	Of subheading 8508.19.9000 or 8508.60.0000	8	20
8509801000	Coffee grinders	8	20
8509802000	Ice grinders	8	20

8509803000	Floor polishers	8	20
8509804000	Kitchen waste disposers	8	20
8509900000	Parts	8	20
8510100000	Shavers	8	20
8510200000	Hair clippers	8	20
8510300000	Hair-removing appliances	8	20
8510901000	Of shavers	8	20
8510902000	Of hair clippers	8	20
8510903000	Of hair-removing appliances	8	20
8511101000	For aircrafts	3	20
8511109000	Other	8	20
8511201000	For aircrafts	3	20
8511209000	Other	8	20
8511301000	For aircrafts	3	20
8511309000	Other	8	20
8511401000	For aircrafts	3	20
8511409000	Other	8	20
8511501000	For aircrafts	3	20
8511509000	Other	8	20
8511801000	For aircraft	3	20
8511809000	Other	8	20
8511901000	For aircraft	3	20
8511909000	Other	8	20
8512100000	Lighting or visual signalling equipment of a kind used on bicycles	8	20
8512201000	Lighting equipment	8	20
8512202000	Signalling equipment	8	20
8512400000	Windscreen wipers, defrosters and demisters	8	20
8512900000	Parts	8	20
8513101000	Safety lamps of a kind used in mining	8	20
8513102000	Flashlights	8	20
8513109000	Other	8	20
8513900000	Parts	8	20
8514101000	For laboratory	8	20
8514102000	For metal industrys	8	20
8514103000	For food industrys	8	20
8514109000	Other	8	20
8514201000	For laboratory	8	20
8514202000	For metal industrys	8	20
8514203000	For food industrys	8	20
8514209000	Other	8	20
8514409000	Other	8	20
8514909000	Other	8	20
8515110000	Soldering irons and guns	8	20
8515190000	Other	8	20

8515211010	Of robot type	8	20
8515211090	Other	8	20
8515212010	Of robot type	8	20
8515212090	Other	8	20
8515213010	Of robot type	8	20
8515213090	Other	8	20
8515219010	Of robots type	8	20
8515219090	Other	8	20
8515291000	Spot welders	8	20
8515292000	Seam welders	8	20
8515293000	Butt welders	8	20
8515299000	Other	8	20
8515311010	Of robot type	8	20
8515311090	Other	8	20
8515319010	Of robot type	8	20
8515319090	Other	8	20
8515391000	AC arc welding machines and apparatus	8	20
8515399000	Other	8	20
8515801000	Ultrasonic machines	8	20
8515802000	Electron beam machines	8	20
8515803000	Laser operated machines	8	20
8515809000	Other	8	20
8515901000	Of welding machines	8	20
8515909000	Other	8	20
8516210000	Storage heating radiators	8	20
8516290000	Other	8	20
8516310000	Hair dryers	8	20
8516320000	Other hair-dressing apparatus	8	20
8516330000	Hand-drying apparatus	8	20
8516400000	Electric smoothing irons	8	20
8516500000	Microwave ovens	8	20
8516601000	Electrical ovens	8	20
8516602000	Electric rice cookers(including with constant warming function)	8	20
8516609000	Other	8	20
8516710000	Coffee or tea makers	8	20
8516720000	Toasters	8	20
8516791000	Electric jar	8	20
8516799000	Other	8	20
8516800000	Electric heating resistors	8	20
8516900000	Parts	8	20
8517691100	HF (high frequency), MF (medium frequency) or LF(low frequency) receiving apparatus	8	20
8517691219	Other	8	20
8517691290	Other	8	20

8517691900	Other	8	20
8517704019	Other	8	20
8517704090	Other	8	20
8518210000	Single loudspeakers, mounted in their enclosures	8	20
8518220000	Multiple loudspeakers, mounted in the same enclosure	8	20
8518299000	Other	8	20
8518309000	Other	8	20
8518400000	Audio-frequency electric amplifiers	8	20
8518500000	Electric sound amplifier sets	8	20
8518909000	Other	8	20
8519201000	Coin- or disc-operated record-players, not incorporating a sound recording device	8	20
8519209000	Other, not incorporating a sound recording device	8	20
8519301000	With automatic record changing mechanism	8	20
8519309000	Other	8	20
8519811000	Transcribing machines, not incorporating a sound recording device	8	20
8519812100	Cassette-players, as defined in Subheading Notes 1 to Chapter 85	8	20
8519812210	For vehicles	8	20
8519812220	Of portable type, other than as defined in Subheading Notes 1 to Chapter 85	8	20
8519812290	Other	8	20
8519812310	For vehicles	8	20
8519812320	Of portable type	8	20
8519812390	Other	8	20
8519812900	Other	8	20
8519813000	Dictating machines not capable of operating without an external source of power	8	20
8519814111	For vehicles	8	20
8519814112	Of portable type	8	20
8519814119	Other	8	20
8519814190	Other	8	20
8519814210	For vehicles	8	20
8519814220	Of portable type	8	20
8519814290	Other	8	20
8519814310	Of reel type	8	20
8519814390	Other	8	20
8519815010	Of reel type	8	20
8519815020	Of disc type	8	20
8519815030	Cassette-type	8	20
8519815090	Other	8	20
8519819000	Other sound recording apparatus, whether or not incorporating a sound reproducing device	8	20
8519891010	Without loudspeaker	8	20

8519891090	Other	8	20
8519892000	Transcribing machines, not incorporating a sound recording device	8	20
8519893000	Decks, whether or not incorporating a sound reproducing device	8	20
8519899010	Other sound reproducing apparatus, not incorporating a sound recording device	8	20
8521101000	Of a width exceeding 12.7 mm	8	20
8522100000	Pick-up cartridges	8	20
8522901010	For audio recording	8	20
8522901020	For video recording	8	20
8522901090	Other	8	20
8522902000	Laser pick-up	8	20
8522909090	Other	8	20
8523210000	Cards incorporating a magnetic stripe, whether or not recording	8	20
8523292211	Those recorded video	8	20
8523292219	Other	8	20
8523292221	Those recorded video	8	20
8523292229	Other	8	20
8523292231	Those recorded video	13.0% or 34won/min (at standard speed)	20
8523292239	Other	8	20
8523292991	Those recorded video	8	20
8523292999	Other	8	20
8523402120	For reproducing sound only	8	20
8523402139	Other	8	20
8523402991	Those recorded video	8	20
8523402999	Other	8	20
8523512910	Those recorded video	8	20
8523512990	Other	8	20
8523529000	Other and parts thereof	8	20
8523592910	Those recorded video	8	20
8523592990	Other	8	20
8523802100	Gramophone records	8	20
8523802910	Those recorded video	8	20
8523802990	Other	8	20
8525501000	Radio-broadcasting apparatus	8	20
8525509000	Other	8	20
8525801010	For video tape recorder	8	20
8525801020	For monitor television	8	20
8525801090	Other	8	20
8526101000	For aircrafts	8	20

8526109000	Other	8	20
8526911010	For aircrafts	8	20
8526911090	Other	8	20
8526912010	For aircrafts	8	20
8526912090	Other	8	20
8526913010	For aircrafts	8	20
8526913020	For vehicles	8	20
8526913090	Other	8	20
8526914000	Loran receivers	8	20
8526919010	For aircrafts	8	20
8526919020	For vehicles	8	20
8526919090	Other	8	20
8526920000	Radio remote control apparatus	8	20
8527120000	Pocket-size radio cassette-players	8	20
8527131000	Of Cassette-type	8	20
8527132000	Of disc type	8	20
8527133000	Combined with Cassette-type and disc type	8	20
8527139000	Other	8	20
8527190000	Other	8	20
8527211000	Of Cassette-type	8	20
8527213000	Combined with Cassette-type and disc type	8	20
8527219000	Other	8	20
8527290000	Other	8	20
8527911010	Of Cassette-type	8	20
8527911020	Of disc type	8	20
8527911030	Combined with Cassette-type and disc type	8	20
8527911090	Other	8	20
8527919000	Other	8	20
8527920000	Not combined with sound recording or reproducing apparatus but combined with a clock	8	20
8527990000	Other	8	20
8528491010	Television monitors specially manufactured for medical purpose	8	20
8528491090	Other	8	20
8528492010	Television monitors specially manufactured for medical purpose	8	20
8528492090	Other	8	20
8528591010	Television monitors specially manufactured for medical purpose	8	20
8528591090	Other	8	20
8528592010	Television monitors specially manufactured for medical purpose	8	20
8528592090	Other	8	20
8528711010	Colour	8	20
8528711020	Black and white or other monochrome	8	20

8528712010	Supporting reception of broadcasting of which vertical resolution is more than or equal to 720lines	8	20
8528712090	Other	8	20
8528719010	Colour	8	20
8528719020	Black and white or other monochrome	8	20
8528721010	Of analog	8	20
8528721020	Of digital	8	20
8528722010	Of analog	8	20
8528722020	Of digital	8	20
8528723010	Of analog	8	20
8528723020	Of digital	8	20
8528724010	Of analog	8	20
8528724020	Of digital	8	20
8528729000	Other	8	20
8528731000	Of the length of fluorescent screen of braun tube under 37 cm in diagnal line	8	20
8528732000	Of the length of fluorescent screen of braun tube not less than 37 cm but under 45.72 cm in diagnal line	8	20
8528733000	Of the length of fluorescent screen of braun tube not less than 45.72 cm in diagnal line	8	20
8528739000	Other	8	20
8529101000	For radar apparatus	8	20
8529109100	For radio navigational aid or radio remote control apparatus	8	20
8529109210	For receiving from satellites	8	20
8529109290	Other	8	20
8529901000	Of radar apparatus	8	20
8529909100	Of radio navigational aid or radio remote control apparatus	8	20
8529909200	Of transmission apparatus for radio-broadcasting ortelevision	8	20
8529909400	Of radio-broadcast receivers	8	20
8529909500	Of television cameras	8	20
8529909610	Tuner for colour	8	20
8529909620	Tuner for black and white or monochrome	8	20
8529909630	Screen for video projector	8	20
8529909641	For plasma display panel type	8	20
8529909649	Other	8	20
8529909650	Other parts for black and white or monochrome	8	20
8529909990	Other	8	20
8530101010	For ground equipment	8	20
8530101090	Other	8	20
8530109000	Other	8	20
8530800000	Other equipment	8	20
8530900000	Parts	8	20

8531101000	Burglar alarms	8	20
8531102000	Fire alarms	8	20
8531103000	Gas alarms	8	20
8531104000	Electric bells	8	20
8531105000	Sirens	8	20
8531109000	Other sound or signalling apparatus	8	20
8531801010	Of mobile telephones for cellular networks	8	20
8531801090	Other	8	20
8535211000	Rated at less than 7.25 kV	8	20
8535212000	Rated at 7.25 kV and more but less than 75.5 kV	8	20
8535291000	Rated at less than 200 kV	8	20
8535292000	Rated at 200 kV and more	8	20
8535301000	Rated at less than 7.25 kV	8	20
8535302000	Rated at 7.25 kV and more but less than 72.5 kV	8	20
8535303000	Rated at 72.5 kV and more but less than 200 kV	8	20
8535304000	Rated at 200 kV and more	8	20
8535400000	Lightning arresters, voltage limiters and surge suppressors	8	20
8535901000	Connector	8	20
8535902000	Electrical terminal	8	20
8535909000	Other	8	20
8536109000	Other	8	20
8536200000	Automatic circuit breakers	8	20
8536300000	Other apparatus for protecting electrical circuits	8	20
8536410000	For a voltage not exceeding 60 V	8	20
8536490000	Other	8	20
8536501000	Rotary type	8	20
8536504000	Of magnet switches (including magnretic contactors)	8	20
8536610000	Lamp-holders	8	20
8536699000	Other	8	20
8536701000	Of plastics	6.5	20
8536702000	Of ceramic wares for laboratory, chemical or other technical uses	8	20
8536703090	Other	8	20
8537101000	Switch boards	8	20
8537102000	Automatic control panels	8	20
8537202000	Automatic control panels	8	20
8537209000	Other	8	20
8538100000	Boards, panels, consoles, desks, cabinets and other bases for the goods of heading 85.37, not equipped with their apparatus	8	20
8538901000	Of switches	8	20
8538902000	Of automatic circuit breakers	8	20
8538903000	Of relays	8	20
8538904000	Of automatic control panels	8	20
8539100000	Sealed beam lamp units	8	20

8539210000	Tungsten halogen	8	20
8539221000	Incandescent lamps	8	20
8539222000	Decoration lamps	8	20
8539223000	Beam lamps	8	20
8539224000	Attracting fish lamps	8	20
8539290000	Other	8	20
8539310000	Fluorescent, hot cathode	8	20
8539321000	Mercury lamps	8	20
8539322000	Sodium vapout lamps	8	20
8539323000	Metal halide lamps	8	20
8539391000	Cold cathode fluorescent lamp(CCFL)	8	20
8539399000	Other	8	20
8539410000	Arc lamps	8	20
8539491010	Of machines and mechanical appliances for making semiconductor devices	3	20
8539491090	Other	8	20
8539492000	Infra-red lamps	8	20
8539902000	Of discharge lamps	8	20
8539909000	Other	8	20
8540110000	Colour	8	20
8540120000	Black and white or other monochrome	8	20
8540201000	Television camera tubes	8	20
8540209000	Other	8	20
8540400000	Data/graphic display tubes, colour, with a phosphor dot screen pitch smaller than 0.4 mm	8	20
8540500000	Data/graphic display tubes, black and white or other monochrome	8	20
8540609000	Other	8	20
8540720000	Klystrons	8	20
8540790000	Other	8	20
8540810000	Receiver or amplifier valves and tubes	8	20
8540891000	Thermionic valves and tubes for transmitters	8	20
8540892000	Discharge tubes	8	20
8540893000	Digitron	8	20
8540899000	Other	8	20
8540911000	Deflection coils	8	20
8540912000	Electronic guns	8	20
8540913000	Shadow mask	8	20
8540919000	Other	8	20
8540990000	Other	8	20
8543100000	Particle accelerators	8	20
8543200000	Signal generators	8	20
8543300000	Machines and apparatus for electroplating, electrolysis or electrophoresis	8	20
8543701000	Electric fence energisers	8	20

8543702010	Medicated water electrolysis apparatus	8	20
8543702020	Electical beauty appliances	8	20
8543702030	Audio mixers	8	20
8543702040	Equalizers	8	20
8543702050	Ozon generator	8	20
8543702090	Other	8	20
8543709010	High frequency amplifiers	8	20
8543709020	Detectors, including optical sensor	8	20
8544111000	Insulating lacquer or enamel insulated	8	20
8544119000	Other	8	20
8544190000	Other	8	20
8544200000	Co-axial cable and other co-axial electric conductors	8	20
8544300000	Ignition wiring sets and other wiring sets of a kind used invehicles, aircraft or ships	8	20
8544421090	Other	8	20
8544422090	Other	8	20
8544491012	For a voltage exceeding 80V but not exceeding 1,000 V	8	20
8544491090	Other	8	20
8544492012	For a voltage exceeding 80 V but not exceeding 1,000 V	8	20
8544492090	Other	8	20
8544499012	For a voltage exceeding 80 V but not exceeding 1,000 V	8	20
8544499090	Other	8	20
8544601010	Plastic insulated wire	8	20
8544601090	Other	8	20
8544602010	Plastic insulated wire	8	20
8544602090	Other	8	20
8544603090	Other	8	20
8545110000	Of a kind used for furnaces	5	20
8545190000	Other	5	20
8545200000	Brushes	8	20
8545901000	Carbons rod	8	20
8545909000	Other	8	20
8546101000	Rated at not more than 1,000 V	8	20
8546102000	Rated at more than 1,000 V	8	20
8546201000	Rated at not more than 1,000 V	8	20
8546202000	Rated at more than 1,000 V but not more than 10 kV	8	20
8546203000	Rated at more than 10 kV but not more than 100 kV	8	20
8546204000	Rated at more than 100 kV but not more than 300 kV	8	20
8546205000	Rated at more than 300 kV	8	20
8546901000	Artificial plastic insulators	8	20
8546909000	Other	8	20
8547100000	Insulating fittings of ceramics	8	20
8547200000	Insulating fittings of plastics	8	20
8547900000	Other	8	20
8548101000	Of subheading 3824.90	6.5	20

8548106010	Of subheading 8107.30	3	20
8548106020	Of subheading 8111.00	3	20
8548107000	Of subheading 8506.10, 8506.30, 8506.40, 8506.50, 8506.60 or 8506.80	8	20
8548109000	Other	8	20
8548909000	Other	8	20
8601100000	Powered from an external source of electricity	5	20
8601200000	Powered by electric accumulators	5	20
8603101000	Coaches	5	20
8603102000	Vans and trucks	5	20
8603901000	Coaches	5	20
8603902000	Vans and trucks	5	20
8604001000	Workshops	5	20
8604002000	Cranes	5	20
8604003000	Testing coaches	5	20
8604004000	Track inspection vehicles	5	20
8604009000	Other	5	20
8605001010	Sleeping cars	5	20
8605001090	Other	5	20
8605002000	Luggage vans	5	20
8605003000	Travelling post office coaches	5	20
8605004000	Hospital coaches	5	20
8605009000	Other	5	20
8607110000	Driving bogies and bissel-bogies	5	20
8607120000	Other bogies and bissel-bogies	5	20
8607191000	Axles	5	20
8607192000	Wheels	5	20
8607193000	Pair of axle and wheel	5	20
8607199000	Other	5	20
8607210000	Air brakes and parts thereof	5	20
8607290000	Other	5	20
8607301000	Hooks	5	20
8607302000	Coupling device	5	20
8607303000	Buffers	5	20
8607309000	Other	5	20
8607910000	Of locomotives	5	20
8607990000	Other	5	20
8608001000	Railway or tramway track fixtures and fittings	8	20
8608002000	Mechanical signalling, safety or traffic control equipment	8	20
8608009000	Parts	8	20
8701100000	Pedestrian controlled tractors	8	20
8701202000	Used	8	20
8701901010	New	8	20
8701901020	Used	8	20
8701909900	Other	8	20

8702101010	New	10	20
8702101020	Used	10	20
8702102010	New	10	20
8702102020	Used	10	20
8702103010	New	10	20
8702103020	Used	10	20
8702901010	New	10	20
8702901020	Used	10	20
8702902010	New	10	20
8702902020	Used	10	20
8702903010	New	10	20
8702903020	Used	10	20
8703101000	For travelling on snow	8	20
8703102000	Golf cars	8	20
8703109000	Other	8	20
8703217000	New	8	20
8703218000	Used	8	20
8703227000	New	8	20
8703228000	Used	8	20
8703231010	New	8	20
8703231020	Used	8	20
8703239010	New	8	20
8703239020	Used	8	20
8703241010	New	8	20
8703241020	Used	8	20
8703249010	New	8	20
8703249020	Used	8	20
8703317000	New	8	20
8703318000	Used	8	20
8703321010	New	8	20
8703321020	Used	8	20
8703329010	New	8	20
8703329020	Used	8	20
8703337000	New	8	20
8703338000	Used	8	20
8703907000	Electric vehicle	8	20
8703909000	Other	8	20
8704211010	New	10	20
8704211020	Used	10	20
8704219010	Freezer and refrigerator vehicles	10	20
8704219020	Tank lorries	10	20
8704219090	Other	10	20
8704221011	New	10	20
8704221012	Used	10	20
8704221091	New	10	20

8704221092	Used	10	20
8704229010	Freezer and refrigerator vehicles	10	20
8704229020	Tank lorries	10	20
8704229090	Other	10	20
8704231010	New	10	20
8704231020	Used	10	20
8704239010	Freezer and refrigerator vehicles	10	20
8704239020	Tank lorries	10	20
8704239090	Other	10	20
8704311010	New	10	20
8704311020	Used	10	20
8704319010	Freezer and refrigerator vehicles	10	20
8704319020	Tank lorries	10	20
8704319090	Other	10	20
8704321010	New	10	20
8704321020	Used	10	20
8704329010	Freezer and refrigerator vehicles	10	20
8704329020	Tank lorries	10	20
8704329090	Other	10	20
8704901010	New	10	20
8704901020	Used	10	20
8704909010	Freezer and refrigerator vehicles	10	20
8704909020	Tank lorries	10	20
8704909090	Other	10	20
8705101000	Of telescopic boom type	8	20
8705102000	Of latticed boom type	8	20
8705109000	Other	8	20
8705200000	Mobile drilling derricks	8	20
8705300000	Fire fighting vehicles	8	20
8705400000	Concrete-mixer lorries	8	20
8705901010	Agicultural spraying lorries	8	20
8705901090	Other	8	20
8705909010	Breakdown lorries	8	20
8705909020	Road sweeper lorries	8	20
8705909030	Mobile workshops	8	20
8705909040	Mobile broadcast vans	8	20
8705909050	Mobile clinics	8	20
8705909060	Telegraphy, radiotelegraphy and radiotelephony transmitting and receiving vans and radar vehicles	8	20
8705909070	Snow-ploughs and snow-blowers	8	20
8705909090	Other	8	20
8706001010	Of those specified in subheading 8701.20 or 8701.90.10	8	20
8706001090	Other	8	20
8706002000	For the motor vehicles falling within heading 87.02	8	20
8706003000	For the motor vehicles falling within heading 87.03	8	20

8706004000	For the motor vehicles falling within heading 87.04	8	20
8706005000	For the motor vehicles falling within heading 87.05	8	20
8707100000	For the vehicles of heading 87.03	8	20
8707901010	Of those specified in subheading 8701.20 or 8701.90.10	8	20
8707901090	Other	8	20
8707902000	For the motor vehicles falling within heading 87.02	8	20
8707903000	For the motor vehicles falling within heading 87.04	8	20
8707904000	For the motor vehicles falling within heading 87.05	8	20
8708100000	Bumpers and parts thereof	8	20
8708210000	Safety seat belts	8	20
8708290000	Other	8	20
8708301000	Mounted brake linings	8	20
8708302000	Brake boosers	8	20
8708303000	Electronic control brakes	8	20
8708309000	Other	8	20
8708400000	Gear boxes and parts thereof	8	20
8708501000	Drive-axles with differential, whether or not provided with other transmission components and parts thereof	8	20
8708502000	Non-driving axles and parts thereof	8	20
8708700000	Road wheels and parts and accessories thereof	8	20
8708800000	Suspension systems and parts thereof (including shock-absorbers)	8	20
8708920000	Silencers (mufflers) and exhaust pipes; parts thereof	8	20
8708930000	Clutches and parts thereof	8	20
8708940000	Steering wheels, steering columns and steering boxes; parts thereof	8	20
8708951000	Air bags	8	20
8708959000	Other	8	20
8708991010	For the motor vehicles falling within heading 87.01	8	20
8708991020	For the motor vehicles falling within heading 87.02	8	20
8708991030	For the motor vehicles falling within heading 87.03	8	20
8708991040	For the motor vehicles falling within heading 87.04	8	20
8708991050	For the motor vehicles falling within heading 87.05	8	20
8708999000	Other	8	20
8709110000	Electrical	8	20
8709190000	Other	8	20
8709900000	Parts	8	20
8711101000	Motor cycles	8	20
8711102000	Mopeds	8	20
8711103000	Side-cars	8	20
8711109000	Other	8	20
8711201000	Motor cycles	8	20
8711202000	Side-cars	8	20
8711209000	Other	8	20
8711301000	Motor cycles	8	20

8711302000	Side-cars	8	20
8711309000	Other	8	20
8711401000	Motor cycles	8	20
8711402000	Side-cars	8	20
8711409000	Other	8	20
8711501000	Motor cycles	8	20
8711502000	Side-cars	8	20
8711509000	Other	8	20
8711901000	Motor cycles	8	20
8711902000	Side-cars	8	20
8711909000	Other	8	20
8712001000	Racing bicycles	8	20
8712009010	For transportation of goods	8	20
8712009020	Tricycles	8	20
8712009090	Other	8	20
8714110000	Saddles	8	20
8714190000	Other	8	20
8714911000	Frames	8	20
8714912000	Forks	8	20
8714919000	Other parts	8	20
8714921000	Wheel Rims	8	20
8714922000	Spokes	8	20
8714931000	Hubs, other than coaster braking hubs and hub brakes	8	20
8714932000	Free-wheel sprocket-wheels	8	20
8714941000	Coaster braking hubs and hub brakes	8	20
8714942000	Other brakes	8	20
8714949000	Parts thereof	8	20
8714950000	Saddles	8	20
8714961000	Pedals	8	20
8714962000	Crankgear	8	20
8714969000	Parts thereof	8	20
8714990000	Other	8	20
8715000000	Baby carriages and parts thereof.	8	20
8716100000	Trailers and semi-trailers of the caravan type, for housing or camping	8	20
8716200000	Self-loading or self-unloading trailers and semi-trailers for agricultural purposes	8	20
8716310000	Tanker trailers and tanker semi-trailers	8	20
8716390000	Other	8	20
8716400000	Other trailers and semi-trailers	8	20
8716801000	Hand-carts	8	20
8716802000	Carts drawn by ox or horse	8	20
8716803000	Sledges	8	20
8716901000	Of trailers and semi-trailers	8	20
8716909000	Other	8	20

8801009010	Balloons and dirigibles	8	20
8805101090	Other	5	20
8805102090	Other	5	20
8805109090	Other	5	20
8805211090	Other	5	20
8805212090	Other	5	20
8805291090	Other	5	20
8805292090	Other	5	20
8903910000	Sailboats, with or without auxiliary motor	8	20
8903920000	Motorboats, other than outboard motorboats	8	20
8903991000	Outboard motorboats	8	20
8903999000	Other	8	20
8904001000	Tugs	5	20
8904002000	Pusher craft	5	20
8904009000	Other	5	20
8905100000	Dredgers	5	20
8905201000	Drilling ships platforms	5	20
8905202000	Production plat forms	5	20
8905209000	Other	5	20
8905901000	Light-vessels	5	20
8905902000	Fire-floats	5	20
8905903000	Floating cranes	5	20
8905904000	Generating vessels	5	20
8905905000	Salvage ships	5	20
8905906000	Work-shop vessels	5	20
8905907000	Drilling ships	5	20
8905908000	Floating docks	5	20
8905909000	Other	5	20
8907100000	Inflatable rafts	5	20
8907901000	Rafts (other than subheading 8907.10)	5	20
8907902000	Tanks	5	20
8907903000	Coffer-dams	5	20
8907904000	Landing-stages	5	20
8907905000	Buoys	5	20
8907906000	Beacons	5	20
9001101000	Optical fibres	8	20
9001102000	Optical fibre bundles	8	20
9001103000	Optical fibre cables	8	20
9001200000	Sheets and plates of polarising material	8	20
9001300000	Contact lenses	8	20
9001409000	Other	8	20
9001501000	For correcting visions	8	20
9001509000	Other	8	20
9001901000	Prisms	8	20
9001903000	Other lenses	8	20

9001909000	Other	8	20
9002111000	For photographic cameras.	8	20
9002119010	For movie cameras and VTR(video tape recorder) cameras	8	20
9002119020	For projectors	8	20
9002191000	For microscopes	8	20
9002192000	For astronomical telescopes	8	20
9002201000	For photographic cameras	8	20
9002209000	Other	8	20
9002901000	For photographic cameras	8	20
9002909010	Of machines and mechanical appliances for making semiconductor devices	3	20
9002909090	Other	8	20
9003110000	Of plastics	8	20
9003191000	Made of or combined with precious metals	8	20
9003199000	Other	8	20
9003900000	Parts	8	20
9004101000	Made of or combined with precious metals	8	20
9004109000	Other	8	20
9004901010	Made of, or combined with, precious metals	8	20
9004909010	Made of, or combined with, precious metals	8	20
9005100000	Binoculars	8	20
9005801000	Monoculars	8	20
9005802010	Reflecting telescopes	8	20
9005802020	Astronomical refracting telescopes	8	20
9005802030	Transit instruments, equatorial or zenith telescopes and altazimuths	8	20
9005802090	Other	8	20
9005809000	Other	8	20
9005900000	Parts and accessories (including mountings)	8	20
9006100000	Cameras of a kind used for preparing printing plates or cylinders	8	20
9006301000	For subaqueous photography	8	20
9006302000	Air survey cameras	8	20
9006303000	For medical or surgical examination of internal organs	8	20
9006304000	Comparision cameras for forensic and criminological purposes	8	20
9006401000	Instant polaroid cameras	8	20
9006402000	Instant sticker cameras	8	20
9006409000	Others	8	20
9006511000	Photographic cameras for special use	8	20
9006519000	Other	8	20
9006521000	Photographic cameras for special use	8	20
9006529010	Cameras of a kind used for recording documents on microfilm, microfiche or other microforms	8	20
9006529090	Other	8	20

9006531000	Photographic cameras for special use	8	20
9006539010	Single use/disposable cameras	8	20
9006539020	Cameras of a kind used for recording documents on microfilm, microfiche or other microforms	8	20
9006539090	Other	8	20
9006591000	Photographic cameras for special use	8	20
9006599010	Cameras of a kind used for recording documents on microfilm, microfiche or other microforms	8	20
9006599090	Other	8	20
9006610000	Discharge lamp("electronic") flashlight apparatus	8	20
9006691000	Flashbulbs, flashcubes and the like	8	20
9006699000	Other	8	20
9006910000	For cameras	8	20
9006990000	Other	8	20
9007110000	For film of less than 16 mm width or for double-8 mm film	8	20
9007191000	For film of less 30 mm width	8	20
9007199000	Other	8	20
9007201000	For film of less than 16 mm width	8	20
9007209010	For film of less than 20 mm width	8	20
9007209020	For film of not less than 20 mm width	8	20
9007910000	For cameras	8	20
9007920000	For projectors	8	20
9008100000	Slide projectors	8	20
9008200000	Microfilm, microfiche or other microform readers, whether or not capable of producing copies	8	20
9008300000	Other image projectors	8	20
9008401000	For the preparation of printing plates	8	20
9008402000	For microfilm	8	20
9008409000	Other	8	20
9008900000	Parts and accessories	8	20
9010101000	For photo-engraving	8	20
9010102000	For microfilm	8	20
9010109090	Other	8	20
9010509000	Other	8	20
9010600000	Projection screens	8	20
9010909000	Other	8	20
9011109000	Other	8	20
9011201090	Other	8	20
9011209000	Other	8	20
9011801000	Polarising microscopes	8	20
9011802000	Metallurgical microscopes	8	20
9011803000	Phase contrast and interference microscopes	8	20
9011804000	Biological microscopes	8	20
9011805000	Comparison microsecopes	8	20
9011809000	Other	8	20

9011909000	Other	8	20
9012101090	Other	8	20
9012102000	Diffraction apparatus	8	20
9012909000	Other	8	20
9013100000	Telescopic sights for fitting to arms; periscopes; telescopes designed to form parts of machines, appliances, instruments or apparatus of this Chapter or Section XVI	8	20
9013200000	Lasers, other than laser diodes	8	20
9013801110	For opto-elecrionic watchs	8	20
9013801130	For televisions	8	20
9013801140	For monitor	8	20
9013801190	Other	8	20
9013801910	For opto-elecrionic watchs	8	20
9013801930	For televisions	8	20
9013801990	Other	8	20
9013802000	Magnifiers, loupes, thread counters	8	20
9013803000	Door viewers (door eyes)	8	20
9013909000	Other	8	20
9014101010	For aircrafts	8	20
9014101090	Other	8	20
9014102010	For aircrafts	8	20
9014102090	Other	8	20
9014109000	Other	8	20
9014200000	Instruments and appliances for aeronautical or space navigation (other then compasses)	8	20
9014901000	For aircrafts	8	20
9014909000	Other	8	20
9015100000	Rangefinders	8	20
9015200000	Theodolites and tachymeters (tacheometers)	8	20
9015300000	Levels	8	20
9015400000	Photogrammetrical surveying instruments and appliances	8	20
9015801000	For use in the field.	8	20
9015802000	For hydrographic use	8	20
9015803000	For oceanographic use	8	20
9015804000	For hydrological use	8	20
9015805000	For meteorological use	8	20
9015809000	Other	8	20
9015900000	Parts and accessories	8	20
9016001000	Direct reading balances	8	20
9016002000	Electronic balances	8	20
9016008000	Other	8	20
9016009000	Parts or accessories	8	20
9017109000	Other	8	20
9017201090	Other	8	20
9017202090	Other	8	20

9017203000	Mathematical calculating instruments	8	20
9017209000	Other	8	20
9017301000	Micrometers	8	20
9017302000	Dialgauges	8	20
9017303000	Vernier callipers	8	20
9017309000	Other	8	20
9017801000	Divided scales, measuring rod and tapes	8	20
9017809090	Other	8	20
9017909090	Other	8	20
9018119000	Parts and accessories	8	20
9018191000	Electro-encephalographs	8	20
9018192000	Audiometers and similar apparatus	8	20
9018197000	Patient monitoring system	8	20
9018198000	Other	8	20
9018201000	Ultra-violet or infra-red ray apparatus	8	20
9018209000	Parts and accessories	8	20
9018310000	Syringes, with or without needles	8	20
9018321000	Needles for injections	8	20
9018322000	Needles for sutures	8	20
9018329000	Other	8	20
9018419000	Parts and accessories	8	20
9018492000	Dental units	8	20
9018499000	Parts and accessories	8	20
9018501000	Ophthalmic instruments and appliances	8	20
9018901000	Pregnancy diagnostic apparatus	8	20
9018909020	Gynaecological or obstetrical instruments	8	20
9018909040	Artificial kidney apparatus	8	20
9018909050	Dialyzers for artificial kidney apparatus	8	20
9018909060	Veterinary instrument and appliances	8	20
9020001000	Gas masks	8	20
9020008000	Other breathing appliances	8	20
9022130000	Other, for dental uses	8	20
9022141020	Angiography units	8	20
9022141090	Other	8	20
9022142000	For verterinary use	8	20
9022191000	For physical or chemical testing	8	20
9022192000	For industrial use	8	20
9022199000	Other	8	20
9022211010	Gamma cameras	8	20
9022211020	Linear accelerators	8	20
9022211030	Cobalt 60 therapy units	8	20
9022211090	Other	8	20
9022212000	For verterinary use	8	20
9022291000	For physical or chemical testing	8	20
9022292000	For industrial use	8	20

9022299000	Other	8	20
9022300000	X-ray tubes	8	20
9022901010	X-ray generators	8	20
9022901030	X-ray high tension generators	8	20
9022901090	Other	8	20
9023001000	Models of human or animal anatomies	8	20
9023009000	Other	8	20
9024101000	Hardness testing machines	8	20
9024102000	Tensile testing machines	8	20
9024103000	Compression testing machines	8	20
9024104000	Fatigue testing machines	8	20
9024105000	Universal type testing machines	8	20
9024106000	Machines and appliances for testing adhesive strength or shear force of ball or wire of printed circuits board, semiconductor device and electronic integrated circuit	8	20
9024109000	Other	8	20
9024801010	Testing machines to detect changes in the dimensions of textile	8	20
9024801020	Abrasion testing machines	8	20
9024801090	Other	8	20
9024809010	Elasticity meters	8	20
9024809020	Plastimeters	8	20
9024809090	Other	8	20
9024901000	Sensor (devices sensing a specific quantity of change, whether or not combined with equipment which convert measured signal into electrical signal)	8	20
9024909000	Other	8	20
9025119000	Other	8	20
9025192010	Optical pyrometers	8	20
9025801000	Hydrometers and similar floating instruments	8	20
9025802010	Mercury barometer	8	20
9025802090	Other	8	20
9025803010	Psychrometers	8	20
9025803020	Hair hygrometers	8	20
9025803090	Other	8	20
9025809000	Other	8	20
9025901900	Other sensor	8	20
9025909000	Other	8	20
9027100000	Gas or smoke analysis apparatus	8	20
9027802050	Exposure meters	8	20
9027901000	Microtomes	8	20
9027909110	Gas sensor	8	20
9027909122	Of smoke	8	20
9027909991	For gas or smoke analysis apparatus and microtomes	8	20
9028101010	Of digital type	8	20

9028101090	Other	8	20
9028102000	Calibrating meters	8	20
9028201010	Of digital type	8	20
9028201090	Other	8	20
9028202000	Calibrating meters	8	20
9028301010	Not less than 50 A	8	20
9028301020	Less than 50 A	8	20
9028302000	Calibrating meters	8	20
9028900000	Parts and accessories	8	20
9029101000	Revolution counters	8	20
9029102000	Production counters	8	20
9029103000	Taximeters	8	20
9029104000	Mileometers	8	20
9029105000	Counters for indicating the working hours of machines	8	20
9029109000	Other	8	20
9029201010	Chronometric system	8	20
9029201090	Other	8	20
9029202000	Stroboscopes	8	20
9029901200	Rotation sensor	8	20
9029901900	Other sensor	8	20
9029909000	Other	8	20
9030201090	Other	8	20
9030202010	Of cathode-ray	8	20
9030202090	Other	8	20
9030320000	Multimeters with a recording device	8	20
9030331000	Voltmeters	8	20
9030332000	Ammeters	8	20
9030333000	Circuit testers	8	20
9030334000	Registance meters	8	20
9030335000	Galvanometer	8	20
9030336000	Frequency measuring apparatus	8	20
9030339000	Other	8	20
9030391000	Voltmeters	8	20
9030392000	Ammeters	8	20
9030393000	Circuit testers	8	20
9030394000	Registance meters	8	20
9030395000	Galvanometer	8	20
9030840000	Other, with a recording device	8	20
9030901100	Electromagnetic sensor	8	20
9030901200	Radiation ray sensor	8	20
9030901900	Other sensor	8	20
9030909090	Other	8	20
9031100000	Machines for balancing mechanical parts	8	20
9031200000	Test benches	8	20
9031491000	Optical surface testers	8	20

9031492000	Optical goniometers or angle gauges	8	20
9031493000	Focimeters	8	20
9031494090	Other	8	20
9031499090	Other	8	20
9031801000	Ultrasonic fish finders	8	20
9031802000	Load-cells	8	20
9031809010	Equipment for testing the characteristics of internal combustion engines	8	20
9031809020	Gear testing machines	8	20
9031809030	Planimeters	8	20
9031809040	Spherometers	8	20
9031809050	Apparatus for checking textile materials	8	20
9031809060	Ultra-sonic thickness measuring instruments	8	20
9031809070	Instruments for detecting faults cracks or other defects	8	20
9031809080	Dynamometers	8	20
9031809099	Other	8	20
9031901190	Other	8	20
9031901299	Other	8	20
9031909090	Other	8	20
9032101010	For refrigerators	8	20
9032101020	For aircraft	5	20
9032101090	Other	8	20
9032102000	Of fixed type	8	20
9032200000	Manostats	8	20
9032811010	For aircraft	5	20
9032811090	Other	8	20
9032812010	For aircraft	5	20
9032812091	Of machines and mechanical appliances for making semiconductor devices	3	20
9032812099	Other	8	20
9032819010	For aircraft	5	20
9032819090	Other	8	20
9032891010	For aircraft	5	20
9032891090	Other	8	20
9032892010	For aircraft	5	20
9032892090	Other	8	20
9032893010	For aircraft	5	20
9032893090	Other	8	20
9032899010	For aircraft	5	20
9032899090	Other	8	20
9032901000	For aircraft	5	20
9033000000	Parts and accessories (not specified or included elsewhere in this Chapter) for machines, appliances, instruments or apparatus of Chapter 90.	8	20
9101110000	With mechanical display only	8	20

9101191000	With opto-electronic display only	8	20
9101199000	Other	8	20
9101210000	With automatic winding	8	20
9101290000	Other	8	20
9101910000	Electrically operated	8	20
9101990000	Other	8	20
9102111000	For the blind	8	20
9102112000	With dials bands or similar of precious metal or of metal clad with precious metal	8	20
9102119010	Battery or accumulator operated	8	20
9102119090	Other	8	20
9102121000	Battery or accumulator operated	8	20
9102129010	For the blind	8	20
9102129020	With dials bands or similar of precious metal or of metal clad with precious metal	8	20
9102129090	Other	8	20
9102191000	Battery or accumulator operated	8	20
9102199010	For the blind	8	20
9102199020	With dials bands or similar of precious metal or of metal clad with precious metal	8	20
9102199090	Other	8	20
9102211000	For the blind	8	20
9102212000	With dials bands or similar of precious metal or of metal clad with precious metal	8	20
9102219000	Other	8	20
9102291000	For the blind	8	20
9102292000	With dials bands or similar of precious metal or of metal clad with precious metal.	8	20
9102299000	Other	8	20
9102911000	Stop-watches	8	20
9102912000	For the blind	8	20
9102919010	Battery or accumulator powered	8	20
9102919090	Other	8	20
9102991000	Stop-watches	8	20
9102992000	For the blind	8	20
9102999000	Other	8	20
9103101000	Travel clocks	8	20
9103109000	Other	8	20
9103901000	Travel clocks	8	20
9103909000	Other	8	20
9104001000	For vehicles	8	20
9104002000	For aircraft	8	20
9104004000	For vessels	8	20
9104009000	Other	8	20
9105110000	Electrically operated	8	20

9105190000	Other	8	20
9105210000	Electrically operated	8	20
9105290000	Other	8	20
9105910000	Electrically operated	8	20
9105990000	Other	8	20
9106100000	Time-registers; time-recorders	8	20
9106901000	Watchmen's telltales	8	20
9106902000	Timers	8	20
9106903000	Parking meters	8	20
9106909000	Other	8	20
9107001000	With synchronous motor	8	20
9107009000	Other	8	20
9108110000	With mechanical display only or with a device to which a mechanical display can be incorporated	5	20
9108120000	With opto-electronic display only	5	20
9108190000	Other	5	20
9108200000	With automatic winding	5	20
9108900000	Other	5	20
9109110000	Of alarm clocks	8	20
9109190000	Other	8	20
9109900000	Other	8	20
9110111000	Battery or accumulator powered	8	20
9110112000	With automatic winding	8	20
9110119000	Other	8	20
9110121000	Battery or accumulator powered.	8	20
9110122000	With automatic winding	8	20
9110129000	Other	8	20
9110191000	Battery or accumulator powered	8	20
9110192000	With automatic winding	8	20
9110199000	Other	8	20
9110901000	Battery or accumulator powered	8	20
9110909000	Other	8	20
9111100000	Cases of precious metal or of metal clad with precious metal	8	20
9111200000	Cases of base metal, whether or not gold-or silver-plated	8	20
9111800000	Other cases	8	20
9111901000	Of precious metal or metal clad with precious metal	8	20
9111909000	Other	8	20
9112200000	Cases	8	20
9112900000	Parts	8	20
9113100000	Of precious metal or of metal clad with precious metal	8	20
9113200000	Of base metal, whether or not gold-or silver-plated	8	20
9113901000	Of plastics	8	20
9113902000	Of leather or composition leather	8	20
9113909000	Other	8	20

9114100000	Springs, including hair-springs	8	20
9114200000	Jewels	8	20
9114300000	Dials	8	20
9114400000	Plates and bridges	8	20
9201101000	Of automatic	8	20
9201109000	Other	8	20
9201200000	Grand pianos	8	20
9201901000	Harpsichords	8	20
9201909000	Other	8	20
9202101000	Violins	8	20
9202102000	Violoncellos	8	20
9202109000	Other	8	20
9202902000	Harps	8	20
9202903000	Mandolines	8	20
9202904000	Banjo	8	20
9202909000	Other	8	20
9205101000	Trumpets	8	20
9205102000	Trombones	8	20
9205109000	Other	8	20
9205901010	Flutes	8	20
9205901020	Clarinets	8	20
9205901030	Saxophones	8	20
9205901040	Recoder	8	20
9205901090	Other	8	20
9205902010	Pipe organs	8	20
9205902020	Reed organs	8	20
9205902090	Other	8	20
9205903010	Accordions	8	20
9205903020	Melodicas	8	20
9205903090	Other	8	20
9205904000	Mouth organs	8	20
9205909000	Other	8	20
9206001000	Drums	8	20
9206002000	Xylophones	8	20
9206003000	Cymbals	8	20
9206004000	Castanets	8	20
9206005000	Maracas	8	20
9206006000	Tambourine	8	20
9206009000	Other	8	20
9207101000	Organs (including synthesizers)	8	20
9207103000	Pianos	8	20
9207109000	Other	8	20
9207901000	Guitars	8	20
9207902000	Accordions	8	20
9207903000	Rythm box	8	20

9207909000	Other	8	20
9208100000	Musical boxes	8	20
9208901000	Fair ground organs	8	20
9208902000	Mechanical street organs	8	20
9208903000	Mechanical singing birds	8	20
9208904000	Musical saws	8	20
9208909000	Other	8	20
9209301000	Of metal wire	8	20
9209309000	Other	8	20
9209920000	Parts and accessories for the musical instruments of heading 92.02	8	20
9209940000	Parts and accessories for the musical instruments of heading 92.07	8	20
9209991000	For musical movements	8	20
9209992000	Metronomes, tuning forks and pitch pipes of all kinds	8	20
9209993000	Mechanisms for musical boxes	8	20
9303100000	Muzzle-loading firearms	8	20
9303201011	Pump-action	8	20
9303201012	Semi-automatic	8	20
9303201019	Other	8	20
9303201020	Shotguns, multiple barrel, including combination guns	8	20
9303201090	Other	8	20
9303209011	Pump-action	8	20
9303209012	Semi-automatic	8	20
9303209019	Other	8	20
9303209020	Shotguns, multiple barrel, including combination guns	8	20
9303209090	Other	8	20
9303301010	Single-shot	8	20
9303301020	Semi-automatic	8	20
9303301090	Other	8	20
9303309010	Single-shot	8	20
9303309020	Semi-automatic	8	20
9303309090	Other	8	20
9303900000	Other	8	20
9304001000	Air guns	8	20
9304009000	Other	8	20
9305109010	Firing mechanisms	8	20
9305109020	Frames and receivers	8	20
9305109030	Barrels	8	20
9305109040	Pistons, locking lugs and gas buffers	8	20
9305109050	Magazines and parts thereof	8	20
9305109060	Silencers (sound moderators) and parts thereof	8	20
9305109070	Butts, grips and plates	8	20
9305109080	Slides(for pistols) and cylinders (for revolvers)	8	20
9305109090	Other	8	20

9305210000	Shotgun barrels	8	20
9305291000	Firing mechanisms	8	20
9305292000	Frames and receivers	8	20
9305293000	Rifle barrels	8	20
9305294000	Pistons, locking lugs and gas buffers	8	20
9305295000	Magazines and parts thereof	8	20
9305296000	Silencers (sound moderators) and parts thereof	8	20
9305297000	Flash eliminators and parts thereof	8	20
9305298000	Breeches, bolts (gunlocks) and bolt carriers	8	20
9305299000	Other	8	20
9305990000	Other	8	20
9401200000	Seats of a kind used for motor vehicles	8	20
9401901000	Of wooden	8	20
9401902000	Of metal	8	20
9403401000	Dinner tables	8	20
9403409000	Other	8	20
9403900000	Parts	8	20
9404210000	Of cellular rubber or plastics, whether or not covered	8	20
9404300000	Sleeping bags	8	20
9405101000	Of filament lamps	8	20
9405102000	Of fluorescent lamps	8	20
9405201000	Of filament lamps	8	20
9405209000	Other	8	20
9405301000	Of filament lamps	8	20
9405309000	Other	8	20
9405401000	Of anti-explosive type	8	20
9405402000	Of flood type	8	20
9405403000	Of street type	8	20
9405409000	Other	8	20
9405500000	Non-electrical lamps and lighting fittings	8	20
9405601000	Of neon tubes	8	20
9405602000	Of filament lamps	8	20
9405603000	Of fluorescent lamps	8	20
9405609000	Other	8	20
9405911000	Of chandeliers	8	20
9405919000	Other	8	20
9405921000	Of chandeliers	8	20
9405929000	Other	8	20
9405991000	Of chandeliers	8	20
9405999000	Other	8	20
9406009010	Of plastic	8	20
9406009020	Of iron or steel	8	20
9406009030	Of aluminium	8	20
9406009090	Other	8	20
9503002110	Of textiles	8	20

9503002130	Of plastics	8	20
9503002190	Other	8	20
9503002910	Garments and accessories therefor, footwear and headgear	8	20
9503003411	Of textile materials	8	20
9503003419	Other	8	20
9503003491	Of textile material	8	20
9503003493	Of plastics	8	20
9503003494	Of metal	8	20
9503003499	Other	8	20
9503003500	Toy musical instruments and apparatus	8	20
9503003700	Other toys, put up in sets or outfits	8	20
9503003800	Other toys and models, incorporating a motor	8	20
9503003911	Balloons, toy balls, kites and the like	8	20
9503003919	Other	8	20
9505100000	Articles for Christmas festivities	8	20
9505900000	Other	8	20
9506110000	Skis	8	20
9506120000	Ski-fastenings (ski-bindings)	8	20
9506190000	Other	8	20
9506210000	Sailboards	8	20
9506290000	Other	8	20
9506310000	Clubs, complete	8	20
9506320000	Balls	8	20
9506399000	Other	8	20
9506401000	Table-tennis tables	8	20
9506402000	Table-tennis rackets	8	20
9506403000	Table-tennis balls	8	20
9506409000	Other	8	20
9506510000	Lawn-tennis rackets, whether or not strung	8	20
9506591000	Badminton rackets	8	20
9506599000	Other	8	20
9506610000	Lawn-tennis balls	8	20
9506621000	Soccer balls	8	20
9506622000	Basket balls	8	20
9506623000	Volley balls	8	20
9506624000	Hand balls	8	20
9506625000	American footballs	8	20
9506629000	Other	8	20
9506691000	Badminton shuttlecock	8	20
9506692000	Baseballs	8	20
9506699000	Other	8	20
9506700000	Ice skates and roller skates, including skating boots with skates attached	8	20
9506910000	Articles and equipment for general physical exercise, gymnastics or athletics	8	20

9506990000	Other	8	20
9507101000	Of glass fibre	8	20
9507109000	Other	8	20
9507200000	Fish-hooks, whether or not snelled	8	20
9507901000	Fish landing nets and other fishing tackles	8	20
9507909000	Other	8	20
9508100000	Travelling circuses and travelling menageries	8	20
9508900000	Other	8	20
9601100000	Worked ivory and articles of ivory	8	20
9601901090	Other	8	20
9601902000	Of horn	8	20
9601903000	Of bone	8	20
9601904000	Of coral	8	20
9601909090	Other	8	20
9602001000	Gelatin capsules	8	20
9602009010	Worked vegetable carving material (for example, corozo) and articles of vegetable carving material	8	20
9602009020	Worked jet (and mineral substitutes for jet), amber, meerschaum agglomerated amber and agglomerated meerschaum, and articles of those substances	8	20
9602009090	Other	8	20
9603100000	Brooms and brushes, consisting of twigs or other vegetable materials bound together, with or without handles	8	20
9603210000	Tooth brushes, including dental-plate brushes	8	20
9603290000	Other	8	20
9603300000	Artists' brushes, writing brushes and similar brushes for the application of cosmetics	8	20
9603400000	Paint, distemper, varnish or similar brushes (other than brushes of subheading 9603.30); paint pads and rollers	8	20
9603500000	Other brushes constituting parts of machines, appliances or vehicles	8	20
9603900000	Other	8	20
9604000000	Hand sieves and hand riddles.	8	20
9605000000	Travel sets for personal toilet, sewing or shoe or clothes cleaning.	8	20
9606100000	Press-fasteners, snap-fasteners and press-studs and parts therefor	8	20
9606210000	Of plastics, not covered with textile material	8	20
9606220000	Of base metal, not covered with textile material	8	20
9606291000	Of shell-fish shell	8	20
9606299000	Other	8	20
9606300000	Button moulds and other parts of buttons; button blanks	8	20
9607110000	Fitted with chain scoops of base metal	8	20
9607191000	Of plastic	8	20

9607199000	Other	8	20
9607201000	Of base metal	8	20
9607209000	Other	8	20
9608100000	Ball point pens	8	20
9608200000	Felt tipped and other porous-tipped pens and markers	8	20
9608310000	Indian ink drawing pens	8	20
9608391000	Fountainpens	8	20
9608399000	Other	8	20
9608401000	Propelling Pencils	8	20
9608402010	Of mechanical type	8	20
9608402090	Other	8	20
9608500000	Sets of articles from two or more of the foregoing subheadings	8	20
9608600000	Refills for ball point pens, comprising the ball point and ink-reservoir	8	20
9608911000	Pen nibs	8	20
9608912000	Nib points	8	20
9608991000	Parts	8	20
9608999000	Other	8	20
9609101000	Pencils	8	20
9609103000	Crayons	8	20
9609200000	Pencil leads, black or coloured	8	20
9609902000	Pastels	8	20
9609903010	For writing	8	20
9609903090	Other	8	20
9609909000	Other	8	20
9610001000	Slates	8	20
9610002000	Black boards	8	20
9610009000	Other	8	20
9611001000	Stamps	8	20
9611002000	Hand printing sets	8	20
9611009000	Other	8	20
9612101000	For typewriter	8	20
9612102000	For EDPS machines	8	20
9612109000	Other	8	20
9612200000	Ink-pads	8	20
9613100000	Pocket lighters, gas fuelled, non-refillable	8	20
9613200000	Pocket lighters, gas fuelled, refillable	8	20
9613800000	Other lighters	8	20
9613901000	Piezo-electric ignition units	8	20
9613909000	Other	8	20
9614001000	Pipes and pipe bowls	8	20
9614009000	Other	8	20
9615111000	Combs	8	20
9615119000	Other	8	20

9615191000	Combs	8	20
9615199000	Other	8	20
9615901000	Hair-pins	8	20
9615909000	Other	8	20
9616100000	Scent sprays and similar toilet sprays, and mounts and heads therefor	8	20
9616200000	Powder-puffs and pads for the application of cosmetics or toilet preparations	8	20
9617001000	Vacuum flasks	8	20
9617002000	Vacuum lunch-boxes	8	20
9617008000	Other	8	20
9617009000	Parts	8	20
9618001000	Tailors' dummies	8	20
9618002000	Automata	8	20
9618009000	Other	8	20